# AT THAT POINT
# IN TIME

# AT THAT POINT IN TIME

*The Inside Story of the Senate Watergate Committee*

FRED D. THOMPSON

*Quadrangle / The New York Times Book Co.*

*Book design: Tere LoPrete*

**Library of Congress Cataloging in Publication Data**

Thompson, Fred D
    At that point in time.

    Includes index.
    1. Watergate Affair, 1972-    2. United States. Congress. Senate. Select Committee on Presidential Campaign Activities.  3. Thompson, Fred D.  I. Title.
E860.T45      364.1'32'0973      74-23290
ISBN 0-8129-0536-9

*To Sarah*

# *Acknowledgments*

I would like to thank all of the many people whose assistance enabled this book to find its way into print. Although I cannot mention everyone by name here, I would like to acknowledge the efforts of several people who have been particularly helpful. First of all, my thanks to the men and women of the Minority Staff of the Senate Watergate Committee; without their diligent work and devotion to duty neither my survival nor this book would have been possible. For their faith, assistance, and advice, I want to express my gratitude to Edwin Barber, Jonathan Segal, and Irv Horowitz. For her long patience and good counsel, special thanks to my wife Sarah. For their typing assistance and good humor during the final hectic days of the manuscript preparation, my thanks to Dorthea Roberson and Sandra Morehart.

And finally, I want to acknowledge the contribution of my mother and father, who, as always, had faith that I could do what I set out to do.

—F. D. T.
Nashville
May 1975

# Contents

# AT THAT POINT
# IN TIME

# Chapter I · The Investigation Begins

Shortly after 10 o'clock on the morning of May 17, 1973, Sen. Sam Ervin of North Carolina banged a gavel on the green felt covering of a large table. The setting was the cavernous Caucus Room of the Senate Office Building, with its marble walls, its huge Corinthian columns, and its delicate chandeliers. The occasion was the first day of public hearings by the Senate Select Committee on Presidential Campaign Activities, created three months earlier to look into the worst political scandal in American history—Watergate.

And there in the midst of it all, seated at the committee table, blinded by the television lights, possessed of the august title of minority counsel to the committee, was a 30-year-old lawyer from Lawrenceburg, Tennessee, six years out of law school: me, Fred Thompson. I "wallowed in Watergate" for eighteen months, from February 1973 to August 1974—a period that changed the course of history and ended with the first resignation of a United States president.

When five men were captured in the Watergate offices of the Democratic National Committee early in the morning on Saturday, June 17, 1972, I had just completed a three-year stint as an assistant United States attorney in Nashville. Ironically I had resigned the day before the break-in. I was about to become an unpaid political worker—the middle Tennessee director of the reelection campaign of Sen. Howard Baker.

The Baker campaign of 1972 was eminently successful. The senator, the first Republican popularly elected to the Senate from our state in 1966, became the first to be reelected, with a 276,000-vote margin that attracted national attention. Preoccu-

3

pied with the campaign, I paid little attention to Watergate revelations in the newspapers and on television. No one I knew discussed it much.

Early in 1973, back in private law practice in Nashville, I attended a luncheon sponsored by the Tennessee Accountants Association that honored Baker as "the man of the year." I decided to say hello to the senator, whom I had not seen since the election, and whom I had grown to respect and admire during the grueling days of the campaign.

After Baker's speech I lingered to get a word with him, and chatted with his aides while he exchanged small talk with the accountants. To my surprise, Baker asked if I would ride to the airport with him. When it appeared that his departure might be delayed by more well-wishers, he said, almost apologetically, "Fred, if you've got an appointment or need to be somewhere we can talk later." I assured him that I would wait.

Finally we got away. The driver was Bill Hamby, the director of Baker's Tennessee field offices, and an old friend of mine. Baker was seated beside him; the senator has a tendency to car sickness, a problem that is aggravated if he rides in the back seat. I sat directly behind Baker and beside Ron McMahon, his press secretary.

It was a short ride to the airport, and the senator came right to the point. "Fred," he said, "I've been appointed vice chairman of the Watergate committee." My mind raced for facts that I felt I should have known. I remembered something in the papers about the resolution that had created the committee.

Baker went on. "I'm considering several people for minority counsel to the committee and you're one of them. I don't know what the pay is, but it won't be enough. It should last a few months, and the minority counsel will have responsibility for supervising one-third of the staff. I want you to understand I'm not offering you the job, but I wanted to see what your reaction would be if we make that decision."

I asked a few questions about the time involved and whether I would have to give up my law practice entirely for the duration of the committee's work. Baker could not be precise beyond his estimate of a few months, but it would indeed mean giving up all private practice while it lasted. I said the job sounded interesting, but that I would have to consult my wife and law partners. I also wanted time to do a little homework on Watergate and the powers and duties of a congressional committee.

For me, as for millions of other Americans, Watergate did not ring many bells in the winter of 1972–1973. The only names I could recall without prompting were Howard Hunt and Gordon Liddy, and my only reaction to the case had been a vague feeling that every political campaign has a few crackpots who cause embarrassment.

The first person I consulted was Jack Butler, my friend and law partner. Jack expressed some reservations, which I shared. "The investigation may turn out to be significant," he said, "but it's a lot of time away from your law practice at a pretty crucial time." Later that night I discussed the matter with my wife Sarah, explaining that the major burden would be hers: she was teaching school in addition to running our household of three school-aged children. But, as always, Sarah said the decision was mine, and she could tell that I was interested. My initial reaction to Baker's offer had been a positive one, and the more I thought about it the more I became convinced that I wanted to take part. I sent a message to Baker: "If you want me for the job, I'll do it."

Late one afternoon in February, Baker called from Washington. "Fred," the senator said, "you're it."

"Fine, I appreciate that. I'll try to do a good job for you."

"I know you will. When can you come to Washington?"

"When do you need me?"

"Tomorrow."

"I'll be there."

The next morning, as I drove to the airport in cold and dreary weather, I recalled our family conference the night before. "I really don't think this thing will last more than a few months at the most," I told Sarah and the kids, "and I should be able to come back and resume my law practice, at least part-time, by June or July. Sometimes these so-called political scandals have a way of playing themselves out after a few days." I spoke with authority.

Actually, I wondered if I had been trying to convince my family or myself that the committee's lifetime would be short. The resolution establishing the committee provided a one-year tenure. And there were hints, from the reading I had done, that a major scandal might really be unfolding. On the other hand, hadn't the president's press secretary called the Watergate break-in "a third-rate burglary attempt"? The press, I speculated, had never liked the Nixon administration and was probably still chafing from his enormous victory the previous November.

Within a few hours I was in Baker's office, confronted with an eight-inch stack of newspaper clippings on the Watergate scandal. That pile, along with notes I had made hastily the night before in the Vanderbilt University Library, constituted the entire documentation then in possession of the Watergate committee.

I knew most of Baker's staff, and I spent part of the first day renewing old acquaintances. "Well, the press department's got you off to a good start," commented Ron McMahon as he pitched a copy of the *Washington Post* across the desk. There was an item announcing my appointment, and a picture of Sam Dash with my name underneath it. "Just stick with me, babe; we'll take care of you," said Ron.

I asked about Dash, my majority counterpart and the man who would select two-thirds of the staff. Baker had mentioned that Dash was a law professor, but I knew nothing of his background. McMahon showed me a press clipping on Dash. As I read his impressive biography I shook my head. "Well," I said, "I can see right now we're going to have to avoid all social functions together."

"Why?"

"I can just see us being introduced now. 'Here's Samuel Dash, professor of law, head of the Georgetown Criminal Law

Institute, author, lecturer, expert on electronic eavesdropping. And here's Fred Thompson, intersection lawyer from Nashville.' "

The rest of the day was taken up with newspaper and television interviews. I spoke guardedly. "Let the chips fall where they may" was probably my most provocative remark. I said I was looking forward to the job, that I was sure I could get along with Mr. Dash, that this would not be a partisan inquiry. It was not a stop-the-presses performance.

It took only a few days to get down to business. My "office" at first was a small table in a corner of one of Baker's offices, in a room shared with two secretaries and two legislative assistants. Its location was strategic: every time someone had to use the rest room I had to move my chair. At this table, euphemistically called a desk, I interviewed many of the key people who later joined the staff; if the surroundings didn't discourage them, nothing would.

Dash came by to introduce himself. Our backgrounds could not have been more dissimilar. Dash was of Russian-Jewish descent and had grown up in Philadelphia, where he began his law practice. He was well known in the American Bar Association for his work on several committees, and he had written a book, *The Eavesdroppers,* which was one of the works I consulted in preparing my senior dissertation in law school on the constitutional right of privacy. Now he was a professor at Georgetown Law School.

I had grown up in Lawrenceburg, Tennessee, a town of 12,000 about seventy miles south of Nashville. After graduating from law school I spent two years in the rough-and-tumble country practice. At 30, I was eighteen years younger than Dash, and, unlike Dash, I had been involved in party politics, having managed a losing campaign for the House of Representatives four years before I worked in Baker's reelection effort.

Dash was much more friendly than his austere photographs indicated, and I got the impression that he was as curious about me as I was about him. He spoke in quick bursts, often changing direction on a sentence two or three times before he completed it. He also appeared a little ill at ease, and I wondered if this was his first encounter with a real live country lawyer. He did not try to impress me with his credentials or assume a commanding role, but I remained a little skeptical. Often, when people say they are nonpartisan, I react the way Baker said he did to Sam Ervin's assertion that he was "just a country lawyer": I put my hand on my wallet.

Dash was having his own relocation problems. He was sharing the office of Rufus Edmisten, a long-time political aide to Ervin and counsel to Ervin's subcommittee on separation of powers. Edmisten is the politician's politician, a personification of the good-old-boy stereotype. Easygoing and gregarious, he was the man to see if you wanted someone to hear your side of an argument. He never disguised his desire to run for office in North Carolina, and he was determined not to make anyone angry with him. Edmisten soon earned the reputation of the "fastest chair on the committee." Almost every time a photograph was taken near the center of the committee table Rufus was in the picture. His office matched his personality—there were old Indian relics, pictures of him with Ervin, and an array of North Carolina mementoes. In 1974 Edmisten was elected attorney general of North Carolina.

Unlike me, Dash had the problem of developing a close working relationship with Ervin, whom he had not known before his appointment and with whom he had little in common. Dash also had to maintain good relations with Edmisten and other veteran aides to Ervin who, like all congressional staff members, strive always to get as close to "the man" as possible.

Edmisten and I developed an immediate understanding. Both of us knew politics and what was involved in working for a senator. It was to our mutual self-interest and, more important, to the self-interest of Ervin and Baker that we get along together, maintain a united front, and protect each other's flanks. It was certain that somewhere along the line our senators would have differences of opinion and that they would even cross swords on occasion. When this happened, Edmisten and I would do battle, fight hard but fair, and protect our respective senators, with no hard feelings afterward. That was the game, and both of us knew the rules.

Although Edmisten's title was "deputy counsel" to the committee, it soon became obvious that he was serving as Ervin's liaison. Thus I had to develop a relationship with Dash similar to the one I had with Edmisten. I was not too pleased when I learned on arriving in Washington that Dash had already asked Baker whether I would "accept assignments" from Dash, as chief counsel. From this it was clear that Dash and I had different views about our roles. There were no real guidelines on the function of a committee counsel, and there were certainly none for a minority counsel. It all depended on our relationship to the senators on the committee and on how much space each of us was big enough to occupy.

The first time I had the opportunity to see Dash and Edmisten together I took up the matter of how the staff would be run. It was clear, from the floor debate on the resolution that established our committee, that the Republicans had fought strenuously to get equal representation. That bid had been defeated. The Republicans had also attempted to expand the committee's jurisdiction to cover presidential elections prior to 1972, but that had also been turned back. Both votes had been almost entirely along party lines. I was concerned about the disadvantages of the minority staff, which was limited to one-third of the total. Why had the Democrats fought so hard on the Senate floor, except to insure themselves the upper hand?

I made my position clear to Dash. "You know, Sam," I said, "it occurs to me that you're probably not quite sure as to whether I've been brought up here to sabotage your efforts, and, of course, I don't know you either. However, there is something you should know. I am partisan in that I am interested in the Republican party. It's my party. I'm working for the Republican members of the committee. However, it's my opinion that the worst thing in the world for the Republican party would be for the Republicans on the Watergate committee to play an obstruction role and look like we're covering up the facts. Frankly, I don't think a full field investigation is going to hurt that much. If it does, it will just have to hurt. Of course, I'm interested in the political implications, but our participation in a good, honest, thorough investigation is the best politics I know of. On the other hand, I'm not naive enough to be blind to the prospects of our having a breakdown somewhere along the line and dividing into opposite camps. Nobody knows what will happen. Because of that, the minority staff is going to have to have a separate identity, answerable to me on the staff level. There will be one investigation, but there will be separate identity. That's essential. I'll hire my people and you hire yours. There should be, and I want there to be, full cooperation across the board. If you need minority staff help, you tell me and we'll help. I'll treat you the same way."

Dash appeared relieved that the ice had been broken. He rose and extended his hand. "Fred, I couldn't agree with you more."

At the next committee meeting, when the subject of committee rules was discussed, I pursued the point. The proposed language of a rule stating that all committee staff personnel would be under the direct supervision and control of the chief counsel was inappropriate, I said, in light of the Senate resolution giving one-third of the committee staff to the minority. I said that Dash and I had discussed the matter and had arrived at an understanding. It was the first purely partisan matter that the staff members had brought before the committee members, and all of them turned to Dash. He said he had no objection to the provision's removal, and this began a good working relationship between us. Dash even invited me to attend his interview for his personal secretary, "to demonstrate our bipartisanship." It was a gesture I appreciated, but not one that I reciprocated when it came time to interview candidates for my secretary.

The next few weeks were hectic as Dash and I set out to organize the investigative effort. We spent our days interviewing prospective staff members, often in hallways outside senators' offices, and assimilating all the available Watergate material. At night we brought ourselves up to date on the enormous volume of factual information on Watergate that the press had been printing for months. Also available to us were the transcripts of the trial of the seven original Watergate defendants, along with preliminary work done by Wright Patman's House Banking and Currency Committee on the money-laundering aspect of the case and by Sen. Edward Kennedy's Judiciary Subcommittee. Getting the material from the Kennedy subcommittee proved to be far from simple. Dash would return from a meeting with a Kennedy staff member utterly exasperated. "They're trying to tell me they don't have anything in writing," he would say. "I ask him about a matter, he says he has a card on it. He goes to that card and it leads him to another card. That leads him to a third card, and a fourth, which neither one of us can decipher." An element of Washington gamesmanship was appearing—the effort either by Kennedy or his staff to reap the benefit of his own work. Some preliminary work by other Ervin committees and sub-committees also appeared to be getting to us very slowly.

Edmisten finally moved out of his subcommittee office and turned it over to Dash. I set up shop in the waiting room of that office until another room could be vacated for me. Three of us—my secretary, another staff member, and I—operated from this single desk for several days, in the midst of visitors and reporters waiting for appointments. Since my desk was a few feet away from Dash's secretary's desk, I knew everyone who entered his office and nearly everyone who called him. He, of course, had the same information about me. However, when my office finally became available, I discovered that I had inherited that most precious of all bureaucratic status symbols, something denied to Dash—my own rest room.

Another part of my Washington education was taking place at the same time—finding an apartment. With the aid of nearly every member of Baker's staff, I located one on Capitol Hill, although it pained me to realize that my monthly rent for four small rooms, in a building more than 100 years old, was the same as the monthly payments on my home in suburban Nashville. And the apartment's furniture had apparently been made for midgets: my six-foot-five-inch frame and the five-foot twin bed were not exactly compatible. But the room involved no reporters, no telephone calls, and no interviews, and at times that made it seem palatial.

Watergate may not have seemed like much of an event in Nashville, but I soon discovered that in Washington the scandal and the Watergate committee were the biggest action in town. Applications for staff positions were arriving by the dozen. Members of prestigious law firms, lawyers to other congressional committees with years of experience, men and women with impressive backgrounds in public relations and administration, young dynamos who regarded the Watergate committee as the vehicle that would banish evil from the face of the earth, political hacks out of a job—all applied to work for us. It was my first experience with the concept of overqualification. I interviewed applicants whose qualifications looked far better than mine, but who would be reluctant to put in twelve- to eighteen-hour days for extended periods without seeing their names in the paper once in a while. This type of applicant was passed over. In addition to competence and stamina, I had one all-important criterion, one that I repeated at every interview: "We're going to try our best to have a bipartisan investigation, but if it comes down to the question of 'us' and 'them' I don't want to worry about who is 'us' and who is 'them.' On the staff level, if you don't feel that your ultimate loyalty can be with the minority, just let me know and there will be no hard feelings."

I had nearly exhausted my list of administrative and secretarial applicants when one of Baker's aides recommended Joan Cole, who was then working for Sen. Robert Griffin of Michigan. She had previously worked for Sen. Len Jordan. Joan knew her way around Capitol Hill; she became my invaluable personal secretary and administrative aide, with the important task of keeping me from making mistakes as I whirled through Washington's bureaucratic maze.

A few days later Don Sanders came aboard. Don, 42 years old, had spent ten years with the FBI and four as chief counsel for the House Internal Security Committee. He was quiet, thorough, and professional, and when he assured me that it would not trouble him to work for a man twelve years his junior, he became deputy minority counsel. Sanders was tough, a man who could handle himself in the infighting that seemed to be inherent in any large staff, and this quality became increasingly important as I watched the majority staff take shape; Dash's choices leaned heavily to young aggressive Ivy Leaguers with liberal Democratic credentials. In the eighteen months he spent on the minority staff, Sanders exhibited another trait that constantly helped our work—his age, experience, and demeanor inspired respect (perhaps it was fear) on the part of everyone he dealt with. This is an intangible that does not appear on a job application, but it was vitally needed in dealing with the majority staff, lawyers for witnesses, the press, and members of other Senate staffs.

Two other minority lawyers who left their marks on the investigation, particularly in areas in which the minority took a leading role, were Howard Liebengood and Michael Madigan.

I needed someone whom I knew well and trusted completely. Liebengood, a close friend since our days at Vanderbilt Law School, was with Neal & Harwell, the law firm of Jim Neal, the Watergate prosecutor. Liebengood agreed to leave Nashville and come to Washington. He proved to have an uncanny ability to develop complex factual situations and to remember the smallest details.

Madigan, a red-haired Irishman, had an impressive record as an assistant U.S. attorney in Washington, D.C. "The mad dog," as we dubbed him, was tenacious, and like Liebengood, possessed a keen sense of humor. The three of us, along with Don Sanders, immediately formed a good close working relationship. By September we had hired fifteen members of the minority staff.

One reason that Washington is like few other places is the whole world of staff members. Capitol Hill is a transient society, full of aggressive young staff members on their way up who come together briefly to make their marks in an arena in which political power is often the only measure of one's place on the ladder. Staff members are unbelievably competitive, often pitting themselves against others in the same office. It is mainly a struggle to see who gets closest to "the man"—the senator or House member for whom they work. And because each staff member's future and prestige are directly dependent on the success of his or her employer, there is also constant competition between the staff of Senator A and the staff of Senator B. It amused me at first when I heard three or four staff members in a discussion, each referring to "the senator," and each meaning a different one. In this atmosphere the ability to make use of the next person often spells the difference between success and failure. It's the major leagues, and the game is fast; victory goes to the roughest and most professional. And the rules cannot be learned in a textbook.

A comment made by Baker several months later illustrated a situation we encountered often. We had just left a heated executive session in which I had tangled, somewhat successfully, with one of the brilliant young Turks on Dash's staff. "Pardon me for saying this," Baker said laughingly, "but I don't think he's afraid you'll overpower him with your intellect as much as he's afraid you just might beat the hell out of him."

As our work grew more intense, Dash and I continued to improve on our good working relationship, the importance of which Baker continually impressed on me. Each morning we met to discuss the progress of organizing the staff and the assignments we were giving to the people we hired. Our aim was to assimilate all the existing information, bring ourselves up-to-date, interview all necessary witnesses, follow the leads produced from the interviews, subpoena all relevant documents—in other words, to follow an orderly building-block approach. That is the way it is taught in the books, and we thought we were doing fine until, as so often happens, events overtook us.

The swift change began on Friday morning, March 23, 1973.

I was leaving Baker's office, on my way to the airport for a long-overdue weekend at home. I saw a young man run up to a Senate staff member in the hall and ask if he had heard about the McCord "bombshell."

It was the day of James McCord's sentencing, and we had considered it a routine matter. McCord had pleaded not guilty to breaking into the Democratic National Committee headquarters; he had declined to take the stand and had given no indication that he possessed any significant information, or at least any information that he was willing to talk about. Now, as I heard from scattered bits of conversation, he had given federal Judge John Sirica a letter stating that he had been pressured to plead guilty and that he was willing to name others implicated in the Watergate break-in.

I threw my bags back into my office, ran out and hailed a cab to the United States Courthouse. When I left the elevator on the fourth floor, I saw a huge throng huddling outside Sirica's courtroom, all trying to peer inside. I identified myself to the guard at the door and was allowed to join those standing inside. The proceedings had just ended and the place was in turmoil. I verified the story with a reporter who was rushing to a telephone, and made my way to the front.

Gerald Alch, one of McCord's attorneys, appeared to be in a state of shock. I asked Alch if McCord would talk to us, and Alch muttered that he might. "Maybe later," Alch said. "I need to talk to him myself." McCord's lawyer was as surprised as everyone else. I noticed that Dash had also arrived; he was on the other side of the room, talking to a lawyer for one of the other defendants. He was getting the same shocked reaction.

Dash and I left the building together and shared a cab back to our offices. "Sam," I said, "I hate to leave now but if I don't get home this weekend you might have to start looking for a new minority counsel." I said I would be back on Monday, and we agreed to make no further contact with any of the lawyers for the principal Watergate defendants until the following week, when we could both be present.

That Sunday, March 25, I was sitting at the kitchen table at my home in Nashville, having my second cup of coffee and contemplating the work that had to be done in the yard, when the phone rang. It was Dash. Bernard Fensterwald, another McCord attorney, had contacted Dash. Dash, McCord, and Fensterwald had met, and I would get a full report the next day. Dash said he had received Ervin's permission to issue a statement about the meeting. I thanked Dash for keeping me informed and said I would see him early the next day. I was somewhat surprised that he was to issue a statement, but since he said he had Ervin's approval I assumed that this was proper procedure and that Ervin had been in touch with Baker.

I soon learned that my assumptions were incorrect. Less than an hour later the phone rang again, and this time it was Baker. "Fred," he asked, "did you know that McCord has been talking to Dash?" I told him of my conversation with Dash. "Well," Baker said, with more than a touch of annoyance in his voice, "he didn't issue a statement, he called a press conference."

"Did he have Ervin's permission for that?" I asked.

"I don't know," Baker said, "but I'm going to find out. When are you coming back?" That usually meant he wanted to see me as soon as possible.

"First thing in the morning."

"Fine. Let's get together first thing in the morning."

By the time I reached Baker's office, he had already arranged a meeting in Ervin's office with Ervin and Dash. For his "press conference" on Sunday afternoon, Dash apparently had called the few members of the Capitol Hill press corps who were then available and told them that he had met with McCord and Fensterwald; Dash said that McCord had given significant information and had "named names."

But there was far more than that in the *Los Angeles Times* that Monday morning: there was a full account of what Mc-Cord supposedly had told Dash. According to the report, Mc-Cord said that John Dean, former Nixon counsel, and Jeb Magruder, deputy director of Nixon's reelection committee, had had advance knowledge of the Watergate bugging operation. It was apparent that this leak—the first major one of dozens that were to flow from the committee—had not helped Baker's disposition as we walked silently from his office, through the tunnel under First Street, to Ervin's office in the Old Senate Office Building.

Dash was in Ervin's office when we arrived. It had not been a pleasant morning for him. Reporters who had not been at the press conference were doubly furious; not only had they missed it, they also apparently suspected Dash of leaking the substance of the McCord interview to the *Los Angeles Times*. They had let Dash know how they felt; now many of them had learned of the Ervin-Baker meeting, and there was a group outside Ervin's door when we arrived.

Ervin, although affable as usual, seemed ill at ease. In my brief encounters with him up to this time, I had come to have affection for the old gentleman. As a law student and a practicing lawyer, I admired his stands on behalf of the rights of individuals in the face of expanding Washington big-brotherism. I knew that some Capitol Hill veterans questioned his press reputation as a great constitutionalist, but I nevertheless believed that I had met an institution as well as a man.

As I was to learn later, Ervin, like many people in public life, has more than one personality. On a personal, informal level, no one could be more charming and unassuming; and no one could tell a joke better. Less than five minutes after we met, I said something that reminded him of a North Carolina farmer. He used the analogy so many times to so many people in the next eighteen months that I concluded that two-thirds of the population of North Carolina must be farmers, with each of them good for at least one story. Ervin was in excellent condition, with remarkable stamina for a man 76 years old. Only his magnificently gnarled hands indicated his age. Frequently he would tell a joke bordering on the off-color, and he would be unable to control his laughter before he finished; the next minute he would furrow his brow, gaze at the ceiling, and cite a line of cases dating back a century to substantiate a legal proposition.

As Baker said later, "Sam is the only man I know who can read the transcript of a telephone conversation and make it sound like the King James version of the New Testament, or speak on abstract constitutional doctrine and the philosophical writings of the Founding Fathers with such authority that you almost suspect he just rode up from Charlottesville with them in his saddlebags."

On that Monday morning, however, things were not serene. Baker, Dash, and I sat in a semicircle in front of Ervin's desk, and Baker spoke directly to Dash. He said there would have to be some changes in the staff's method of operation; he was not going to tolerate getting from a newspaperman his first information on a significant committee development. Baker told Dash the news conference the previous day had been a mistake.

"Senator," Dash interjected, "I received permission from Senator Ervin to make a statement about the matter."

"Yes," Baker replied, barely allowing Dash to finish his sentence, "but you didn't leave it at that. You called a press conference and now it's all over the newspapers this morning." I had never seen Baker this tough; he kept leaning farther and farther forward in his chair as he made his points. "From now on," he said to Dash, "I want an assurance that no staffer will call a press conference. If that's going to be done, it should be done by members of the committee."

Dash replied, "Senator, you're right. It was a mistake. And I want to assure you that as far as I'm concerned, it will never happen again."

I sympathized with Dash. We both now realized that we were in a completely new situation, and an action that might be appropriate in federal court in Nashville or in a committee of the American Bar Association was not necessarily appropriate in dealing with seven senators and the toughest, most tenacious reporters in the country—particularly when every step might have legal and political ramifications.

The air had been cleared for the moment. Ervin had been obviously uncomfortable while Baker spoke, but he fully agreed with him. Ervin, however, was known to be unusually solicitous of his staff members. He voiced general concurrence with Baker's sentiments and said he was sure we could all work in harmony from then on. Shortly afterward, Baker and I left.

Half a dozen reporters gathered around us in the hall, wanting to know what had gone on in the meeting. All of them, aside from those from the *Los Angeles Times,* had heard from their superiors that morning and they appeared eager for anything that was anti-Dash. "What about Dash's press conference?" they asked. "What about the leak? What did you say to Dash?" As I followed him down the hall, Baker would say only that he had full confidence in Dash and that he was not going to criticize the chief counsel. As the elevator door shut, he mentioned that there would be some "procedural changes."

Walking back to his office, Baker had little to say about the matter but appeared relaxed and in good humor. The meeting not only set the tone for his relationship with Dash, it also defined more precisely his position with Ervin, which had always been good. Baker had always deferred to Ervin, his senior by almost thirty years, but that morning he had chewed out Ervin's man, in Ervin's presence. More important, he had followed that by defending Dash to the press. The message was not lost on either Ervin or Dash.

That afternoon at an executive session, all seven members of the committee were present. Underneath the usual good-natured kidding and small talk, excitement was in the air. The leak of McCord's interview was relatively insignificant when weighed against the information that McCord might be willing to give. It was the first solid indication that Watergate indeed might turn out to be something more than a "third-rate burglary," and if McCord's intention was to entice the committee to get at his testimony, he had succeeded admirably. There was a quick consensus that Dash and I should meet with McCord as soon as possible. It was suggested that Judge Sirica might be asked to postpone McCord's sentencing until we had interviewed him in detail. That idea made me uneasy; in my experience, federal judges did not appreciate unilateral contact of

*Senator Ervin, Sam Dash, Senator Baker, and I meet in Ervin's Office to set up committee ground rules. The ability of Ervin and Baker to work together was of vital importance throughout the Watergate investigation.*

THE NEW YORK TIMES/GEORGE TAMES

any kind. I expressed my view and Sen. Daniel Inouye agreed. We would proceed separately and hope for the best.

Later that night Dash and I met in his office at Georgetown Law School, the interview site that Dash had arranged with Fensterwald for McCord. With us was Harold Lipset, Dash's chief investigator. Lipset, one of the first people hired by Dash, had a reputation as a topflight private investigator; he was supposedly the inventor of the bug-in-the-martini-olive, and Dash had met Lipset while researching his book on eavesdropping. Lipset was friendly and easygoing, with an ample supply of expensive cigars in his breast pocket that I often took advantage of. I considered him the epitome of the inner-city private eye; he was the "let's cut out the crap" type.

McCord was late. While waiting, we experienced the same

anticipatory excitement that had been evident earlier at the committee meeting. What if McCord changed his mind? What does he know? Did his shift of attorneys to Fensterwald, who was best known in Washington as a conspiracy buff and head of the Committee to Investigate Assassinations, have any significance?

Finally, nearly an hour behind schedule, McCord and Fensterwald arrived. Fensterwald, a small and rather debonair man, appeared friendly but somewhat restrained when I introduced myself. McCord seemed even more restrained, even toward Dash, whom he had met before. Having seen several unflattering newspaper pictures of McCord, I was surprised to discover that he could pass for an insurance salesman, or even a Sunday school teacher, not the sort of man who could change history.

Fensterwald, maintaining his soft, low-key approach, told us that the leak of McCord's interview with Dash had caused him severe problems. If "certain elements" were told in advance what McCord would say, they could prepare their defenses and attempt to discredit him, he said. They didn't want to talk to us; they would speak to the full committee or not at all. Dash insisted that he had not leaked the information. Since Fensterwald's approach implied that it was Republicans, especially those associated with the reelection committee, who might be damaged by McCord's testimony and might seek to discredit it, I asked if the real reason for his refusal to be interviewed was my presence.

Fensterwald turned in his chair, paused for a minute, and said, "Well, actually, yes, that's it."

I said, "Okay, what if I agree to leave the interview and let Dash ask the questions?" I had no intention of leaving, but I was interested in his answer. Fensterwald appeared surprised by the suggestion, and he replied that well, that would not resolve all of McCord's problems.

"We'll just meet before the full committee," he said.

I decided to spare him my "I'm just interested in a bipartisan investigation" line because it was apparent that these two men had other ideas. McCord sat silently for the most part, with his arms folded, giving quick glances at Fensterwald, then Dash, then me, as though he were in a subway full of pickpockets.

The idea that an appearance before the full committee would prevent leaks was one of the most ludicrous I had heard, but I began to detect Fensterwald's strategy. The first McCord interview had been staged to set up Dash. Either McCord or his associates had leaked the substance of the interview to the press in order to make McCord irresistible to the committee. In addition, the sequence of events gave Fensterwald an excuse to demand an audience with the full committee, a meeting that would cause the public, and perhaps Sirica as well, to attach even more importance to McCord's testimony.

We were thus exposed to the committee's first "irresistible witness," one whose information was so important that he might receive special concessions to give it: immunity from prosecution perhaps, or favorable publicity, or a more lenient sentence as the one who "broke the case." Dash's interview with McCord, and the publicity that followed it, had whetted the committee's appetite, and McCord and Fensterwald knew that the committee would come back for the second course.

The following morning, in executive session, the committee swallowed the bait; it was unanimously agreed that McCord should appear before the committee the next day. That night the staff went over every shred of information we had that pertained to McCord or that McCord might illuminate. At the morning session, Ervin advised the committee of the death of his brother in North Carolina, and said he was leaving immediately for the funeral. It was apparent that he wanted to delay any action until he returned, but the committee's sentiment was to move immediately.

It was almost standing room only in Ervin's office the next morning. Six senators were present, and each had brought along at least one staff member; several members of Dash's staff were present as well. The committee members, Dash, and I sat around a long table facing McCord at the other end; other staff members filled most of the room.

In Ervin's absence, Baker presided. First Dash and I would interrogate the witness, then each senator would pose questions. In the interview, which lasted four and a half hours, McCord said that Gordon Liddy (a former White House aide and counsel of the Committee to Re-elect the President) had told him that John Mitchell (former attorney general and CRP director) had approved the bugging plan and that Jeb Magruder and John Dean had prior knowledge of it. He gave details of his involvement in the operation and of the planning for the entry at Democratic headquarters. His testimony was damaging, but the parts of it that incriminated Mitchell, Magruder, and Dean were all hearsay, from Liddy. Most of us had heard Liddy stories—how he once held his hand over a candle, burning himself severely, to impress a woman companion; and how he had life-sized posters showing him leading a raid in his days as a district attorney in New York state. Liddy might not be the most credible witness around, but he certainly had been in a position to know a lot.

Baker, perhaps surprised by the turnout and seeing the handwriting on the wall, concluded the session by admonishing everyone in the room that the information we had heard was to be held in the strictest confidence; he recited the committee's rules on the subject. McCord, in his testimony, had read from a written statement and had given a copy of it to the committee. As everyone was getting ready to leave, Baker asked if there were any other copies. Fensterwald said there was only one, which he had given to Edmisten before the meeting, when Edmisten escorted Fensterwald and McCord to Ervin's office. Edmisten said he had returned the copy to Fensterwald during the meeting, but Fensterwald said he did not recall getting it back. There was an awkward silence, after which Baker instructed everyone to look for it. For the next few minutes, senators, lawyers, and other staff members opened their briefcases and their jackets, all proclaiming their innocence. Finally Baker, looking somewhat exasperated, said, "All right. Rufus, it seems to be between you and Mr. Fensterwald. I want each of you to hold up your right hand. I'm going to put you under oath." Edmisten's hand went up in a flash, but Fensterwald was still fumbling in his jacket. Finally, from the recesses of an inner pocket Fensterwald pulled out the missing document and turned it over to Baker.

The senator could have saved himself the trouble. The press had gathered outside the office all day, and each time the committee recessed for a Senate vote the reporters spread like a covey of quail, each one focusing on the senator or staff member deemed most likely to reveal what McCord was saying. The next morning the front page of the *Washington Post* carried the full story of McCord's testimony, complete with all his accusations. The fact that his information was mostly hearsay was alluded to only briefly.

This account of the McCord interview seemed to set off a chain reaction in the press corps. It began a procedure that lasted for months, in which a group of reporters would perch doggedly outside even the most insignificant committee meeting, and every news gatherer would feverishly seek to establish a "contact" within the committee. Every reporter needed an exclusive story every day. Each of them had an apoplectic editor who hated to be scooped, and many of them indicated they would be fired if they didn't get their share of leaks.

I watched this performance with disbelief. No one seemed even to consider that the committee's rules strictly forbade the dissemination of information, not to mention the inherent unfairness of spreading damaging hearsay statements across the nation's front pages. Several times, as the investigation continued, a witness would appear before a grand jury and give testimony; had a grand juror made it public, he would have been subject to imprisonment for a criminal offense. The same witness would come before our committee or staff with the same information, and the damaging facts would be solicited by reporters and provided by an investigator with impunity, with the evidence appearing in print the following day.

Some senators wanted good press relations. Some staff members, accustomed to anonymity at the low level of a huge law firm, were flattered by the attention they were receiving from the big names in the news media. Before long, reporters had advance notice of interviews that were to be held. A few times I was called to confirm a change in the site of an interview before I knew there had been a change.

All this was foreign territory to me, and I found it hard to adjust. During my three years as an assistant United States attorney I had presented evidence in numerous cases to grand juries, and our office was involved in hundreds. I saw reporters nearly every day, on the job and at social functions, and never had there been a leak from one of my cases.

In addition to leaks, I was bothered by occasional sarcastic comments from Republicans about our "bipartisan investigation." The language varied, but the implication was clear: "The Democrats on the committee are doing a hatchet job on us and you're just sitting there."

At this stage of the investigation the press was the power broker—the only benchmark the public had to evaluate the performance of the senators and the staff members. From this feverish jockeying for position, it was inevitable that a man came forward who felt destined to occupy center stage—Sen. Lowell Weicker of Connecticut.

The tenor of my relationship with Weicker was set on the first day we met, shortly after my arrival in Washington. I went to his office to pay my respects and become acquainted. I was operating under the theory that, even though Baker had been responsible for my appointment, I was representing all three minority senators—Baker, Edward Gurney of Florida, and Weicker. If differences arose within the minority there was no question about where my loyalty lay and whose directions I would take, but I believed that I should try to respond to the wishes of Weicker and Gurney in every possible way.

As I entered Weicker's office I noticed that he had summoned one of his aides to join us. His handshake was firm; there was no smile. It is always a momentary shock to meet someone as tall as I or taller, and Weicker and I are almost exactly the same height. I wondered if he had a similar sensation. I had expected my call to be a brief social call, but it turned out to be a Weicker lecture. We had to push this investigation farther and harder than the Democrats; it was the only way we could come out with a plus. If we allowed the Democrats to take the lead, they would screw us and also get the credit. Ervin was too old to be chairman and he was a partisan first and foremost. Weicker spoke rapidly, gesturing for emphasis.

I agreed that we had to pursue the investigation vigorously and in good faith, and said I did not know that anyone had suggested otherwise.

After I left Weicker's office I wondered if this was his true nature or whether he had staged a special performance for me. Was he trying to impress me with his toughness? Did he think I was there to do the bidding of the White House? Or perhaps it was just a matter of personality.

Weicker was the son of a wealthy industrialist. He grew up on Park Avenue and developed a fondness for opera. I was told later by a staff member that after I left his office that day he remarked, "Did you see what he was wearing—cowboy boots! He's got a lot of brass coming to see me with cowboy boots on." Actually they were not cowboy boots, but they were shoes not often seen on Park Avenue or in Yale secret societies. I was also told that prior to our first meeting he had had a report prepared on me and my background. His informants were former employees of Ray Blanton, a congressman I had worked against in two campaigns. One man's dossier is another man's report, I mused.

Our relationship did not improve significantly in the weeks that followed. I read in the *Washington Post* one morning that he was going to conduct his own independent investigation and was hiring a special staff for the job.

An arrangement was worked out with Richard Kleindienst, then the attorney general, that Ervin, Baker, Dash, and I would have access to raw FBI data. As a result, Dash and I began to spend several hours a day at the Justice Department, checking these files. Weicker was angry from the start that he had been denied similar access, and I would visit his office periodically to brief him on any significant revelations that we were turning up. At a meeting with Ervin, Baker, Dash, and me, Kleindienst insisted on strict safeguards of the FBI material, known in the Bureau as FD-302s. Having dealt with them as a federal prosecutor, I knew the damage that could arise from the dissemination of material from raw FBI files. Ervin readily agreed to the restrictions as reasonable.

Shortly after we began to examine the FBI files, Bill Wickens approached me in the Senate Office Building. He was heading Weicker's independent investigation, having been loaned from Sen. Robert Taft's office. After reading of his appointment, I told Wickens that the committee staff would conduct the investigation and that what he did for Weicker was not my business, but that if he ever developed anything significant that he wanted to pass on to the committee staff, we would be glad to listen. This did not seem to please him, and we had had no contact for several days. But on this occasion he said he was chasing a hot lead and gave me the names of two people who had been interviewed by the FBI. "I need to know what's in their 302s but I can't tell you why or give you any details right now," he said.

I laughed and walked away, heading directly for Baker's office. I described the conversation to Baker and told him he could expect a call from Weicker. Within an hour Weicker was in Baker's office complaining about my failure to cooperate with his people. Baker told Weicker what Wickens had told me: that he could not tell me anything about why he needed my help. That fact was news to Weicker, and he said it shed a different light on the matter. After the meeting, Baker told me about it, pointing out that this would probably be a continuing problem, but that I should do my best to get along with Wickens.

Meanwhile, Weicker was issuing public statements that were getting good coverage in the press. On March 27, the *Washington Post* quoted him as saying he had "independently established" facts showing that White House aides were involved in the Watergate bugging as well as other espionage activities, and that preliminary information alone "is sufficient to come forth with some sort of sensational disclosures." Similar comments were attributed to "sources familiar with the Weicker inquiry." *The New York Times* quoted Weicker as saying that, although he was sure the president had nothing to hide, he had always been convinced that others in the White House knew of political espionage.

At this time, Ervin and Baker were negotiating with John Ehrlichman, Nixon's former chief domestic affairs advisor, on the ground rules under which White House aides might testify before the committee. Nixon had announced that none of his aides would testify and that he would invoke the doctrine of executive privilege. The committee, in response, unanimously backed the position—one that I considered correct—that executive privilege did not apply to matters involving possible criminal conduct. The senators believed that, because of the committee's united front and other publicity unfavorable to the White House, the president appeared to be relenting. Ervin and Baker were both convinced that Ehrlichman was acting in good faith, and that he was urging the president to compromise.

In parallel secret negotiations with Leonard Garment, Nixon's lawyer, Dash and I were receiving the same impression. We met periodically with Garment in the stately Blair House across from the White House, where dignitaries are housed while visiting Washington on official business. I was discovering the truth of what Baker had told me about Garment: the so-called White House liberal was a capable, fairminded man whose instincts were probably telling him that the committee's legal position was correct. The major point that I kept pressing with Garment was that there could be no halfway position on the testimony of White House aides once a prima facie case of wrongdoing was established; such persons must testify completely. "If the members of the committee ask a White House aide, before a nationwide television audience, if he and the president discussed plans to break into the Watergate and you claim executive privilege for that answer because it's a private communication with the president, you're ruined," I said, although I was sure he didn't need to have that pointed out to him. If the White House had any idea that I would be its defender within the committee, I thought, the negotiations with Garment must have dispelled the notion.

Although Dash and I seemed to be making progress in our meetings with Garment, the press leaks and public statements like Weicker's were a hindrance; they were constantly cited to us as evidence of the committee's bad faith. Ervin and Baker were also aware of the impact of these incidents on the committee's credibility. On one occasion Ervin said, "Well, Howard, it looks like some of our brethren are having a little trouble restraining themselves." Then the two senators moved away to discuss the situation privately.

Two days after McCord's testimony to the committee had been leaked, the *Washington Star* added a new dimension to our problem: it reported that McCord had told the committee that Charles Colson, another White House aide, also knew of the plans to break into the Watergate. In this instance, the report was hearsay twice removed, since McCord was quoting Liddy quoting Magruder quoting Colson.

That same afternoon, I received a call from Dick McGowan, Weicker's former press secretary, who was on special assignment to Weicker during the Watergate investigation. He asked about a new development in our inquiry. In his testimony to the committee, McCord said Liddy had told him of meetings in the office of Attorney General John Mitchell at which Liddy, Dean, and Magruder had discussed plans for political espionage. McCord said Liddy had also reported that he prepared a large chart to explain his operational plans to Mitchell; McCord said that Sally Harmony and Sylvia Panarites, both reelection campaign secretaries, might have seen Liddy's charts. In addition, we were aware that Robert Reisner, Magruder's aide, logged Magruder's appointments and thus might be aware of the meetings with Dean and Mitchell. As chairman of the committee in Ervin's absence, Baker instructed me to issue subpoenas to Harmony, Panarites, and Reisner. The other members of the committee were notified and Lipset and Sanders were directed to serve the subpoenas.

McGowan was calling to verify that the subpoenas had been issued, and I told him they had. That information appeared in the *Washington Post* the following morning, and I learned later that it reached the news media within forty-five minutes of my conversation with McGowan. The disclosure, of course, meant that the witnesses could be contacted by the press, friends, and relatives, not to mention former personnel of the reelection committee who might be damaged by their testimony.

The leak infuriated me. I told Joan Cole, my secretary, to call McGowan and give him the following information: that two of the three subpoenas had been served the previous night and that one had not, and that the witnesses were to appear the following Wednesday, April 4, at 1:30 P.M. Actually, none of the subpoenas had been served at the time, and they called for the witnesses to appear the following Monday, April 2. I did not consider the erroneous information sufficiently significant to cause problems if reported in the press.

Hours later, at 1:43 P.M., the following dispatch was moved by the Associated Press:

WASHINGTON (AP)—Convicted Watergate conspirator James W. McCord told Senate investigators that Presidential Aide H. R. Haldeman "had to be aware" of plans to wiretap Democratic national headquarters, a source close to the Senate Watergate investigation said today.

The source also said that McCord had refused to answer four or five questions about possible involvement in other espionage activities on grounds of possible self-incrimination, during a 4½-hour appearance before the committee Wednesday.

Meanwhile, subpoenas were served Thursday night on two former employees of President Nixon's re-election campaign committee as part of the panel's check on McCord testimony about the alleged involvement of high White House officials in the Watergate bugging. Efforts by federal marshals to serve a third former employee of the committee were unsuccessful, the source said. The witnesses were ordered to appear next Wednesday afternoon.

Not only was the information that I had provided to Mc-Gowan reported in full, the same "source" had evidently added yet another dimension to McCord's testimony—that McCord said Haldeman "had to be aware" of the wiretapping plans.

The reference to Haldeman apparently was based on a question by Weicker, who asked McCord if the witness felt Haldeman "knew what was going on at the Committee to Re-elect." McCord's answer was yes. The question, as posed, could have covered Haldeman's knowledge of anything from the bugging operation to the possessers of washroom keys; the answer did not indicate that Haldeman had prior knowledge of illegal activity. In fact, as we learned later, McCord had no idea of Haldeman's knowledge of the bugging plans. Based on the information we had, the conclusion was worthless and unfair, but it made a good story.

I decided to take the weekend to ponder the problem. Reading the Sunday papers in my apartment, I could see that a lot of people were still hard at work. *The New York Times,* apparently having found more responsible "sources," quoted some of them as saying that McCord had said that Haldeman was fully aware of the espionage operations, and others who said that Weicker merely asked if Haldeman knew McCord was working for the committee and if Haldeman knew what was going on. *The Times* also reported that Weicker's independent investigation had carried him to his home state of Connecticut to interview Alfred Baldwin, the burglars' lookout on the night of the break-in. The *Washington Star* had a front-page story, based on "Senate sources," that cited apparent contradictions between McCord's testimony and testimony that Mitchell had given earlier. Had I been in a less sour mood, I might have been amused when I saw on another page in the same newspaper a column headed "Panel's Credibility Is Endangered," a reference to the events of the last few days.

The following morning I went to Weicker's office and gave him a full account of my dealings with McGowan. The senator seemed somewhat taken aback, not so much by the information as by the fact that I would confront him with it. "Well," he said, "McGowan's not a lawyer, and I'm sure he didn't know that this information about the witnesses was not to be given out." He summoned McGowan to his office. "As a matter of fact," Weicker went on, "I'm a lawyer and I didn't know that myself." I pointed out that the committee had rules on the subject and that I assumed anyone working with the committee knew the rules. I had not thought, I said, that a rule was necessary to point out the problems inherent in releasing to the press the names of prospective witnesses. McGowan, angry, declared that Joan Cole had told him he could make the information public. "Well, there you are," Weicker said, his voice rising. "Come on now, let's be fair about this thing. She told him he could release it."

I knew this was not so, but I saw no need to prolong the discussion. It was pointless to observe that McGowan was undoubtedly the source of the Haldeman information as well. As I left the meeting, I realized that I had been naive to believe that I could force a senator to muzzle one of his aides or to temper his own comments. I knew now that I would not be called by Weicker's office again to supply information, but I also knew that I could abandon hope of improving my relations with Weicker. But I believed action was necessary to curb what James Reston of *The New York Times* called "trial by leak and hearsay"—especially when I had been used as part of the practice.

The next day Weicker continued his attack, calling publicly for Haldeman's resignation. That afternoon, while I was conferring with Baker, a messenger came in with the draft of a press release. Apparently prepared by Ervin, who wanted Baker's concurrence, it said that the committee had no information indicating that Haldeman was guilty of any "improprieties or illegalities." Baker agreed to join in the statement, but he had a problem; he had to catch a plane and he wanted to advise Weicker in advance of its release. I volunteered for the job and went directly to Weicker's office to inform him and to explain why Baker could not tell him personally.

Weicker understood immediately that the statement was directed at him because of his remarks. He seemed surprised but not angry, as I had expected; it was more that his feelings were bruised. "I guess I know when I've been zapped," he said.

Amid the bombshells, the leaks, and the crossfire, our staff was taking shape. One of Dash's assistantships was given to Terry Lenzner, 33, a former assistant United States attorney in New York who had helped convict Bill Bonanno, the crime syndicate heir. He was best known in Washington for his short, unhappy stint as head of the Office of Legal Services for the antipoverty program in 1969 and 1970. Lenzner had been dismissed from that job after an internal dispute, and he departed with an attack on the president: "The Nixon administration has made it clear that it will trade the right of the poor to justice for potential voters." He had also worked as defense counsel for the Berrigan brothers. Lenzner and I viewed each other with mutual suspicion, but our personal relations were usually good. We got along well enough to engage in some mutual ribbing. "Terry," I would say, "with your background you certainly ought to be an objective investigator of this administration. I understand that Helen Gahagan Douglas will be your chief assistant." He would mutter something about the consequences of "hillbillies coming north."

One of the investigating team was a near-legend: Carmine Bellino, 67, who had spent twenty-five years working for a number of congressional committees. He was an intimate of the Kennedys, and he was known particularly for helping Robert Kennedy in the anti-James Hoffa campaign. Bellino appeared easygoing and kindly in private conversation, but he gave me the impression that inside he was tough as a pine knot. He was seldom seen, and he conducted his part of the investigation—

33

accounting was his specialty—by himself. He had his own contacts and never appeared to be disturbed by the whiz kids young enough to be his grandchildren.

Bill Shure joined our minority staff on the recommendation of Weicker, whom he had served as a political aide. Baker had urged me to accommodate Weicker whenever possible, and I hired Shure on his assurance that he would consider himself part of the minority team. Shure was able and intelligent; he could dictate a memorandum and brief Weicker and me with extraordinary speed and competence. But the problem of divided loyalty was constant.

As the staff grew, bureaucratic difficulties developed. Each staff member seemed to be going in his own direction. Interviews would not be written up for several days, and investigators were scheduling interviews without notifying anyone else on the staff. Such a practice could be disastrous to the minority: with only a third of the total staff, it was all we could do to monitor majority-staff interviews under ideal conditions. We were constantly concerned that information was being withheld from us, either deliberately or because of inept coordination. Don Sanders was particularly upset. The FBI, where he had worked for years, had ironclad procedures and schedules for conducting interviews, putting them in writing, and distributing them to the appropriate personnel. At my suggestion, Sanders prepared a memorandum outlining these procedures in detail, and I took it to Dash, urging its immediate adoption. I also asked for an understanding that the minority staff be notified of every interview scheduled by the majority, and I said that our staff would reciprocate. Both staffs met, and the new system was put into effect. We were finally achieving order.

The investigation was divided into three categories: the Watergate break-in and its aftermath, "dirty tricks" and political espionage, and campaign finances. Staff members were assigned to each area, with individuals on the majority and minority staffs designated to keep their counterparts advised of developments. A card system was set up, listing the name of a witness and the date of his interview, its dictation, its transcription, and its distribution. Dash and I kept master files of all interviews.

As the daily interview reports crossed my desk, I began to understand the significance of McCord's testimony. Sylvia Panarites, a reelection campaign secretary through February 1972, remembered a meeting attended by Liddy, Mitchell, and Magruder. She also remembered seeing a wrapped package, four feet by three feet, that Liddy secreted in his office and forbade her to look at. It sounded like it was the chart that Liddy supposedly used for what Dash called the show-and-tell presentation to Mitchell. In addition, Lenzner had discovered that Reisner's log and the appointment book of Vickie Chern (another Magruder aide who worked in the reception room) indicated that Magruder had met with Mitchell, Dean, and Liddy on the dates mentioned by McCord. Sally Harmony, the Liddy secretary whose first interview had produced little, was questioned a second time. Sanders had received an anonymous call that she had additional information, that she was upset and was seeking advice from others who worked for the reelection committee. At the second interview Harmony remembered typing transcripts of conversations given to her by Liddy on paper that had "Gemstone" written across the top. The conversations appeared to be the result of wiretaps.

The investigation was beginning to take on shape and substance. Interviews were scheduled with all the major and secondary officials of the reelection committee, as well as with their secretaries. There was one more leak—on April 11 the *New York Daily News* reported that "Senate investigators" had a witness to corroborate McCord's testimony that Mitchell and Dean met to discuss plans for the Watergate break-in. After the massive hemorrhage of information two weeks earlier, however, this seemed like no more than a cut finger.

Just as it appeared that we had weathered our first heavy storm and were moving calmly, there was another thunderclap. On April 13 it became known that Lipset, our chief investigator of illegal electronic surveillance, had himself been con-

victed of the same crime—illegal electronic surveillance—in
New York in 1966. Edmisten nearly ran through the door of his
office to type Lipset's resignation.

Dash, who knew of the prior conviction, came under heavy
fire from all sides. Edmisten, one of whose primary jobs was to
protect Ervin from embarrassment, was particularly critical.
The day after Lipset resigned, Edmisten went to Baker and
suggested other dire consequences; but Baker telephoned Dash
to express his confidence, and the minority staff was given the
word that there would be no comments on the matter. The
excitement ended quickly, and we returned to work. Some of
the columnists who had denounced our early efforts were
beginning to speak of a "determined smooth inquiry."

On April 17, Nixon summoned the White House press corps to
announce that "major developments" had been uncovered by
an investigation that the president himself had conducted.
Nixon, who had stated on March 15 that no member of his staff
would be permitted to testify before our committee, now said
that "all members of the White House staff will appear voluntarily." And he noted that Ervin, Baker, Dash, and I had been
meeting with White House aides to work out the details. The
announcement took us completely by surprise; although we
believed that our negotiations were making progress, there had
not been so much as a phone call from the White House to
indicate any change of position or to check on details of the
agreement to prevent a possible misunderstanding later. Baker
was in the Soviet Union at the time, on business of the Joint
Atomic Energy Committee.

Nixon's reference to "major developments" turned out to be
an understatement. Through the press, we all learned that the
action now was centered on the Watergate grand jury. Magruder was said to have testified that Mitchell and Dean had approved and helped to plan the Watergate bugging operation.
Television film showed a broken John Mitchell entering the
grand jury room, where he reportedly admitted that he, Liddy,
Dean, and Magruder had discussed bugging operations but
that Mitchell had dismissed the entire plan. This story was in-

consistent with his prior position, and it struck me that he was about as likely to be believed as if he had walked out of the grand jury room carrying a "Rap Brown for President" poster on a stick. Speculation in the press had it that Haldeman was in possibly serious trouble, along with Ehrlichman, Colson, Fred LaRue (a former White House aide and Mitchell's assistant at CRP), Gordon Strachan, and others.

Nixon announced that no one would receive immunity from prosecution, whereupon Dean issued a press statement that he would not be made a "scapegoat." The word we were getting on Capitol Hill was that the White House staff was in turmoil, with each member pointing a finger at someone else. At almost the same time, our own interviews confirmed that all was not well on Pennsylvania Avenue. Bart Porter, a reelection committee staff member, told us of Magruder's attempt to have Porter perjure himself at the trial of the Watergate burglars in connection with the money paid to Liddy. It was also becoming increasingly clear that Strachan, Haldeman's top aide, had probably received reports on the buggings and dirty tricks operations. The focus had turned to the cover-up aspect of the case: Amid all the excitement and pressure, my first, small-minded reaction was that I didn't know which I resented more, the White House culpability or the fact that Weicker was being proven correct about Haldeman.

I had additional misgivings. The more I examined the FBI data, the more I wondered about the adequacy of the federal investigation. Why had there been no follow-up interviews of witnesses as additional material was gathered? Why were those accused by Magruder called by the grand jury before he was? Was there an effort to discredit his testimony? It took no legal genius to draw conclusions from the fact that the president appoints the attorney general and that the attorney general controls all United States attorneys.

Attorneys for both Dean and Magruder contacted Dash, describing their clients' stories in general terms. As Dash passed the information to me privately, Dean's position began to become clear: he had told Nixon material facts about the break-in shortly after it occurred. On the night of April 25 I wrote in my journal: "The focus is on the president now. The word 'impeachment' is beginning to creep into Capitol Hill conversation. A Gallup poll shows that about a third of the American people believe he 'knew.' Many believe the entire White House staff will go. The key issue is now crystallized: when did the president first know? Presumably after the break-in."

All these events had a devastating impact on administration loyalists, and I had considered myself a member of that group. At home for the weekend, tossing pebbles into the black waters of my little creek one night, I thought of the U.S. attorney's office in Nashville, where my office wall carried my certificate of appointment, signed by Attorney General John N. Mitchell. I remembered all the restrictions that had been placed on us, justifiably, to prevent even the appearance of impropriety. And then I had to live with the fact that the head of the United States Department of Justice had sat in his office and entertained plans for political espionage.

My wife and I, raised in Democratic families, became Republicans in the mid-1960s primarily because we thought our new party respected the law and our national institutions and because it stood for integrity of the individual and the decentralization of power, not the absorption of power in the hands of a few. And now, I thought, the party in which we had invested so much time and faith was being irreparably damaged because a few people had betrayed the very principles that we considered the foundation of Republicanism.

For the first time I began to think the unthinkable: Could the president himself have been aware of the break-in? Could he have participated in, perhaps even directed, the cover-up? If Haldeman was indeed Nixon's alter ego, would he not have found out what had gone on and relayed to the president everything he learned? For a Republican loyalist, those were no longer idle thoughts; they were matters of profound concern.

It now appeared that we were going to set out on at least several weeks of public hearings under the most intense national scrutiny. I had to reexamine my own role in the proceedings; until then I had been comfortable with the notion that there was no White House involvement, and that an intense investigation of a few weeks would prove this point. Now that each day brought new revelations of White House wrongdoing, what should be the role of the Republicans on the committee, and of the committee's Republican lawyer? Two alternatives were apparent: to act as a self-appointed defense counsel for the White House, a role Gurney had staked out for himself, or to seek to outdo the Democrats to come down on Republican Watergate malefactors harder and faster than the other party, which evidently was Weicker's strategy.

After some consideration, I decided that I was probably placing too much importance on my own role in the process. It was not necessary that I reach personal conclusions. I was not a national review board or a syndicated columnist, but a lawyer with clients—the Republican members of the committee, no matter how diverse the views and attitudes of Baker, Gurney, and Weicker. I would try to walk a fine line between a good-faith pursuit of the investigation and a good-faith attempt to insure balance and fairness. As a lawyer, I did not especially love most of the people I had defended, nor did I hate those I prosecuted. My personal feelings had always been relatively unimportant.

As I reflected further, I convinced myself that Nixon had not had prior knowledge of the break-in, nor of the cover-up that followed. Even if culpability reached dangerously close to the president, I reasoned, surely his top aides would have shielded him from damaging information, not just to protect themselves, but also to allow him to tell the nation, in the best of faith, that neither he nor his chief advisors were involved. At this stage even Weicker agreed that Nixon was not culpable. I decided not to take the line of the president's most vocal critics, interpreting every facet of the case to put Nixon in the worst possible light; neither would I map out a strict plan for my future conduct.

Above all, I could not permit myself to be incapacitated by fears and doubts about what might lie ahead.

On the afternoon of May 2, 1973, the committee met in executive session in Ervin's office. The staff had been interviewing witnesses around the clock, with a minimum of attention and public disclosures. It was evident from the moment we arrived that Weicker was agitated. Dash reported that he had received information that Haldeman and Ehrlichman had removed a number of files from the White House; he proposed that a subpoena be issued immediately to produce the two men and the documents. There was no opposition, and Ervin signed the subpoenas. Baker asked that a subpoena also be issued for Dean and his documents, and that too was approved without dissent.

Then Weicker was given the floor. He wanted to know when the committee members would receive reports of the interviews then being conducted. "I have never agreed to let the committee staff conduct confidential interviews without the members of the committee being notified and being given an opportunity to attend if they desire," he said. "I want to know the times, places, and persons, whenever anyone is being interviewed." Weicker addressed Dash, his voice rising; but Ervin, who realized that he was the real subject of the complaint, gave the reply. He quietly pointed out the problem of press leaks. It never ceased to astound me that, in executive sessions, senators avoided head-on confrontations whenever possible. They would express anger at a fellow senator by rebuking a staff member, such as Dash, or by phrasing their words to make them apply generally rather than specifically. Ervin was, in effect, telling Weicker that he didn't want him or other senators at the interviews because he was sure they would tell everything they heard; but he framed his remarks so artfully that, even though it was obvious what he was saying, no one could take direct offense.

Weicker sidestepped Ervin's rebuttal and tried another tack. He objected to his lack of access to raw FBI files. Referring to himself as "the junior senator from Connecticut," something he

*Senators Weicker, Baker, and Gurney made up the Minority team I was chosen to represent.*

did frequently, he said he had as much right as anyone else to see the files. He said he should have been invited to a meeting with Attorney General Richard Kleindienst, a session that only Ervin, Baker, Dash, and I attended.

At this point, Ervin exploded. "That meeting was totally at the invitation of the attorney general. He asked to meet with Senator Baker and me." His voice louder than I had ever heard it before, Ervin said the committee had no power to subpoena FBI files and was seeking the best accommodation possible. Kleindienst had set the terms, Ervin went on, and they seemed reasonable.

Weicker interrupted Ervin, and they engaged in heated argument. Apparently taken aback by Ervin's uncharacteristic harshness, Weicker switched course again, renewing his demand that we interview key witnesses at public sessions. Dash, with Ervin's permission to speak, responded. Such procedure would prevent the committee from getting many valuable leads; the staff should be able to follow leads before giving information to the press; witnesses would be less than fully candid if their initial interviews were open to the public. Dash cited all the arguments that everyone in the room, including Weicker, had heard before. In my opinion, Weicker knew the committee would never adopt a proposal so contrary to sound investigative procedure, but it was always good to be on the side of "full disclosure" and "full public view" particularly if the press somehow learned who had espoused that position.

Senator Montoya, ignoring Weicker's point, proposed a compromise on access to FBI files. He moved that the committee ask the attorney general to make its files available to the committee "or any of its members subject to the committee and its members individually respecting the privacy in these particular files not to disclose any material therein except within the confines of the committee proper." Montoya's motion carried; the committee also voted to take initial steps to offer immunity to Liddy, Magruder, and four of the Watergate burglars—Bernard Barker, Frank Sturgis, Eugenio Martinez, and Virgilio Gonzalez.

The next evening marked the annual dinner of the Washington Press Club; one of the periodic social affairs, temporary respites from pressure, for which the capital is famous. Baker was the principal speaker. He was preceded by Rep. James Symington and Sen. Walter Mondale, both of whom gave brief, lighthearted talks about national affairs.

Baker told jokes about Ervin, Tennessee law practice, and Watergate. "It's a little hard," he said, "to just come off the campaign trail with echoes of 'four more years' ringing in your ears and get used to the new popular chant: 'not less than two, nor more than ten years.'" He said his friend, Rep. Jimmy Quillen from Tennessee's Republican first district, had called him and said, "Howard, you know during the campaign we were telling the folks we were going to win this election and we were going all the way, that we were going from the courthouse to the White House. Now they've got everything all wrong. They're taking him from the White House to the court-house." Such jokes could not have been told, that night, by a Democrat; but given Baker's impeccable Republican credentials, he could tell them and get away with it.

Midway through Baker's speech, which turned from jokes to a serious dissertation, I noticed Nixon's press secretary, Ron Ziegler, and his wife at a nearby table. Ziegler did not appear to be enjoying himself. After Baker's speech, as I passed Ziegler's table, I extended my hand and introduced myself. "I thought Symington's speech was in good taste," he snapped, "but I thought we were going to wait until the hearings started before we heard about Watergate." At first I could not believe that Ziegler was serious in his objection to Baker's speech, but he persisted. Finally I said, "All right, Ron, I'll deliver the message."

Later that night, as we relaxed at Baker's home, I described the conversation to him. He seemed untroubled by the thought that Nixon was getting Ziegler's version of his speech perhaps at that moment. Despite what appeared to be Baker's preoccupation with the presidential "mystique" during the hearings—an atmosphere that he considered a prime contributor to Nixon's isolation—he never seemed to hold the presidency in great reverence. And Baker was never afraid to express his views. During the battle over executive privilege, Baker sought out Nixon at a White House reception and impressed on the president the necessity that White House aides testify before our committee. I have always believed that Baker's private discussion of the issue did more than anything else to cause the president to abandon his hardline position.

It was at the same reception, I was told, that Nixon asked Baker, "Who is this Fred Thompson?" The senator's pungent reply prompted the gift that I received from Baker's staff that Christmas: two brass spherical objects mounted on a rectangular platform with the inscription, "You've got 'em, kid, you've got 'em." I was not surprised, in reading the transcripts of the White House tapes, that Nixon could never quite figure Baker out.

The next morning, when I arrived at my office, Joan Cole told me that Ziegler had called. I called back, expecting a continuation of the tirade. But Ziegler said, "Fred, this is Ron. I want to apologize for last night." Everyone at the White House was under a lot of pressure, he said, and the day before had been particularly bad. He meant no disrespect to the senator, and he hoped that I understood. I told him I appreciated his comments, and said that I had been a bit edgy myself.

When I reported the chat to Baker, he asked what I made of it all. It was my opinion that Ziegler had told his boss about the exchange and that he had received, in turn, an elementary lesson in Capitol Hill politics: You don't unnecessarily antagonize the vice-chairman of the committee that is investigating you.

And from the White House point of view, that investigation could not have looked pleasant.

# Chapter II · The Select Committee

The United States Senate has often been called the most powerful deliberative body in the world. Its 100 members possess as many different personalities, abilities, and interests as the 213 million people they represent. Almost without exception, senators are men of drive and ambition who have been elected through the expenditure of enormous amounts of sweat, energy, and money. A senator organizes and a senator fights, and sometimes he wins office solely by virtue of his intelligence and capability, but just as often because of his indomitable will and intuition.

The Senate Watergate committee—more properly, the Senate Select Committee on Presidential Campaign Activities—consisted of seven United States senators who banded together for a limited time and for a limited purpose. Their mandate, under the Senate resolution by which the committee was formed, was to "conduct an investigation and study of the extent, if any, to which illegal improper or unethical activities were engaged in by any persons acting individually or in combination with others in the presidential election of 1972."

The seven men represented constituencies that ranged from the plains of New Mexico and the farms of Georgia to the campus of Yale University. They became members of the committee by different routes; they represented, of course, both major political parties and also both the liberal and conservative wings of each party.

The Senate's Democratic leadership settled early on the chairman, Sam Ervin of North Carolina. The other Democratic members of the committee, Herman Talmadge of Georgia,

Daniel Inouye of Hawaii, and Joseph Montoya of New Mexico, were chosen for a variety of reasons. Geographical balance was one; a more important reason was the belief that none of the three appeared likely to be a presidential candidate. Senator Talmadge is widely regarded as one of the most intelligent members of the Senate, and some say that he manifested that intelligence from the outset when he attempted to decline the assignment. He was—and is—chairman of the Senate Agriculture Committee, a time-consuming post and one that he obviously considered more important to Georgia than exploring Watergate wrongdoings. However, a senator seldom turns down an important request from his party leadership, so Talmadge came aboard.

Senators Inouye and Montoya were less reluctant to serve. For the Democrats they provided not only representation from important ethnic minorities (Inouye is a Japanese-American and Montoya a Spanish-American) but also in the person of Inouye a member whose very personal appearance was a constant reminder of courage and patriotic sacrifice: the Senator's right arm had been amputated as a result of World War II injuries.

The Republican leadership in the Senate, like the Democratic, had an immediate choice for the party's ranking member—Baker of Tennessee. The two other Republican members, Edward Gurney of Florida and Lowell Weicker of Connecticut, had actively sought membership on the committee. Gurney, a handsome man, considered television his medium, an opinion he passed along to his fellow Republicans in the Senate. Weicker was said to have been so eager to join the committee that he had discussed taking the issue to the floor of the Senate if he were denied a position.

In the three months of work that preceded the committee's public hearings, we on the staff became accustomed to the speech and mannerisms of the committee members. At executive sessions, the conversation flowed from the soft drawl of Talmadge to the clipped Southwest accent of Montoya to the smooth, slightly oriental tones of Inouye, which reminded some of us of the interrogation room in the movie *Bridge on the River Kwai*. It was almost like a session of the United Nations, except that everyone spoke English.

I met Senator Gurney shortly after my arrival in Washington. He was a New England native who had moved to Florida, and his diction reflected his origins. Like Inouye he had suffered severe war injuries. During his World War II service as a tank commander, his back and hip had been shattered by enemy gunfire, leaving him with a partly withered leg and a permanent limp. He was constantly in pain, and he carried a thick cushion to sit on. Late one afternoon, on my second visit to his office, he was having a drink. He explained to me, somewhat off-handedly, that although he took medication, a shot of whisky was really the only thing that helped to relieve the pain. It was obvious to me that he did not indulge in excess because he appeared to be in excellent health otherwise, and his appearance belied his 60 years of age. He never again mentioned his pain to me, although occasionally I would see him pull up the trouser of his injured leg and rub the leg vigorously. Otherwise, only his eyes would indicate discomfort on a bad day.

Gurney made it no secret that he was a Nixon defender, a role he had filled previously in proceedings before the Judiciary Committee, of which he was also a member. There are two sides to every case, and considering the emphasis placed on making a case against the president, even within the committee's Republican ranks, it seemed only natural for Gurney to support the other side of the issue. Philosophically, he was comfortable there.

Because Gurney and I were seated side by side at the committee table during the hearings, we held numerous whispered discussions about the proceedings. However, Gurney dealt with me at arm's length, as he seemed to do with everyone. He was always polite, but always aloof. At committee meetings he usually had little to say, often casting a vote to make an action unanimous when he would have preferred to dissent. I never saw much camaraderie between Gurney and the other senators. I had heard that he had a violent temper, but I never saw him display it. An aide to Baker told me of attending a meeting at which Gurney had torn the hide off a Justice Department official over a school-busing decision. The way I heard it, Gurney's merciless attack made Sen. Strom Thurmond of South Carolina, who is vehemently opposed to busing, appear like the personification of moderation.

I have already described Weicker's determination to conduct an independent investigation with his own staff members. Thus, it was obvious from the start that the Republicans could never equal the Democrats in maintaining a united front. The Democrats adhered strictly to the unarticulated congressional maxim that one always goes along with his leadership on party matters, and also to the long-established understanding that chairmen of powerful committees pretty much run the show. In the case of Ervin, both these practices came into play. A man basically reluctant to apply undue pressure, Ervin had only to announce his stand on a matter and the other Democrats on the committee almost invariably followed his lead. On occasion, Talmadge would voice serious reservations about an Ervin proposal; then he would excuse himself because of other pressing business and leave his proxy vote with Ervin, who would cast it in favor of the proposal, as Talmadge knew he would. Actually, most of the committee's actions were unanimous, but often not until after an exhaustive effort to achieve that unanimity.

At work the committee presented a study of democracy in action, primarily because of the special qualities of Ervin and Baker. Ervin always asserted firm positions, but he never treated them as though they were etched in stone. He and Baker not only respected each other, each senator appeared to understand the other's thinking. Baker's east Tennessee and Ervin's North Carolina were more than adjacent territories. Their populations shared dialect, interests, and background; and many of the committee's executive sessions were preceded by the swapping of stories, by Ervin and Baker, about moonshiners, sheriffs, and courthouse characters. The other senators, more familiar with Greenwich or Honolulu than Knoxville or

Kannanopolis, would sit in amused silence, smiling when they thought it appropriate, but never fully appreciating the down-home humor. This boy from Lawrenceburg enjoyed it.

Baker's temperament was ideal for the role he had been assigned. Slow to anger and always thinking of the big picture, he would work for a compromise whenever he felt such action was appropriate. Usually he would defer to Ervin on procedural matters; Baker always called Ervin "Mr. Chairman" at committee meetings, reserving "Sam" for the informal sessions. And Baker often protected Ervin from the chairman's first reactions, such as to dispatch an immediate letter to Nixon or to make a public statement on the committee's plans at a time that we needed to retain a variety of options. Baker never lost sight of the fact that an open quarrel among committee members would be to no one's benefit. Frequently, after Ervin had announced his position on a matter, Baker would state his agreement with those parts he considered acceptable and then say, "It seems to me that we may have to do just that, but I wonder if it might not be better if first we . . ." and present his own proposal. After the other senators had expressed their views Baker would amend his proposal and lead in the discussion that followed until a position was established that all agreed to, a position that frequently bore little resemblance to Ervin's original suggestion.

Had Baker reacted to Ervin's proposals head-on, calling for a vote on a counter-idea, he could never have counted on a majority. By diplomatic negotiation that avoided confrontation Baker often was able to get three-quarters of a loaf on issues in which a less skillful strategy might have left him with none.

Any fears I might have had that the Democrats on the committee would try to use me as a foil were dispelled after the committee's first few meetings. Talmadge was mostly silent; Montoya and Inouye were friendly. In addition, their knowledge that any action I took probably had the approval of Baker made for a smooth relationship. Montoya, almost always smiling, would bound into an executive session sporting his large silver-and-turquoise ring and shake hands and chat with everyone. He was always immaculately dressed, with the frequent exception of short argyle socks whose elasticity appeared to have been spent somewhere on the campaign trails of New Mexico. Moving around the room and chatting as if he were still running for the office he won narrowly in 1972, he quickly became a favorite of the staff.

Inouye's friendliness was more low-key, but he had a keen, dry sense of humor. Early in our meetings, to relieve the anxiety of anyone who felt uneasy at the sight of his empty right sleeve, which was always tucked neatly in his jacket pocket, he told a Sam Rayburn story. When Inouye was a freshman House member, he said, and first met with venerable "Mr. Sam," the long-time Speaker, Inouye eagerly introduced himself. "Oh, I know who you are," Rayburn replied. "How many one-armed Japs do you think we have in the House?" Inouye smiled broadly and then everyone laughed, as if waiting for his cue.

On May 16, 1973, the day before the opening of the public hearings, I walked through the tunnel to the Old Senate Office Building and into the Caucus Room for the first time. This historic room, with its marble walls, high ceilings, and impressive chandeliers, had been the scene of the hearings on the Teapot Dome scandal and for the battle between Sen. Joseph McCarthy and the army. Sen. Estes Kefauver had conducted the investigation into organized crime from this room in 1950 and 1951. Many political careers had been made and broken here. The room lived up to all my expectations; if this was indeed to be another historic occasion, we certainly had the perfect setting.

The committee had voted almost routinely to permit television cameras and still photographers to cover the hearings, but it was not until I saw the room and watched the cameras being installed that I realized the implications of being televised coast to coast. For a moment, the idea of working every day in the full view of millions of people, including thousands of my fellow lawyers, was awesome. After a little thought though, I decided that after the networks had received the first wave of complaints from outraged viewers deprived of their soap operas and game shows, all of us would be TV has-beens almost as soon as we had begun.

Staff members busied themselves preparing detailed information on the first group of witnesses. Dash had proposed that we start with persons of lesser stature who could give background on the operations and organization of the Committee for the Re-election of the President and the White House. Some committee members wanted to begin directly with the "name" witnesses, but Dash's suggestion was approved. So organization charts were prepared on the Committee to Re-elect and the White House. Interviews, newspaper reports, and computer printouts were assembled and collated. Dash provided all committee members with a witness sheet. In addition, our minority staff provided for the Republican members a folder on each witness with appropriate tabs for separate sections on his background, his interviews, comments about him by others, and suggested lines of inquiry. This grueling chore, however, was abandoned after several weeks. Weicker's personal staff was working around the clock preparing areas of inquiry for him. And Baker, after examining the folders and expressing his approval would ignore my carefully assembled package and pose a series of questions based on his memory and overall knowledge of the case. Often he would wait until seconds before his turn to question, jot down two or three words on a piece of paper and open a dialogue with a witness that gave the impression that he had been rehearsing his remarks all night.

On the morning of May 17, 1973, three months after we started our work in Washington, Senator Ervin pounded his gavel on the huge table in the Caucus Room for the first time. Then each senator stated his views on the work of the committee to those in the crowded room and to the millions watching on television around the country.

At first, the view from the committee side of the table was a conglomeration of distractions. The brightness of the TV lights was almost blinding. And the still photographers, who had won their fight against being confined to fixed locations, scampered

*This scene became familiar to millions of people around the world: the Senate Select Committee on Presidential Campaign Activities assembled in the Caucus Room of the Senate Office Building.*

THE NEW YORK TIMES/GEORGE TAMES

back and forth in front of the table, clicking away from every possible angle. The press had been allotted a good portion of the available space, and reporters were jammed around several long tables directly in front of us. They would alternately write, frown, chuckle, whisper to colleagues, or give knowing looks to those on our side of the table. Beyond the press tables was the area set aside for the public, with the first few rows occupied by wives of senators and special guests. There was constant jockeying among Senate offices for extra tickets down front. The remaining seats and the standing room were allotted on a first-come, first-served basis, and it appeared that half of the Capitol Hill police force was on hand to shepherd in and out the steady flow of spectators who had lined the walls of the building waiting to get in. Behind us at the committee table, various staff members clutched documents and waited to offer assistance at the turn of a senator's head.

The drama began. As the first witness, Rob Odle, office manager for Nixon's reelection committee, responded carefully to questions about the CRP's organization setup, each interrogator became accustomed to the sound of his voice as it emanated from the microphone before him and bounded back from the high walls and ceilings of the cavernous room. Soon the many distractions faded into a blurred background as we concentrated on the witness before us, and even the realization that we were being watched by millions of people lost its fascination. For one thing, it is impossible to comprehend fully such a vast audience; for another, we had to keep up with the questioning.

Although each of the witnesses had been interviewed earlier, much as in the trial of a lawsuit, no one on the committee knew what questions would be asked by the person preceding him. Each man guarded his own questions zealously, and there was no attempt at coordination to avoid duplication, so it required alertness and a bit of agility to keep up. Almost invariably I followed Dash. I would enter the room with notes on various areas of inquiry, and then, as Dash proceeded, I would eliminate the areas he was covering and make new notes on points that I believed needed further discussion and analysis. As the hearings continued, it became more like any other job than I had suspected. The long hours of staff preparation, conducted in virtual isolation, made the first few days of the hearings seem much less an event to me than they were to many people around the nation.

As the days passed, the committee clung to its building-block approach to the inquiry. The first "name" witness, Mc-Cord, told his story, which was a bit of an anticlimax after the deluge of press reports about what he would say. Sally Harmony, Liddy's secretary, testified that she had typed secret reports on Gemstone stationery, but for the most part she displayed a very poor memory. As Ervin mentioned to Baker with a chuckle, "If there's anything better than a good memory, it's a good forgettery." Sally Harmony remembered little that she had heard and nothing that she had typed. The joke around the committee table was that she would probably receive job offers from lawyers and businessmen all over the country.

The Caucus Room seemed to become more crowded, and each day's line looked longer than the one the day before. Those waiting were mostly young people. Many spectators attended every day, arriving at the Old Senate Office Building at 4 or 5 in the morning.

There was a constant flow of notes from staff members, and occasionally from reporters, about developments that were taking place outside the hearing room. At the end of each session everyone hurried back to his office to get the full picture of what had transpired that day while he had been in the Caucus Room.

At first, the hearings began at 10 in the morning and continued until 5 or 6 P.M., with a two-hour lunch break that the staff usually devoted to preparing for the afternoon's witnesses. Often I went days at a time without reading a newspaper. This not only saved time, but I also knew that everything that interested me was taking place in the Caucus Room, or that I would have heard about it before it appeared in the papers. It was a unique situation of being almost totally isolated from the outside world while simultaneously having a direct pipeline to nearly all the information that pertained in any way to our all-consuming endeavor.

We were hardly unaware of newspapers, however, because confidential information continued to leak to the press. Dash had established elaborate procedures to protect the secrecy of our information. Secretaries destroyed their typewriter ribbons; excess papers were shredded. (When Senator Ervin questioned Odle he expressed surprise and some indignation at the testimony that CRP had had a shredder in its office. Staff members behind him chuckled; the chairman was obviously not aware that the committee's staff used a shredder every day.) Uniformed guards, who required all persons to sign in and out, were stationed outside the converted auditorium that housed most of the staff. All committee documents were supposed to be placed in a caged area, under lock and key. No sanctions, however, were imposed on anyone who wanted to tuck away an extra copy of an interview, or, simpler still, to give his information from memory to a friendly reporter. And, of course, there was no control of information once it reached a senator's office.

Leaks from senators' offices proved a particularly troublesome point for Bill Shure. Following Weicker's instructions, he attended interviews and reported both to me and to the senator's office. That office, as Bill well knew, had become a sieve. Although Weicker seldom requested copies of interviews, members of his staff did, and Bill, who was extremely conscientious, was concerned about the leaks. He was constantly hunting for an excuse to deny material to a Weicker staff member. Later I learned from Bill that someone in Weicker's office had gotten into his unattended briefcase and removed an interview transcript without Bill's knowledge; the interview appeared in the *Washington Post* the next day. Bill said he had already told the reporter how the document had been obtained, much to the reporter's chagrin. Even before I learned of this I told Bill he could not attend any more interviews without my special authorization and that he should relay that directive to Weicker so that Bill would not be blamed for his nonattendance. I braced myself for the reaction, and I didn't have to wait long.

Weicker telephoned me, his voice as angry as I had expected. Where did I get off, he asked, telling one of his staff members what to do. I reminded him of our conversation at the time Bill was hired, and of Weicker's assurances that Bill would work with the minority staff the way everyone else did and be bound by the same rules. Weicker exploded; he said he would send Shure where and when he pleased and that I would not interfere. When I described several incidents in which confidential material had "found its way" out of his office, he said this was not true. If he didn't know what was going on in his office, I replied, he was the only person on Capitol Hill who didn't. The conversation continued going downhill, and before long I was standing at my desk engaged in an all-out shouting match. Weicker listed Shure's virtues, and I concurred. (I didn't know that Shure and several of

Weicker's other staff members were gathered around Weicker's desk listening to his end of the conversation.) I told the senator he was placing Shure in a hopeless position and that if Weicker forced me to, I would fire Shure. If Shure was to answer only to Weicker, I said, Weicker should pay him. "Fire him," the senator said, "go ahead. It will be on your shoulders." Under those circumstances, I replied, Shure should depart under an arrangement that would be of minimum embarrassment to him, because he was blameless. "No deals," Weicker said. "Just go ahead and fire him." I said, "Do you mean that you would do that to Bill? You won't even help me do it in such a way that it won't hurt him? How could you do this to him?"

Weicker ignored the question, saying that he wanted it understood that I did not represent him and that he had no confidence in me. "And another thing," he said, "don't you ever say anything about another one of my staff members."

"I'll say any damn thing I want to about any staff member," I answered, by this time shouting at the top of my voice. And so we continued, each almost incoherent with anger and each cutting off the other in mid-sentence. Finally Weicker slammed down the telephone.

A few minutes later Joan Cole, my secretary, walked in, looking pale. Through the closed door, she had heard every word I said. "I've only heard one other staff member talk to a senator that way and I've been here a long time," she said. I asked her if that other staff member still had a job.

I telephoned Baker, described my conversation with Weicker, and told him that he would probably be getting a call from Weicker. Baker, who had been reading disparaging remarks about himself in the press, attributed to anonymous "sources" inside the committee, did not appear very concerned. He said he would let me know what happened. To Weicker's credit, he never called Baker—and I never fired Shure. It is foolhardy enough for a staff member to say he will walk over a United States senator; it is even more foolish to actually try.

After this incident, Weicker and I never had another cross word; as a matter of fact, our relationship improved somewhat.

In the Caucus Room, and in executive sessions, he appeared to avoid having his eyes meet mine. On the occasions that I had to consult with him, it was strictly business. Later, Weicker questioned H. R. Haldeman about a Haldeman memo, written before I had been chosen minority counsel, that expressed a desire that the committee not get a soft-headed old man for minority counsel, but a "real tiger." Commenting on the memo, Weicker said, "We got a real tiger all right." I interpreted that as a conciliatory reference to our verbal duel, and from that point we had a tacit understanding not to attack each other.

Now and then when we emerged from our Watergate cocoon, we discovered, to our amazement, that all of us were becoming nationally known personalities. Until then, I had not fully appreciated the power of television or the fact that anyone who gets sufficient television exposure as a newscaster, an actor, or the Pillsbury doughboy, is an overnight celebrity. This was certainly true of the committee members, and Dash and I were getting our share of attention. Baker, with his youthful looks, melodious voice, and incisive questioning, and Ervin, with his grandfatherly demeanor and his constitutional homilies, became sensations. The public reaction was extraordinary. Every office on Capitol Hill, I was told, had at least one TV set tuned to the hearings; viewers were abandoning their soap operas, and businessmen were watching the nightly reruns on public television. Even for senators accustomed to the limelight it was unusual; for those of us who had never even run for office, it was unbelievable. Outside the Caucus Room the crowds gathered at every recess, and often I would be called by name and asked for an autograph. Senators who had been on the Hill for decades walked the halls all but unnoticed while those of us associated with Watergate in any way attracted tremendous attention. At restaurants, maitre d's always had tables, and waiters gave superb service. Even I, with my trial lawyer's egotism, was taken aback one night when Sarah and I walked into a restaurant and several young couples broke into applause.

At the start of the hearings I chided Joan about opening my

personal mail. Within a few days the mail chore had become enormous, and once Joan walked in with a large stack of letters marked "personal" and a self-satisfied look on her face. "Okay," I said after examining a few, "you win. Open them." About a third of the incoming letters were marked "personal"; invariably, they contained such "personal" information as news clippings and a request to be placed on the committee's mailing list.

All this attention was a pleasant reward for the pressure and long hours of work. However, as I told Sarah after the ovation at the restaurant, on Capitol Hill I frequently saw the lonely figures of former congressmen. Some of them were now lobbyists, but many of them simply appeared anxious to be close to the glory that once had been theirs. Not long before, they too had been cheered by thousands.

Like millions of other Americans, I sometimes watched the reruns of the hearings at night. It was a painful experience; I always felt I could have done better, asked more incisive questions. My children, on the other hand, rarely watched; they preferred to play ball. On the nights that I visited Baker's home while the hearings were in progress, he refused to allow the TV set to be turned on.

Watergate bugs, coloring books, games, and other trinkets were coming onto the market and receiving an enthusiastic public reception. The Watergate office complex, where the break-in took place, became a nationally known landmark. Senator Ervin fan clubs were forming around the country. Uncle Sam sweatshirts were on sale and people were wearing Uncle Sam watches that had all the Watergate bad guys clustered around the dial. There were Watergate parties given by members of the media. From Washington, it appeared that the entire nation was involved in decrying or celebrating all that was known as Watergate.

I basked in my temporary fame with something less than a totally clear conscience. I thought of the witnesses who had appeared. Many were young men my age—innocents like Rob Odle, whose idealism still burned brightly as he delivered a ringing defense of Nixon, and the bewildered Hugh Sloan, at the pinnacle of power politics. And there were young men who were not so innocent, men like Bart Porter and Jeb Magruder, who had had a look at the big time and had permitted personal ambition and misguided loyalty to sear their consciences. At a time when they could have begun to realize their dreams, these dreams and aspirations had seemed to disappear. And I remembered the faces of their wives, who, though blameless, were enduring at least equal agony. I thought of the witnesses' parents, and I thought of the witnesses' children. I could imagine the comments the children must be hearing at school and the price that all of them were paying because of a foolish adventure. I could not help wonder what I would have done had I been in their position.

Even more tragic, perhaps, were the older men like John Mitchell and Maurice Stans. They were old enough to be my father, with years to spare. They had spent their adult lives building professional reputations and then, at the peak of power and prestige they were the objects of public ridicule. From Stans' attorney I knew that at the very time Stans appeared before the committee his wife was critically ill. And Mitchell's problems with his wife had been the subject of national gossip for months; his friends indicated that the full extent of those problems was known to only a few. As the personal tragedies unfolded there were whispered references to possible suicides. As I was signing autographs, appearing on talk shows, and collecting lecture fees, I concluded that if ever I really began to enjoy my job I would not deserve to hold it.

# Chapter III · John Dean, The Accuser

From the time Watergate hearings began, one overriding question was on the minds of most everyone who followed our proceedings closely, a question shared by comittee members and the staff: what would John Dean say? In mid-April 1973, Dean issued his statement asserting that he would not be made the scapegoat in the scandal. By the end of April, press reports were appearing from sources in the Dean camp that said Dean not only had damning information on Watergate, but information about other illegal activities in the Nixon administration dating to 1969. The stories flowed regularly in the newspapers and news magazines, usually implicating Haldeman and Ehrlichman in the cover-up. Each had the effect of a minor bombshell. This represented the first round of a strategy by Dean and his associates to achieve one goal—immunity from prosecution. It was becoming obvious that Dean had been deeply involved in the cover-up, and it was becoming equally obvious that Dean was possibly the only person who could point the finger at higher-ups, who at this stage were Haldeman and Ehrlichman. The Dean strategy was to titillate the prosecutors with glimpses of what he might say. In addition to leaks to the press, information was being relayed to the federal prosecutors by Dean's attorneys, so the information could not be used against their client if a proposed deal fell through.

The emerging information was dynamite. Along with giving information about the cover-up, Dean was the first to tell the prosecutors of the burglary of the office of Dr. Louis Fielding, Daniel Ellsberg's psychiatrist, and of the destruction of FBI files by Patrick Gray, then FBI director. The "Dean stories" appeared to be punched by a network of "well-informed sources," code words for "friends and associates of Dean."

The decision whether to grant immunity to Dean was not an easy one for the prosecutors, who were under extreme pressure. If they offered immunity to Dean, they could be accused of allowing the real culprit to go free. If they prosecuted Dean and he refused to cooperate, they might be accused of a cover-up themselves, and of passing up what might be their only opportunity to reach the big fish.

When it became apparent that the prosecution had serious reservations about a deal, Dean began round two of his campaign. If the prosecution would not grant immunity, perhaps the Watergate committee would. On Saturday, May 12, just five days before our hearing began, Charles Schaffer, Dean's lawyer, called Dash and said Dash could talk to Dean in Schaffer's office. At that session, Dean told Dash essentially what he had said to the prosecutors, but now he was beginning to imply other, more enticing, things. Having struck out when he used Haldeman and Ehrlichman as bait, Dean now began to dangle a larger prize—the president. News stories indicating that Dean would implicate Nixon began to trickle out.

When the committee met on Tuesday, May 15, Dash made his pitch. He said Dean had given "significant information" that was sufficient to justify immunity, but there was one problem: Dash could not report what Dean had told him because he had agreed not to. Dean, Dash said, was particularly fearful that once his story became known to the committee's Republican minority members the White House would be alerted in time to prepare a defense to Dean's charges. So the committee was being asked, in effect, to grant immunity to Dean without knowing his testimony, without being able to consider its value. If the prosecution had been asked to buy a pig in a poke, the committee was not being given a chance even to see the poke.

Gurney was outraged. Dean was "taking the committee for a ride," he said, and he would have nothing to do with it. Baker expressed "strong reservations." The committee, he said, had already been too free with its grants of "use" immunity. Under the law, use immunity provided that testimony given to a committee by a witness cannot be used against him in a later criminal proceeding. Therefore, the committee lived with the possibility that its efforts to get at the truth might seriously jeopardize future criminal action, an eventuality that Ervin, for one, did not find overwhelmingly objectionable. As a former prosecutor, I felt that the liberal grants of immunity and the enormous amount of pretrial publicity in the case were making the prospect of successful prosecution less and less likely. Theoretically, the same information for which the committee was granting use immunity was available to the prosecution from other sources, such as other witnesses or documents, and such information could be used against a defendant. For that reason, Dash always argued, we were not really jeopardizing prosecution by granting use immunity. However, these discussions appeared to be mere legal toe-dancing in the face of the rushing torrent of events.

Dean was gambling that the committee could not resist his offer, and on his terms—and he was correct. Most committee and staff members were all but salivating at the prospect of Dean's testimony. Baker, having satisfied himself that there was no alternative, moved for a grant of immunity. Gurney, seeing the way the vote was going, followed suit; but he said he wanted the record to show that he thought the committee was "making a serious mistake." Weicker made it unanimous for the minority, saying that he had no reservations. I wondered if Weicker knew something the rest of us did not. Not only had Weicker privately interviewed Dean, who was his neighbor in Virginia (he later bought Dean's house), but he and Dean were also known to have shared beer and pretzels on occasion.

Now Dean had two shots at acquittal. He had use immunity and the additional possibility that his testimony before a national, ever-increasing television audience would generate sufficient pretrial publicity to preclude a conviction. This prospect of prejudicial pretrial publicity was so real that Archibald

Cox, who had just become the Watergate special prosecutor, attempted to have the hearings postponed until after Dean was tried. The day before Dean's appearance before the committee, Schaffer made a long and eloquent argument, urging the committee not to subpoena his client to appear before the television cameras. This argument was entirely for the record: Schaffer knew well that pretrial publicity might be the very thing to set his client free.

Afterward, when Dash asked jokingly what Schaffer would have done if the committee had granted his request to quash the subpoena, Schaffer laughed with the rest of us. Clearly, he would have responded the way William Buckley did when asked what he would have done if he had been elected mayor of New York—demanded a recount. It was a game, and all of us were players; it was played again and again by the lawyers for other witnesses. We all knew that it would be months or years before it was determined whether, after all the work and effort, we had engaged at least partly in a self-defeating exercise by perhaps insuring that those brought before the committee in public session could never be prosecuted successfully. By the middle of 1975, however, none of the Watergate defendants had won a legal decision on this point.

After Dean was granted use immunity, Schaffer continued his contact with Dash; and he was able, in effect, to set the ground rules for the committee. I told Dash that I had no objection to his unilateral contact with Dean, but that I reserved the same right should others wish to confide in me alone. I regarded the Dean-Dash relationship as something that could strengthen my hand in the future, if the need arose, and something that could protect me from charges of partisanship. I had only one demand—that Dean be brought in early enough so that I could question him on the crucial issue of presidential involvement. Dash agreed.

Weeks passed before my demand was met. On June 18, a few days before his public appearance, Dean and his lawyers came in for questioning by me. Dean was quiet and casually dressed, in stark contrast with Schaffer, who was always austere and wore correctly conservative suits and ties. Dean resembled a thousand kids I had seen on college campuses. Was this the man, I wondered, who was going to bring down the president of the United States? Usually I have an immediate personal reaction to anyone I meet, but with John Dean it was different. To me, he was neutral; everything about him—his looks, his speech, his mannerisms—was neutral. He chain-smoked and drank Pepsi-Cola from a can while answering questions, almost, it appeared, by rote. He was obviously very well rehearsed.

Dean was responsive and friendly in replying to my questions. Schaffer, however, was stern and tough, interrupting my interrogation with occasional remarks that challenged my motivations. He and I fenced verbally. Although Schaffer was making no substantive progress, he was taking the heat away from Dean and trying, with some success, to make his client emerge as the good guy. I admired Schaffer's technique.

I asked Dean how he had distributed the "hush money" that had been given him to handle. He described the amounts and the recipients, and volunteered the fact that $4850 had been left over. When I asked him what he did with the leftover money, he replied that he had spent it on his honeymoon.

When I got to the issue of presidential involvement, Schaffer interrupted again. Certain matters concerning the attorney-client privilege with regard to Dean and Nixon, he said, and certain questions touching on national security had to be resolved before Dean could go into these matters. Even at this late date we were not able to explore this most important issue. We agreed to adjourn and to contact the president's office about a possible waiver of these privileges, if any in fact existed. Later, Nixon waived any claims of privilege.

The following day there was a leak to the press on the portion of Dean's testimony that dealt with his use of the hush fund for his honeymoon; the disclosure obviously damaged Dean's credibility. Schaffer informed Dash and me that, because of the leak, his client would submit to no further interviews. Although I had not leaked the information, the implica-

tion was clear that I had. The disclosure was interpreted on
Capitol Hill as a White House-inspired plot to discredit Dean,
but it was my assumption that the material had been leaked by
Dean or his associates, both to lessen its impact when it was
brought out at the hearings and to provide an excuse to refuse
further interrogation of Dean. In a heated conversation with
Schaffer, I cited the pattern of leaks of testimony before the
committee, noted that Dean had offered nothing on the most
crucial part of his story—the issue of presidential involvement—and said I believed that Dean was using the committee
to bolster his own position. If it was up to me, I said, I would
force Dean to return for further questioning under the threat of
a contempt citation. Schaffer heard me out, but left without
relenting.

That night there were more press leaks, and they came from
both directions—pro-Dean and anti-Dean. Nearly everything
Dean had testified to appeared in print, including material
accusing the White House and additional detail about the
honeymoon money. I concluded that Gurney's office and
Weicker's office were engaging in a duel of leaks. The committee, meanwhile, did not even meet to consider Dean's refusal to
testify further in closed session. It seemed obvious that the
committee members considered Dean such an important witness that it was unwise to risk his displeasure. And that was not
the only advantage Dean obtained in his dealings with the
committee: not until the morning of his public testimony did
we receive his 245-page statement and the fifty documents he
submitted with it. As a result, we found ourselves racing
through the material he offered at almost the same time that he
was reading it to the nation. There was no chance to analyze it,
or to prepare questions based on it.

My irritation was heightened as Dean continued to read his
lengthy statement. A second part of Dean's plan was unfolding: the statement contained the names of many individuals
who had little relation to Watergate, and nearly all of it was
based on hearsay. This provided needless embarrassment to

many individuals, and it also served to make his testimony even more sensational.

Dean also attempted to discredit Baker and Gurney. Soon after the committee was formed, Baker met with Nixon in an effort to persuade the president to relax his stand on executive privilege and to permit members of the White House staff to testify. Describing this session in his testimony, Dean implied that Baker was a defender of the president; Dean's underlying message, as we saw it, was that if we leaned on him too hard, he might have further ammunition against Baker. Dean referred repeatedly to the White House belief that it could count on Gurney to support its position. Gurney's attitude was hardly a secret, but Dean's repetition of the point was an obvious but skillful bid to neutralize the senator from Florida. His statement thus managed to raise questions about the motivations of those he considered to be his chief antagonists—Baker, Gurney, and me.

Furthermore, Dean was getting cream-puff questions from the Democrats, particularly Ervin, who protected the witness like a housemother watching a college freshman, and who attempted to rehabilitate Dean every time he ran into trouble. I could not believe Dean's accusations about Nixon; I could not conceive that Nixon would permit a subordinate such as Dean to place him in a compromising position. In this supercharged atmosphere of intense pressure and partisan politics, I began to adopt a position that continued for almost the duration of the committee's life—a concern with form, rather than substance. At that time, I realize now, I was worried less about Nixon's culpability and more about the way Dean had used the committee for his own ends.

So, in the short time we had available to question the witness, I decided to focus on Dean's background. Dean's handling of the hush money intrigued me; I could not believe that he had spent $4,850 on a honeymoon. I wondered how he actually had spent it. During his questioning he said he had intended to take several weeks for his honeymoon, and that he had planned to spend that amount. Checking the records at the

White House travel office, we discovered that Dean had made reservations for only a four-day trip.

During the lunch break on the second day of Dean's testimony, Howard Liebengood and I were in my office on our hands and knees, going over the White House travel records and additional information on Dean, which were spread out on the floor in front of us. Someone knocked softly at the door, and there was John Dean. "Pardon me, Fred," he said, "may I use your restroom?"

Trying to appear nonchalant, I said, "Of course," and Dean had to tiptoe in and out of his own records. The episode had the trappings of a grade C movie.

After the questioning resumed, Dean could never explain, at least to my satisfaction, what he had done with the money. Nor could he explain why, if he had put a check in the safe to cover the money, as he said he had, he had torn it up, since that would have been the only evidence to support his story that he intended to return the money to the safe. This was the first time in three days of testimony that I saw Dean even slightly disturbed, and not even Ervin's efforts to help him recoup appeared entirely successful: Dean and Schaffer even engaged in a colloquy in an effort to explain why the check had been destroyed. But these were only jabs delivered in the final minutes of the tenth and last round. Dean had clearly been the winner of the first nine and a half. And the matters I raised were minuscule when weighed against the thrust of his testimony: that the president had been aware of the cover-up as early as September 15, 1972, three months after the Watergate break-in.

It was a bad week for me from start to finish. By the time John Dean testified, the lines outside the Caucus Room wound around the hallway, down the stairs, and outside the building. Before the last day of his testimony I was walking into the Caucus Room with Sarah when a girl, who appeared to be about 18 or 19, stepped out of the line and said in a loud voice, "Please, I've been waiting for you for weeks and weeks. Could I please have your autograph?" I gallantly signed her autograph

*A comment to Senator Baker. Such remarks had to be brief so that we wouldn't miss the witnesses' testimony.*

THE NEW YORK TIMES/GEORGE TAMES

book as the crowd milled around me and my wife beamed as she looked on. As I finished my signature the young lady clutched her autograph book to her breast without looking at it, turned to her boyfriend and exclaimed, "Just think, Senator Weicker!" I hurried into the Caucus Room to the sound of guffaws.

The tender loving care accorded Dean by the committee's Democratic majority was in sharp contrast to the treatment that side gave to Richard Moore, a witness two weeks later. I had been advised by Fred Buzhardt, then the White House counsel, that Moore, a White House aide who enjoyed almost universal respect, had information that was substantially different from Dean's. Dean, in his testimony, said that he had talked to Moore, whom he regarded as something of a father-figure, about his concern over the president's inaction in stopping the Watergate cover-up. Because Moore's testimony would touch directly on the issues discussed by Dean, we called Moore to testify. The day before Moore's appearance, I arranged to interview him in the office of his attorney, Herbert Miller, who later served as Nixon's postresignation lawyer. Terry Lenzner of the majority staff, who had interviewed Moore previously, was assigned to accompany me. In my questioning of Moore I learned, for the first time, that Moore's earlier interview had contradicted Dean; it appeared that information corroborating Dean's was being relayed through channels much more quickly than information to the contrary.

Moore was a kindly man who looked and acted older than his 60 years. As I questioned him in Lenzner's presence, he appeared to have important testimony; he stated flatly that Dean had indicated to him that the president was not aware of the cover-up before March 21, 1973, six months after the date Dean had cited in his own testimony. Moore said Dean had told him that the president was not aware of the facts and that he (Dean) was going to tell the president the facts. Moore also said that Dean had told him following the Dean-Nixon meeting of March 21 that the president had been surprised at Dean's information. My interview with Moore was relatively brief, and it covered only these few crucial points.

When Moore took the stand the following afternoon, Lenzner opened the questioning. His first question was, "Do you have a recollection of a meeting on March 14, 1973, at 8:30 in the morning, also attended by Mr. Kleindienst and Mr. Mitchell?" Moore, who had previously expressed to us his concern that he had been called to appear on such short notice, was obviously taken aback by the question, which had nothing to do with the subject matter of the previous day's interview. He smiled meekly, gazed at the ceiling, and paused for a long time before replying that he did not remember. The balance of Lenzner's interrogation was a series of questions on matters unrelated to the main issues. It was an effective trial lawyer's tactic: challenge the witness's memory on collateral matters; if he does not remember those, perhaps his memory can be challenged on the matters at issue. Moore began to take on the appearance of Ed Wynn with a bad case of amnesia. As Lenzner pressed him again and again on peripheral, insignificant details, Moore—"the president's witness"—took long, thoughtful pauses while gazing at the chandeliers in the Caucus Room.

I thought someone should set the record straight and report that we had indicated to Moore the previous day that he would be questioned only on matters regarding the president's culpability and on his conversation with Dean following the Dean-Nixon meeting on March 21. But I decided that Moore was not a client. The scenario of the young, tough, fast-talking prosecutor sniping at the befuddled gray-haired gentleman ran its course.

The next morning, after Moore had had a chance to regain his composure, I questioned him about his meeting with Dean; his testimony was clear and, I thought, significant. He repeated what he had said in my interview with him.

In the next few days thousands of letters and telegrams arrived in Washington denouncing Lenzner's questioning of Moore. William Safire took the same position in *The New York Times*. Lenzner appeared bewildered at this intense public reaction to what he considered a wholly justifiable, lawyer-like technique. In a way, he was correct—if you regarded a committee hearing as an adversary proceeding of "us against them," protecting your witnesses and trying to annihilate the opposition's. This partisan point of view was affecting more and more of the daily affairs of the committee.

# Chapter IV · The Tapes

Friday the 13th was a particularly eventful day in July 1973. It was 6 P.M., at the end of a long week, and a few staff members, along with a few of the ever-present corps of reporters, were relaxing over a beer across the street at the Carroll Arms, a hotel, restaurant, and cocktail lounge, which was famous as the place where Bobby Baker cut a few deals. Friday afternoon was the time that the sages of Capitol Hill gathered to decide who was lying, who was telling the truth, and whether Nixon was involved in the cover-up.

It was two weeks after Dean had dropped his depth charges, implicating the president in the cover-up as early as September 15, 1972. The general opinion was that if Dean's testimony was corroborated, the president was finished. My reporter friends, who professed to take no side and wanted only a headline-grabbing story, were complaining that the first major opportunity to corroborate Dean and "get" Nixon had already been missed—in the testimony of John Mitchell.

A month earlier Mitchell had telephoned United Press International and said, "Somebody has tried to make me the fall guy, but it's not going to work." Martha Mitchell had been issuing regular pronouncements to the same effect. There was a large body of opinion that this meant Mitchell would turn on Nixon, his former boss and law partner, and that this would end the game.

But the man that Ehrlichman called "the big enchilada" did no such thing. Mitchell said that neither he nor the president was guilty, and he gave the impression that fifteen years of hearings would not alter his story. As for Dean, well, Mitchell said, the boy was all right but he must be lying—at least in the areas of which Mitchell had direct knowledge.

Now there was general agreement that Haldeman and Ehrlichman, soon to appear publicly before the committee, would take the same approach. The case was taking on the dimensions of a conventional lawsuit, a situation I had seen many times; the issue was simply one of "who's lying?" The pattern was the familiar one of matching the word of someone on the inside who had decided to cleanse his soul, usually receiving immunity from prosecution for his action, against the word of those he accused, who insist that their accuser is a new Judas seeking to save his own skin. The major difference in the Watergate case, of course, was that the decisions would be made not by a jury of twelve men and women from middle Tennessee, but by the entire nation.

Mitchell testified on July 10–12. My experiences with him that week aroused mixed emotions, but mostly feelings of emptiness. Eighteen months earlier I had been an assistant U.S. attorney in Nashville; the certificate of appointment on my wall was signed by John Mitchell. Our office always received copies of Attorney General Mitchell's speeches on crime and the administration of justice. I first met the man in the committee's offices on the day he was indicted in New York in connection with Robert Vesco's contributions to the 1972 Nixon campaign. Mitchell's hands were shaking so badly that he could hardly hold his pipe. I asked myself if this man, for whom I had once worked and whom I had respected, could actually have sat in the office of the attorney general and entertained plans for illegal wiretaps, muggings, and kidnappings. I tried to get the thought out of my mind, but I could not help musing, as I avoided looking at him, how far and how fast a man can fall. In our three-hour interview his voice broke from time to time, but he cleared his throat and continued, always looking his interrogator straight in the eye.

When Mitchell appeared before our committee, however, he had undergone a miraculous transformation. His hand was steady, his voice was clear and strong, and his collar appeared only about an inch too large for his neck, not the three inches I had observed at the staff interview. His performance before the committee, in which he rejected all suggestions of impropriety and illegality, was described by the columnist William S. White, hardly a Mitchell sympathizer, with these grudging words of admiration: "Whatever his faults and shortcomings—and perhaps only Martha Mitchell could count them fewer than very many—John Mitchell stands up to his hips in midgets among the other Watergate characters. . . . He had courage. He had resolution in adversity and the capacity to finish in manliness even if he did not and could not finish in style." Mitchell withstood all of the committee's assaults with equanimity and surprising good humor, even though he must have known that the majority of those watching him thought he was lying in his teeth—a viewpoint shared by the jury that convicted him in the cover-up trial the following year.

For Howard Baker, the first day's questioning of Mitchell caused mixed emotions. About a year earlier, the attorney general, at Baker's request, had traveled to Tennessee to address the Tennessee Bar Association. Moreover, although few people knew it, Mitchell, a few years before, had offered Baker a post on the Supreme Court. Men like Baker who grow up in the mountains of east Tennessee do not forget things like that. Nevertheless, Baker pressed Mitchell continuously: "Why had he not told the president the facts?" he asked. "What is the constitutional basis for arrogating unto yourself . . . a presidential decision?" Mitchell conceded that there was no such basis. He eventually attempted to justify his conduct by saying that if he had told the president, Nixon would have taken action detrimental to his own campaign, and Mitchell placed the president's reelection above all other considerations. Ever since, this statement by Mitchell has been cited as perhaps the epitome of the "Watergate mentality."

Wednesday afternoon, with the hearings in recess, we relaxed in Baker's office. The senator, who looked like a man who had just finished a necessary job without enjoying it much, had little to say. While we were discussing the day's developments

*Bill Shure, at left, and Bob Silverstein, with pen in hand, both Minority staff members, discuss with me the testimony of John Mitchell.*

and the next day's schedule, the senator's secretary, Doris Lovett, entered the room with a bewildered look on her face. Doris had worked for Baker a long time; she almost never interrupted our post-hearing meetings.

"Senator," Doris said, "uh, Mrs. Mitchell is on the phone."

"Who?" Baker asked.

"Mrs. Mitchell. Martha Mitchell. She says she has to talk to you."

"About what?"

"I don't know."

Baker looked at me with a half-smile of disbelief. "I can't talk to her," he said.

"I'll talk to her, Doris," I said, and looked at Baker to see if he would veto the idea. He did not, so I picked up the phone at the other side of the room, introduced myself, and explained that the senator could not talk just then. Was there anything I could do for her? I braced myself for an attack on Baker's treatment of her husband, but it did not come.

"Well," said Mrs. Mitchell, "I just wanted to tell Howard that he did a fine job today and tell him what he should do tomorrow."

"Well, it's nice of you to call," I said. I was unable to think of anything else to say.

"You tell Howard to get John so mad tomorrow that he will just blurt it all out, just blurt the truth all out."

"Blurt what out, Mrs. Mitchell?"

"You know. You know what I mean."

"No, ma'am," I replied, in my best southern-gentleman manner. "I'm afraid I don't."

"You know what he's doing, you know who he's protecting, just get him so mad he'll tell the truth."

By this time I could see the headlines in the next day's papers: "MARTHA SAYS SHE'S COLLABORATING WITH BAKER ON HOW TO HANDLE MITCHELL." I said, "Mrs. Mitchell, I'll tell Senator Baker exactly what you said and I'm sure he'll handle the situation the best way he can. I certainly appreciate your calling."

"Well, you just tell him, you just tell him what I said," she replied, and she hung up.

Taking advantage of the senator's look of consternation, mixed with some amusement, as he listened to my end of the conversation, I pretended that Mrs. Mitchell was still on the line. "In that case, Mrs. Mitchell, I'm sure the senator will want to talk to you about John," I said, and extended the phone toward Baker. Then I broke into a laugh and hung up.

"Man, don't do that," Baker said with a smile.

Fifteen minutes later, with Baker out of the room, Doris buzzed me on the intercom. "Mrs. Mitchell is on the phone for you this time," she said. Allowing curiosity to take advantage of my judgment, I picked up the phone.

"Fred," Mrs. Mitchell said, "I just wanted to make sure you understood my message."

"Yes, ma'am, I think I got the message."

"You know what I mean. Did you see that survey that came out recently showing that 90 percent of all lawyers were crooks?"

"No, ma'am. I don't believe I've seen that one," I said, thinking that most people I knew wouldn't put it much higher than 75 percent.

"But you understand a wife has to stick by her husband, no matter what."

"Yes, I understand that."

"Fred, you know you and I are southerners; we understand each other and we've got to stick together. Now you and Howard make sure you get John real mad."

"Where are you, Mrs. Mitchell?" I asked. I recalled that Mitchell's attorneys had indicated that they were trying to put some distance between John and Martha at this time.

"I'm down in God's country."

"Oh, I didn't know you were in Tennessee."

"Oh no, no," she said. "Not there, but I'm not going to tell you where."

"Well," I said, "I'll tell Senator Baker what you said and we'll handle the matter the best way we can."

"Okay, just remember what I told you."

"Yes, ma'am, goodbye."

We didn't hear from Mrs. Mitchell again.

Mitchell's first day of testimony made it appear that the committee would never be able to resolve the major conflicts in the case. This opinion was held by several members, who feared that our hearings would produce nothing more substantive than criticism of them for trying to grab headlines. The following morning, an hour before Mitchell was to resume his testimony, the committee assembled in executive session. Talmadge, removing what appeared to be a $2 cigar from his mouth, got to the point at once: We should expedite this phase of the hearings. "We can complete this break-in and cover-up business before the August recess if we *and the staff* use a little more restraint in the questioning of witnesses," he said.

Dash and I looked at each other; each thought the senator must have been referring to the other.

Inouye suggested evening sessions, but Dash pointed out that interviews were being conducted at night and that we needed some time to prepare for the next day's hearings. There was general agreement that we should wind up as soon as possible; after the overwhelming early public approval, the committee's performance was starting to get mixed reviews. As Baker said, "If people get the impression that we're deliberately trying to drag this thing out, that big public tiger can turn and devour us."

Nevertheless, everyone agreed that on certain matters involving the White House we would have to stand fast. The committee needed certain papers that the president was refusing to release; Haldeman and Ehrlichman were to testify soon, and Ervin voiced the opinion that we would not be able to question either of them effectively without access to some documents.

Baker suggested that Ervin write a letter to the White House, stating that the committee had authorized issuing a subpoena for the documents but that the chairman would like to talk to the president to work something out before the subpoena was issued. "We're faced with the same kind of situation we were faced with in calling for members of the White House staff to appear before the committee," Baker said. "The president relented then, and I think he may relent again. But we don't want to go around issuing subpoenas for the president until we've gone that extra mile."

This discussion took place long before the issuance of a subpoena on the president became almost a daily occurrence on Capitol Hill. Realizing the partisan implications of his remarks, Baker continued, "In case there's any doubt in anyone's mind, I'll pledge to this committee that if we go that extra mile and he doesn't come across, I'll make a public statement that I think the president's wrong and furthermore that he is not immune to a subpoena from this committee." Then he turned to Ervin and said, "Look, Sam, why don't you pick up the phone and call the president and tell him that you and I want to meet with him; that you believe we can work this thing out."

Ervin appeared a bit startled. I was certain that he had never considered direct contact with Nixon, the man with whom he had been pictured on magazine covers, usually showing the two at each other's throats. Ervin looked around the room, and found that his colleagues were either shaking their heads affirmatively or giving no reaction whatever. The decision was Ervin's.

"All right," he said, "I guess we could do that."

It was agreed that the committee would deliver a letter to the White House, informing the president that Senator Ervin would call Nixon when the committee reconvened at 1 o'clock that afternoon.

Shortly after 1, Rufus Edmisten called William Timmons, the president's congressional liaison, to determine Nixon's availability. Edmisten was given another White House number. Ervin dialed that number; after a brief pause he began to speak to the president.

"Mr. President, this is Senator Ervin. Our committee had a meeting this morning and we sent you a little note. I suppose you got it. . . . I don't know how it got in the paper. . . ."

( Our letter, "For the president's eyes only," had been carried by the wire services before it even reached the White House.)

"We just don't agree with your interpretation with respect to presidential papers. We don't want to have any confrontation about it. The committee thinks that we ought to have some arrangement. . . . We recognize it's such a thing as executive privilege. . . .

"Yesterday I discussed with former Attorney General Mitchell that I recognized the president does have executive privilege and I took the position that it does not cover criminal acts and did not cover political acts and Mr. Mitchell sort of agreed with me. . . ."

For the first time Ervin reminded me of a country lawyer talking over a case with a rival lawyer. Although he attempted to state his position firmly, his tone was friendly.

"The committee is hoping that they can work out some arrangement that some member of the committee staff and some member of the White House staff . . .

"I agree that is right . . .

"The question was not so much . . .

"We feel that we cannot adequately examine Ehrlichman and Haldeman and other members of the White House staff without access to the papers. We would hope that . . ." (At this point Baker interjected, "Ask him if you and I can come down and talk to him.")

Senator Ervin continued: "Maybe Senator Baker and I can come down and talk to you about this . . .

"I was at home when your letter was written and I didn't get back until Tuesday. There was a death in my family and I had to stay there . . .

"Well, Mr. President, we have got these witnesses under subpoena, and this four-day proposal . . . I don't know how we can continue hearings . . . Next week . . . Week after next . . . We can't give you a detailed request for papers when we don't have access and can't describe. We want any papers that are relevant to any matters that the committee is authorized to investigate.

"Mr. President, if nobody can go through them . . . if we can't see the papers, we can't identify them. Then the general attitude is that any papers . . . All except those that are of a purely confidential nature . . . anything that reflects wrongdoing, on the part of any of the White House aides . . . We are not out to get anything, Mr. President, except the truth. (Pause) We are not out to get anybody."

Ervin's face grew flushed. It was obvious that the president had charged that Ervin was trying to get him. There was a long pause while Ervin listened. Nixon was engaged in a tirade. Ervin attempted to change the subject.

"I don't know whether the committee . . . how long they will, they will be willing to wait. . . .

"Well, Mr. President, frankly, I don't believe there is much hope for us working out anything . . . frankly, from what you say . . . I'll have to report to the committee that you are willing to see me sometime next week if it is convenient and sort of defer to the wishes of the committee. . . .

"As far as I am concerned and as far as the committee is concerned, we are not out to get anyone. There is nothing that would give me greater delight than to be able to say that there is nothing in the world to connect you with the Watergate in any way and I would be happy if the committee could reach that conclusion. . . ." Ervin hung up the phone.

He looked like a man who had been relieved of a great burden. "Well," the chairman said, "he's standing pretty fast. The only papers he's willing to turn over are those that involve communications with other agencies. He didn't sound too agreeable." He looked at Baker and grinned.

"Howard," he said, "the president said he'd see me but he wouldn't see anybody else, even Senator Baker."

"Well, I guess I get the message," Baker said.

The meeting adjourned and everyone walked out silently. All of us seemed to realize that the "historical confrontation" everyone had been discussing was becoming a reality. In addition to the problem of what was the right thing to do, there were now newer, more dangerous considerations of public relations for the committee and each of its members. And we were no closer to the truth about Watergate.

All this had made for a busy, frustrating week, and now it was Friday afternoon at the Carroll Arms. I was kidding with my fellow Tennessean, Jim Squires of the *Chicago Tribune*. As usual he was telling me that he needed a good news story and that our long-time friendship had not helped him much. Actually, Jim didn't need me for anything; he was good enough to get what he needed on his own, as I knew, and as he knew I knew.

As we continued the mutual needling, Don Sanders, the

deputy minority counsel, walked in. He looked concerned; but Don always looked concerned. Don sat down and ordered a beer. About twenty minutes later he said he wanted to talk to me a minute. Outside. I hadn't seen Don all day, which was not unusual. On hearing days I tried to isolate myself as much as possible. After all the witnesses had been interviewed, all the documents analyzed and summarized, and all the memorandums prepared to show the relationship of the testimony of that day's witness to that of other witnesses, I had to sit alone and study it all. Sometimes this process would begin at 8:30 in the evening and continue until 2 or 3 the next morning, with the testimony scheduled to resume at 10 that morning. During such periods as these, Don did not see me, except for regularly scheduled staff meetings, unless a matter was urgent. One of his major tasks was to make certain that our minority staff covered, if possible, every interview scheduled by the majority staff; with three or four simultaneous interviews on some days, I did not want a blow-by-blow account of the interviews unless there was a direct relation to the witness we were examining at the public hearing.

Sanders suggested that we walk across the street to the grassy lot across from the New Senate Office Building. After we arrived, he looked all around, even behind trees and over his shoulder. Just as I was beginning to think the pressure had finally become too much for him, he gave me the whole story in one succinct sentence: "All of the president's conversations in the Oval Office and his office in the Executive Office Building are on tape."

The discovery of the tapes was a classic case of serendipity. Sanders and Howard Liebengood had lunched together that day at the Capitol Hill Club. Liebengood had been present the previous day at an interview of Fred Fielding, who worked in John Dean's office. Majority staff members asked Fielding several questions about the duties of a man named Alexander Butterfield, and Liebengood learned later that day that Butterfield had been scheduled for an interview the next day. Sanders and Liebengood were trying to decide the importance of the But-

terfield interview; in fact, they were trying to learn who Butterfield was. The two men decided that, because of the interest
in Butterfield on the part of the majority staff, the minority
should be represented when he was questioned. Liebengood
had other commitments, so Sanders said he would attend.

At this point in the inquiry most staff interviews of "big
name" witnesses resembled a carnival. Any staff member could
attend—lawyers, nonlawyers, investigative assistants—and few
could restrain themselves from asking questions, often interrupting another interrogator with a line of inquiry that bore no
relation to what had been asked before. Sanders, who loathed
this procedure, always waited until the majority staff members
had finished their questioning before he began his; and he
demanded that he not be interrupted.

At the Butterfield hearing, however, only three interrogators
were present: Scott Armstrong and Gene Boyce of the majority
staff, and Sanders. Boyce and Armstrong were a study in
opposites. Boyce was one of Edmisten's "good old boys" from
North Carolina, one of a group Edmisten had brought up to
enhance his political standing at home and to add a little
balance to the crew known to us as Dash's whiz kids. Armstrong,
in my view, should never have been on the staff. Although very
capable, he was a close friend, from their days at Yale, of Bob
Woodward of the *Washington Post,* which was then running
exclusive Watergate stories almost daily based on "informed
sources" within the committee. Armstrong was Woodward's
best man when he married several months after the Watergate
hearings. More than once I accused Armstrong of being Woodward's source. After *Rolling Stone* magazine published an
article that characterized almost every member of the staff—
except Armstrong—as incompetent or worse, Armstrong admitted to Sam Dash that he had provided information for that
article.

Armstrong questioned Butterfield for three hours on the
manner in which presidential logs were maintained and compiled (it turned out that that had been Butterfield's job in the
White House) and on the procedures for preparing the notes

and memorandums relating to staff conversations with the president. In Sanders' judgment, Butterfield, while outwardly responsive, was giving no more detail than absolutely necessary. It occurred to Sanders that Butterfield might be concealing something.

Before Dean testified, Fred Buzhardt, White House counsel, had called me and given me in great detail the White House version of Nixon's conversation with Dean and others. I had prepared a memorandum of my conversation with Buzhardt and given it to Dash, who in turn distributed it to the members of the committee. Armstrong had brought a copy of the memorandum to the interview. Sanders considered the detailed nature of the information Buzhardt had related and he reviewed mentally the testimony of other witnesses that the committee had heard.

After Armstrong concluded his questioning, Sanders said, "John Dean has testified that at the end of one conversation with the president he was taken to a side of the Oval Office and addressed by the president in a very low voice concerning a presidential exchange with Colson about executive clemency. Do you know of any basis for the implication in Dean's testimony that conversations in the Oval Office are recorded?"

Even before Butterfield replied, it was apparent that Sanders had struck home. With a look that was part consternation and part relief, Butterfield said that he had thought this question might be asked and that he had wondered how he would answer. He was most concerned, he said, about the effect on national security and international affairs, in addition to his own role as the one to make the disclosure. However, he went on, he considered it his obligation to tell the truth in this staff interview, just as though he were under oath. Then he proceeded, with no further prodding, to detail the entire White House recording system.

After Butterfield left the interview room, Sanders, who was well aware of Armstrong's reputation as a source for leaks, reminded Armstrong and Boyce that, if this testimony were leaked, it would have to come from someone in that room, in which case all of them would be held accountable. Armstrong and Boyce agreed, whereupon Sanders came immediately to me while Armstrong and Boyce hurried to Dash's office.

The following morning Capitol Hill was all but deserted. Liebengood and I were waiting for Baker at his office when he arrived at about 9:30. We told him of the new development; he thought a moment and then raised the question I heard him ask many times when something new came to light: "What does it mean?"

Baker needed little help in determining the significance of a new fact, but he invariably asked the opinions of those around him before stating his. From my knowledge, he never substituted someone else's judgment for his own, but sometimes he used the opinions of others to sharpen his own perceptions. Almost always, however, he instinctively knew what was significant; on the campaign trail, for example, he could always sense the importance of some new issue or new factor, often in the face of contrary opinions from his advisors.

On Friday night, after hearing Sanders' story, I noted in my journal that the discovery of the tapes could either prove Nixon's innocence or lead to his impeachment. I voiced this opinion to Baker, and it led to a lengthy, speculative discussion of the significance of the tapes. Baker thought it inconceivable that Nixon would have taped his conversations if they contained anything incriminating. I agreed. I subscribed to the general theory about Nixon—whether you agreed or disagreed with his policies or his motives, he was above all a consummate politician who would never put himself in an inextricable position. The more I thought about what had occurred, the more I considered the possibility that Butterfield had been sent to us as part of a strategy: the president was orchestrating the whole affair and had intended that the tapes be discovered. Then he would produce the tapes, or perhaps play them publicly; there would be nothing incriminating, and John Dean's testimony would be utterly discredited. It was some time before my theory—and I was not alone in holding it—proved totally wrong.

## The Tapes

In retrospect it is apparent that I was subconsciously looking for a way to justify my faith in the leader of my country and my party, a man who was undergoing a violent attack from the news media, which I thought had never given him fair treatment in the past. I was looking for a reason to believe that Richard M. Nixon, President of the United States, was not a crook.

Had I analyzed the situation sufficiently, I would have realized that the facts did not point toward a setup. First of all, the White House had no control over the timing of Butterfield's interview, or even the fact that he was interviewed at all. That had been a staff decision. Second, Butterfield went through three hours of interrogation without mentioning the existence of the tapes, a point he could easily have volunteered during this time without making it seem obvious. Sanders said later that Butterfield had appeared genuinely concerned about having to make his information known.

After twenty minutes of discussion, Baker reached only one conclusion: that Butterfield's testimony be made public before the committee as soon as possible. When Liebengood and I went to Baker we thought we might be overemphasizing the importance of the tapes; after seeing him, we were convinced that our initial reaction had been correct.

Saturday night was hot and muggy. I walked from my apartment to the Monocle restaurant, and I ate dinner alone. I thought about almost nothing except the tapes. How should we handle the mechanics of getting Butterfield to testify on Monday? Had we been set up by the White House? What if, in fact, there was no taping system? Then it occurred to me that the committee's work might be finished in thirty more days: if everything was on tape, they were the best possible evidence, and we might not need any additional testimony; the contradictions might be resolved immediately. There was an aura of unreality, something like the feeling one gets when he is the first to see a major accident on the highway. Was I actually sitting there in the possession of information, known to only a handful of people in the world, that might ultimately mean the impeachment, the downfall, of the leader of the most powerful nation on earth?

Later that evening I called Sarah in Nashville. I rarely discussed nonpublic Watergate business with her, especially over the telephone. Not only did this protect her, but I always operated on the assumption that my telephone was tapped. It was a thought I would never have entertained a few months earlier, but I found a paranoia about wiretaps in Washington; I decided not to dispute the assumptions of those who had been in the capital much longer than I. I didn't mention the tapes to Sarah, and our conversation was dominated by the problems of a damaged bicycle and a lost puppy. I was ready with my all-purpose statement for such domestic crises: "Don't worry about it, honey, I'll take care of it next weekend when I get home."

After sleeping late on Sunday, I was back at my desk that afternoon. I had two prime considerations. First, I wanted to be certain that the tapes were not a trap for the committee or that there was a significant bit of missing information that we lacked; experience had taught me that matters of this importance do not usually fall into your lap without more complications that are immediately apparent. Second, if our information was legitimate, I wanted to be sure that the White House was fully aware of what was to be disclosed so that it could take appropriate action. Legalisms aside, it was inconceivable to me that the White House could withhold the tapes once their existence was made known. I believed it would be in everyone's interest if the White House realized, before making any public statements, the probable position of both the majority and the minority of the Watergate committee. Even though I had no authority to act for the committee, I decided to call Fred Buzhardt at home. Buzhardt was the only White House staff member with whom I had had any substantial contact. He had been unassuming and straightforward in his dealings with me. He never tried to enlist me in any White House strategy, to suggest that I relay confidential information to him, or to do any of the things that were probably assumed by many of the so-called sophisticates in Washington.

"Fred," I said, "I hate to bother you on Sunday."

"Oh, that's all right," he replied. "I'm getting used to it."

"Fred, the committee is aware of the fact that every conversation in the White House is on tape. I know you realize the significance of that. It's not my place to give you advice, but I think that if I were you I'd start making plans immediately to get those tapes together and get them up here as soon as possible."

There was a short pause. Then Buzhardt said, "Well, I think that is significant, *if it is true*. We'll get on it tomorrow."

His tone was completely casual. If he was giving me a message, I was not sure I was reading it. He left the distinct impression that he was not aware of any taping system, but I felt I could not ask him that directly. If he were under orders not to discuss it, I did not want to put him in the position either to defy his orders or to lie to me. The remainder of our conversation was general and shed no additional light on the matter. Evaluating the chat, I concluded that I had made no progress in determining whether the White House was playing a game with the committee; but I was certain that when Buzhardt related our conversation the next day the White House would understand that it could expect no substantial support within the committee if it decided to withhold relevant tapes.

On Monday morning, July 16, Ervin, Baker, Dash, and I conferred. The senators agreed at once that Butterfield should be called in immediately. Jim Hamilton was assigned to contact Butterfield, requesting that he be present at the committee's interview room at the noon recess. We returned to the hearing room and resumed the testimony of Richard Moore, the White House aide who had contradicted Dean. But I was preoccupied, knowing what was to come that afternoon. The word about the discovery of the tapes was being passed to the other senators at the table, and I knew that the press would have the story within minutes, but that didn't matter much at that stage.

At the noon recess Ervin, Baker, Dash, and I conferred with Butterfield in the interview room. When Butterfield was informed that he would take the witness chair that afternoon, he was upset. He complained about the treatment he was receiving from the committee and said he had not had time to consult a lawyer. This struck a sensitive chord in Ervin, who told Butterfield that he could get counsel immediately, that we would wait for him to consult, but that we wanted his testimony that day if possible. Butterfield thought it over, and conceded that he might as well get it over with, that he didn't see that much need for an attorney. Then the four of us went over his testimony for the first time, and he responded willingly and fully. Dash had suggested that I be the one to question Butterfield, and, working from notes I had written earlier, I went over every question I would put to him in the public session.

When we left the interview room, we encountered a large group of reporters; they could smell a new development the way sharks smell blood. As we went our separate ways, each of us was followed by two or three reporters, a tactic we had come to refer to as the full-court press. Butterfield stayed in the room until the reporters dispersed. The press was in full cry: "Who is the witness? Is it a surprise witness? What is he going to say?" About twenty minutes later the word came to me that the reporters had Butterfield's name, but that they didn't know who he was. A few minutes after that, they had his job—federal aviation administrator—but they could not relate it to Watergate. It was not until 1:50 P.M., ten minutes before the hearing was to resume, that CBS had gathered all the tidbits; Daniel Schorr was reporting the discovery of the tapes. This sequence satisfied a perverse curiosity I had shared with some associates—how long it would take the reporters to put together a story. But we had kept the information secret almost down to the wire, which was a new indoor record for the committee.

The committee was called to order, and Butterfield was sworn. He was tall, handsome, and somewhat ill at ease; central casting could not have come up with a better man for his role. Butterfield was articulate, and just slightly disdainful of

*Sam Dash advises Senator Ervin. Though he seemed sometimes to prefer a different approach, Ervin almost always supported Dash's proposals.*

the committee. The touch of resentment in his voice reassured me that his testimony was genuine, and that it would be believed.

When I started to interrogate him, he cut me off:

"I would like to preface my remarks if I may, Mr. Thompson, with a statement. Although I do not have a statement as such, I would simply like to remind the committee membership that whereas I appear voluntarily this afternoon, I appear with only some three hours' notice and without time to arrange for permanent counsel or for assistance by a temporary counsel."

I knew, of course, that he had been given an opportunity to call counsel. I had to decide immediately whether to argue the point with him or to proceed with the questioning. I chose the latter course, and he loosened up.

"And what were your duties at the White House?"

He was in charge of its day-to-day administration.

"Mr. Butterfield, are you aware of the installation of any listening devices in the Oval Office of the president?"

There was not a sound in the crowded Caucus Room.

"I was aware of listening devices, yes, sir."

From that point it was all downhill, and we knew he would be completely responsive. There were listening devices, he testified, in the Oval Office, the Executive Office Building, and the Cabinet Room. Moreover, there were devices on the telephones in the Executive Office Building, the Lincoln Room, and the phone on the president's desk in Aspen Cabin at Camp David. The Camp David installation was particularly sensitive because Aspen Cabin was sometimes used by foreign dignitaries; Butterfield said the device was removed prior to the cabin's occupancy by a chief of state or other high-ranking foreign officials.

After a few more questions regarding the nature of the devices and how they were activated, I got to the heart of the matter: "And as far as you know, those tapes are still available."

"As far as I know, but I've been away for four months, sir."

This meant, of course, that either the tapes were still in existence or that they had been destroyed after the creation of the Watergate committee.

I left the room while reporters scrambled for telephones. I was convinced that we had finally found a way to resolve all the conflicts in the testimony and to determine, in Baker's words, "what did the President know and when did he know it."

Looking back, I wonder how I could have failed to realize at once, that Friday afternoon, the significance of the tapes. Even later I failed to appreciate their full importance. As a trial lawyer, I focused on the fact that the tapes could resolve conflicts in testimony; I did not foresee the extraordinary constitutional confrontations that emanated from them. We know now that the discovery was the key that opened the lock in the most publicized congressional hearing in the nation's history. For the White House promptly adopted a position I never believed it would: it refused to voluntarily produce relevant tapes. And this, in turn, led to two historic lawsuits against the president, one by the committee and one by the special prosecutor; to the so-called Saturday Night Massacre in which the special prosecutor, the attorney general, and the deputy attorney general left office; to a landmark Supreme Court ruling on the limits of presidential power; to impeachment proceedings in the House of Representatives; and, finally, to the resignation of the president of the United States.

Almost a year later, when I read *All the President's Men* by Bob Woodward and Carl Bernstein of the *Washington Post,* I learned several illuminating facts about the tapes' discovery and its significance.

Woodward and Bernstein, said Ben Bradlee, executive editor of the *Post,* considered the tapes' disclosure a "B plus" story. In their book, the reporters wrote, "By May 17, 1973, when the Senate hearings opened Woodward and Bernstein had gotten lazy. Their nighttime visits were scarcer and increasingly they had begun to rely on a relatively easy access to the Senate committee staff investigators and attorneys."

That the Watergate staff leaked to these two reporters, and dozens of others, was hardly a surprise; it was the worst-kept secret in Washington. What fascinated me was the Woodward-Bernstein discussion of Butterfield and his role. They wrote that they were curious about Butterfield's position, which CRP treasurer Hugh Sloan described to them as being in charge of "internal security" at the White House. Woodward had tried several times to have committee staff members interview Butterfield, the book says, and finally, on Saturday, July 14, "Woodward received a phone call at home from a senior member of the committee's investigative staff." The conversation is described as follows:

" 'Congratulations,' he said. 'We interviewed Butterfield. He told the whole story.'

'What whole story?'

'Nixon bugged himself.' "

When I read this account I could only laugh and shake my head. Armstrong had struck again! And we had been feeling so smug that on this one occasion the staff had kept a secret, through fear or through choice. I now knew that the *Post* had had the story but had chosen not to run it, either because its editor felt it was insufficiently significant or because he had been unable to corroborate the information.

To make matters worse, in the draft prepared by the majority staff for the committee's final report, the discovery of the tapes was described in great detail and the credit for asking Butterfield the crucial question was given to Scott Armstrong. I told Dash I would make sure this assertion would never appear in the final report; Dash did a little checking and agreed.

The incident, which was central to the entire Watergate investigation, is a classic example of faulty perception. Both Ben Bradlee and I thought at the outset that we were dealing with a "B plus" incident; now staff members of the committee are still arguing over who asked the witness which question to assure themselves a small niche in history.

In hindsight, I have come to believe that the discovery of the tapes may prove to be an historic event in more than one way. At a time when the United States government acknowledges that 2 million conversations were overheard by authorized eavesdroppers in a twelve-month period, and at least an equal number were being recorded by private detectives, suspicious spouses, corporate spies, special agents, and blackmailers; at a time when people like me conduct their lives under the assumption that their telephone lines are tapped; and at a time when devices such as the bug-in-the-martini-olive are proliferating, the disastrous consequences that flowed from Nixon's fateful decision to record White House conversations may serve to awaken the nation to the threat posed to the little privacy that remains to us.

# Chapter V · The Defenders

The steady drift toward what I regarded as unfair treatment of witnesses reached its culmination during the testimony of John Ehrlichman. From the beginning of our work, Ehrlichman together with Haldeman (we rarely referred to one without mentioning the other) were considered focal points of the entire Watergate inquiry. But Haldeman, primarily because of his reputation as a man-eater and his position of power as the White House chief of staff, was suspected of cover-up involvement some time before Ehrlichman was. Ervin and Baker had negotiated with Ehrlichman in their effort to get the president to waive his insistence on executive privilege and to allow White House aides to testify before the committee. More than once Baker expressed his pleasure that in Ehrlichman, at least, the White House had at least one top-level administrator who was untouched by scandal and who would listen to reason; this opinion of Ehrlichman was widely held. Once, while briefing Weicker after I had examined some FBI files, I said that Ehrlichman had told the FBI that he knew nothing about the Watergate matter. Weicker replied that he was certain this was true, that without a doubt Ehrlichman was clean.

Ehrlichman's downfall originated with Dean's testimony, which charged him with participation in the cover-up. Dean also disclosed the break-in at the office of Daniel Ellsberg's psychiatrist in Los Angeles, which was part of the operations of the plumbers' unit in the White House. The plumbers were headed by David Young and Egil Krogh; Krogh was Ehrlichman's assistant.

On May 4, 1973, Haldeman and Ehrlichman arrived at our

offices in room 1448 of the New Senate Office Building for a staff interview. As always, in those days, they were together; and as always, they were trailed by cameramen taking pictures and reporters asking questions to which there were usually no answers. The appearance of Haldeman and Ehrlichman before our staff was an important occasion. Secretaries combed their hair, applied makeup, and strained eagerly for a glimpse of the two celebrities. When the witnesses entered, they were suntanned and appeared almost jovial. They were accompanied by their lawyers, John Wilson and Frank Strickler. They obviously had decided early in the inquiry that their best strategy was to stick together as closely as possible; that was the basis for their decision to choose the same counsel, a decision that greatly surprised me. Not only did this give an impression that they were "getting together" on their stories, but also, in my experience, there was almost never the likelihood, in a situation as complex as this one, that the interests of two men were entirely compatible.

Whatever their reasoning, it appeared from the start that Haldeman and Ehrlichman were in good hands. Their principal attorney, John Johnston Wilson, a small, dapper, pink-faced man of 72, had been practicing law in Washington for almost fifty years. He was the senior partner in the Washington firm of Whitford, Hart, Carmondy, and Wilson, which he joined in 1940. He had represented a Swiss concern whose American assets had been confiscated. He had represented the steel companies against President Truman after the president ordered the companies seized to prevent price increases. He had represented Sen. Barry Goldwater in his libel suit against Ralph Ginzburg, the New York publisher. And he had won all those cases. In addition to being capable and having a reputation for inexhaustible energy and a love for his work, he was ideologically perfect for the assignment. A fellow lawyer in Washington described his politics as somewhat "to the right of McKinley."

Haldeman, Ehrlichman, and their lawyers entered the room for their interview looking and acting like old friends on vacation who had dropped by for a brief chat. There were several sessions, some of which ran late into the night. But they never pleaded fatigue or pointed to the clock, even though some interrogations lasted four or five hours. I found it difficult to keep in mind that our witnesses had been forced to resign two of the most important appointive jobs in the nation, and that they must despise the sight of our rather spare staff offices, not to mention their questioners.

But it occurred to me that this was part of Wilson's technique. Haldeman, Ehrlichman, and their lawyers were disarmingly friendly and given to small talk. In addition, it slowly became apparent to us, in the staff interviews, that a switch in roles was taking place on the part of the two witnesses, a switch that intensified when they appeared before the committee a few days later. Haldeman was supposed to be the "heavy," with a reputation for dressing down staff members and treating senators with equal cold-bloodedness; Ehrlichman was considered Mister Nice Guy. But in the interviews, Haldeman looked and acted like a boy in uniform who had just been called on to recite the Scout's oath for assembled parents. When asked a pointed question, he appeared hurt to discover that anyone could consider he could have done anything wrong. Ehrlichman, on the other hand, would alternately lean back to look down at Dash or lower his head and eyebrows with a look of deep concern as he shook his head at Dash's questions. Although his responses were well modulated and polite, he gave the appearance of forced friendliness: it was a significant preliminary to his later encounters at the hearing with Ervin and Dash.

As we interviewed Ehrlichman, I thought back to a day weeks earlier when we had interviewed former Attorney General Richard Kleindienst. We were the first to inform him that Ehrlichman had taped some of his telephone conversations with Kleindienst and had turned over the transcripts to our committee. Kleindienst was shocked that the taping had taken place without his knowledge; he kept repeating "that son of a bitch, that son of a bitch." And he was equally shocked when we were the first to tell him that Patrick Gray had burned a file, acting, Gray said, at the instruction of Ehrlichman.

At our interview it was decided that Ehrlichman would be questioned first. ("I've been following him around for years—now he can follow me," Ehrlichman said with a laugh.) He was escorted to Dash's office while Haldeman was led to mine, where he sat in a straight-back chair reading religious material for three or four hours while waiting his turn. He asked Joan Cole, with great politeness, to remove any confidential papers from my desk so there could be no question about impropriety. He told her, with a little grin, that recent experience had taught him a person couldn't be too careful.

I remember the stories I had heard about Haldeman blistering his subordinates for such offenses as having mustard put on his sandwich. If he was conning us, the performance was so good I almost enjoyed it.

In all the interviews Wilson struck the same pose. He sat in a chair at the side of the room, crossed his fingers in front of him, slouched slightly, and rested his chin on his chest. With his thick eyeglasses, it was often difficult to determine if he was awake or asleep. At first it appeared that the grueling hours might be too much for the old gentleman and that he was, indeed, drifting off. Then Dash asked Ehrlichman about a presidential conversation. "That's still covered by executive privilege, Mr. Dash. We can't answer that," Wilson said, lifting his head but making no other movement. His remark had been made before Ehrlichman even had a chance to answer. Wilson took no notes; all the facts were in his head. For hours he maintained the same posture, apparently reviving only to snap out a brief reply at an appropriate point or to characterize someone whose name was mentioned in passing during an occasional informal discussion while the interview was taking place: "That fellow's a snake, a snake in the grass."

During breaks in the questioning and before and after the interviews, Wilson was a charmer, especially with the women. There was a stream of compliments, witticisms, and self-deprecating statements. At the lunch break on the first day, we sent out for sandwiches, producing an unlikely scene as Haldeman, Ehrlichman, Wilson, Strickler, Dash, and I gathered around a small table with the secretaries to make our selections. Wilson expressed a yen for chocolate candy, and from then on he was never without an ample supply, provided by Joan. For the women staff members, the candy merely accentuated the sweet-little-old-man image. To them he was lovable, like a baby walrus with horn-rimmed glasses. To us lawyers, on the other side of the door, the emerging image was somewhat different.

When Haldeman appeared before the committee, he took a soft line, as he had when questioned by the staff, because his fate was dependent on his credibility. The question of his involvement was essentially his word against John Dean's, and he had to appear more believable, more likable. Ehrlichman, on the other hand, had a more complicated problem: he had to explain and defend the break-in at Ellsberg's psychiatrist's office. The committee had a document showing that Ehrlichman had approved a "covert operation" with his own written notation "as long as it's not traceable." Against this evidence, Ehrlichman fashioned a double defense. First, he had not known that the "covert operation" involved a break-in, and second, the break-in itself might have legal justification. He and Wilson must have known that the second position would come under severe attack, particularly from Ervin, for whom constitutional rights were a lifelong passion; so they had to be aggressive, and never let it appear that their confidence was shaken. Ervin's outrage at this defense soon manifested itself, and when the questioning of Ehrlichman became too heated Wilson entered the debate.

It was evident from the outset that we were to be treated to a jousting match between Ehrlichman and Dash.

Dash asked, "So there came a time when you were administering an investigative unit."

"Yes, in a literal sense that is true."

"A literal sense?"

"Yes sir—not in an actual sense."

"Not in an actual sense?"

"Well here I am dueling with a professor."

"I'm not dueling with you, I'm just trying . . ."

"Professor, if you say actual it's actual."

Later, Dash asked, "Did you, Mr. Ehrlichman, authorize the taps which you have just discussed or have any part in authorizing them or any other wiretaps?"

Ehrlichman replied, "Would you break that question down for me, Mr. Dash; it is very compound."

Subsequently Dash asked, "Now, did you become aware or did you play any role in the creation of the Committee to Re-Elect the President?" Ehrlichman chided him again: "Well, that's two questions. Yes, I became aware of it, and no, I didn't play any role."

Although I was somewhat amused at the sight of a witness unwilling to roll over and play dead before the committee, it was obvious to me that there were glaring weaknesses in Ehrlichman's testimony.

I asked Ehrlichman a series of questions based on the president's statement of May 22, 1973. "Therefore," the statement said, "I instructed Mr. Haldeman and Mr. Ehrlichman to insure that the investigation of the break-in not expose either an unrelated covert operation of the CIA or the activities of the White House investigative unit. . . ." It seemed to me that in these remarks the president was admitting that he had, indeed, ordered at least a limited cover-up, for what Nixon contended to be a legitimate purpose, and that he had instructed Haldeman and Ehrlichman to limit the investigation. Ehrlichman, on the other hand, was denying that he had limited the investigation in any manner, which appeared to be a direct contradiction of the president's statement. Repeatedly I asked Ehrlichman when those instructions had been given to him by the president. After a torturous exchange, Ehrlichman's reply appeared to be that the president had given him no such instructions.

A front-page article in the *Washington Star-News* the next

day focused on the apparent inconsistency between the president's statement and Ehrlichman's testimony.

Later, at a recess, Daniel Schorr interviewed me outside the Caucus Room and implied that I had leaned on Ehrlichman a bit heavily. He asked if this posture did not seem strange to me in my role as counsel for the Republicans on the committee. I replied that there was no Democrat or Republican way to conduct the investigation, as long as it was done fairly. But it was growing increasingly apparent that fairness was a word that was vanishing from the committee's vocabulary.

Ehrlichman testified that it was his understanding that the money sent from the White House to the reelection committee for the original seven Watergate defendants was not hush money, but expense money comparable to defense funds that were often established for defendants in a criminal case. Ervin was fidgeting in his seat, obviously eager to get his chance at the witness. "Mr. Ehrlichman," he asked, "do I understand that you are testifying that the Committee to Re-elect the President and those associated with them constituted an eleemosynary institution that gave $450,000 to some burglars and their lawyers merely because they felt sorry for them?" The question provoked an immediate burst of laughter from the audience, followed by applause that appeared to continue for a full minute.

Ervin had imposed a twenty-minute limit on the questioning time of each senator, and he was sputtering out questions, some of them unintelligible, as fast as he could. Wilson interrupted with an appeal to the chairman to permit the witness to answer the questions.

Then Ervin engaged Ehrlichman in a discussion of the desirability of recording telephone conversations, which delighted the audience. Ervin concluded the exchange: "Well, I have about fifteen telephones and none of them came with any kind of machine like that on them and I haven't put any on them either." More laughter.

The pattern was set. Ervin, the matador, with his cape and

99

*John Ehrlichman testifies while his attorney, John J. Wilson, sits at his side. I kept waiting for Wilson, with his stern demeanor and dark glasses, to make the committee an offer it couldn't refuse.*

THE NEW YORK TIMES/MIKE LIEN

his sword, was battling with the bull while the multitudes cheered. When Ervin scored points or made a clever comment—sometimes on a matter that was irrelevant to the inquiry at hand—the audience applauded. Ehrlichman's responses were met with moans, groans, and hisses. Each morning, as Ervin entered the hearing room, the crowd applauded as he walked to his seat. The proceedings appeared to be disintegrating before our eyes. Once or twice I heard Baker quietly mention these disruptions to Ervin, who whispered back, quite audibly, "Well, I don't think we can put a stop to it. I just don't see how we can put a stop to them." Had anything resembling this occurred in even the lowest court I ever practiced in, the judge would have acted immediately, and an overenthusiastic rooter might have found himself in jail for contempt of court. Ervin, in his opening statement, made a reference to "judicial-type" proceedings; later he commented occasionally that nearly all the evidence accepted by the committee would have been inadmissible in a court of law. Now, any illusion that this bore any resemblance to a "judicial-type" proceeding was being shattered. I would not have been surprised if I had arrived one morning to find a barker selling peanuts and cotton candy.

As the hearing grew more and more uproarious, I watched John Wilson closely. At first he was impassive, and at times I thought I could even detect a slight smile on his face. Perhaps he thought, the atmosphere being what it was, that Ehrlichman would become an abused victim, and even get sympathy from some viewers. Then, as matters became more and more acrimonious and partisan, Wilson, almost as if on cue, changed from the kindly, gentle old man to the indignant, fulminating, razor-sharp courtroom lawyer. He had seen as many sunrises as Ervin, and once he decided to lock horns he gave not an inch. He distracted attention away from Ehrlichman, challenged Ervin to a debate on constitutional law, and, from most objective accounts, emerged the winner. Twice Ervin adjourned the proceedings at times when it appeared that Wilson was scoring heavily.

As George Higgins, a former assistant U.S. attorney, described the confrontation in the April issue of the *Atlantic*, "It was awful to watch, and it was also grand. . . . The only thing missing, as he (Wilson) waltzed them around, was 'Roses from the South.' "

Alone in my office late on the night after the first day of Ehrlichman's testimony, I was at a low point, physically and mentally. All of us had spent many nights working until 1 or 2 in the morning; these hours, along with the pressures that made it difficult to sleep or to sit down and enjoy a quiet meal, were beginning to show. We were working under the scrutiny of millions, beleaguered at every turn by reporters who constantly raised questions about our motivation and who seemed to revel over every tidbit that could be used to belittle a committee member or a staff member, and the effect was taking its toll. The self-analysis that followed every new development, the effort to both pursue a vigorous investigation and still insure fairness and balance, the constant infighting among the staff—all these were intensified by fatigue and demoralization. A man thinks about such things as missing his son's entire baseball season.

The staff was growing increasingly haggard and short-tempered. Its members were still working elbow to elbow in the converted auditorium, and the lack of privacy exacerbated the problem. I found myself avoiding Dash so as not to converse with him about anything, even to engage in friendly small talk. One night Dash knocked at my door, opened it, and walked in; I was sound asleep in the middle of the floor, and he nearly stepped on me. His appearance was not much different from mine; his eyes were constantly red, and his rapid-fire conversation, which had slowed considerably, would sometimes trail off in the middle of a sentence.

The more the complexion of the hearings changed and the atmosphere deteriorated, the more upset I became. I had attempted to play the game fairly. Before the public hearing began, when Fred Buzhardt visited my office to make some points for the White House side of the case, I agreed to listen, but I told him that any substantive information that I received would be considered information for the committee. Buzhardt replied that he understood, but nevertheless he apparently expected that I would not pass on information about Nixon's conversations with Dean, but retain it for use in cross-examining Dean. Instead, I prepared a memorandum, which was distributed to the entire membership of the committee, and which was later used by the committee as an official White House statement. This so-called Thompson-Buzhardt memo later received considerable notoriety, and proved a considerable embarrassment to Buzhardt and the White House. On another occasion early in the investigation, to avoid any hint of impropriety, I declined to converse with Charles Colson, a White House aide, when both he and his lawyer, David Shapiro, were on the telephone with me, each on a separate extension. If there was any possibility that Colson would appear before the committee, I said, I could not speak with him; I would deal only with Shapiro. Colson immediately hung up and I continued my conversation with Shapiro.

At the same time, Dean and a number of Watergate lawyers were constantly in unilateral contact with Dash. Leaks to the press that damaged a number of persons, both legally and personally, continued to appear; it reached the point where those accused were no longer bothering to issue denials. In the staff offices, members of the majority staff had anti-Nixon slogans pinned on the wall, as well as cartoons lampooning various White House aides. One of these pictured Colson being dragged by an automobile in a most uncustomary manner with this caption underneath: "When you've got 'em by the ——— their hearts and minds will follow." One staff member had a ticket to the impeachment of Andrew Johnson tacked on his wall. This did not exactly square with the language of my standard form letter of reply to many citizens, which repeated my desire and expectation that the committee would "conduct a fair and nonpartisan investigation."

Now, it appeared, the high and mighty of the White House were being brought low, and the "public" was being avenged; it did not seem to matter that the witnesses appearing before the committee were at a far greater disadvantage in many ways than someone accused of murder or bank robbery. Our witnesses were not entitled to a bill of particulars that spelled out their alleged offenses, to allow them to prepare for their examination. They had no right to discover any evidence in the possession of the government that might help them. They were confronted with the hearsay accusations of prior witnesses. They were not given an opportunity to face their accusers. Some of the people who were the most vigorous in pushing the Watergate investigation had, on prior occasions, attacked congressional investigations as villainous because of their trampling on individual rights. Walter Lippmann once called congressional investigations "legalized atrocities"; but that was back in the days of McCarthy. Now, it struck me, many of these critics maintained a discreet silence while the crowds jeered, hissed, and cheered.

I decided to change my approach, and I momentarily sought an altruistic motive. Would I not be helping the committee, I thought, enhancing its credibility, by chiding the Democrats for their excesses and bringing out any favorable points that administration witnesses might have, particularly when the Democratic side and Weicker were pounding hard at anti-administration arguments? Basically, however, I knew that this was not my real motive; my side was being "had," and I was permitting it to happen. This was foreign to my nature, and that I had allowed it to occur, possibly because I did not want to risk alienating the press and most of those watching on television, made me first angry and then disgusted. I walked home to my apartment, but I could not sleep.

The following morning Ervin and Wilson resumed their political debate. Both old war-horses had primed themselves. I later learned that Wilson had stayed up the entire night reviewing legal precedents. It may be difficult for men their age to gear themselves for battle, considering all that both had experienced in their long and active lives, but they were at the top of their game, and a jury of millions was watching. They performed brilliantly, displaying arcane technical knowledge, playing to the gallery, employing humor and righteous indignation, all with exquisite timing. Had I not been there because it was my job, I would have paid admission to watch.

The crowd, however, was just as unruly as the day before. As Ervin walked into the room, he was applauded lustily; the audience was relishing the prospect of a second course. During one of Wilson's monologues, I leaned over to Baker and said, "Yesterday was a complete disaster. I never spent a worse night in my life." Baker needed no elaboration. He straightened up and touched the eraser end of his pencil to his lips for a few seconds. Then he tapped Ervin on the sleeve and huddled with him. I could not hear the conversation, but it was apparent that Baker was expressing an opinion very forcefully. He had tried previously to have Ervin act to control the audience, but always in an offhanded, gentlemanly manner. This time, I could see, he was "leaning" on the chairman. Ervin nodded his head affirmatively; Baker straightened up again and looked straight ahead at the witness.

Later, in questioning Ehrlichman, Talmadge observed that "down in my country" people believe that "no matter how humble a man's cottage that even the king of England cannot enter without his consent." Once again the crowd broke into applause. Shortly afterward, one of Ehrlichman's answers aroused raucous laughter. Finally Ervin pounded his gavel. "On behalf of the committee," he said, "I want to make a request of the audience and that is that the audience refrain from expressing its approval or disapproval of anything which occurs in connection with the interrogation of the witness." Talmadge expressed his agreement, and Baker noted that the committee's job was made "infinitely tougher if we are cast in the role of conducting a circus or entertainment. I compliment the chairman in making the observation." In typical Baker style, he was complimenting the chairman for taking an action that Baker had had to repeatedly urge on him. As we left the room that day, we overheard spectators and reporters praising Ervin for cutting off his own cheering section.

The only blemish in Wilson's virtuous performance occurred two days later. Outside the hearing room, a reporter asked if he had taken offense at some of Weicker's questions; Wilson responded that it wasn't Weicker who bothered him, "it's that little Jap." Wilson obviously believed that his remarks were off the record, but in those days he should have known that a sneeze in the men's room was not necessarily off the record. His remarks were reported, and Wilson was bombarded with criticism. The letters and telegrams that poured in from Hawaii made it appear that a natural disaster had struck the state.

Unfortunately for Inouye, the target of Wilson's remark, the senator from Hawaii committed a gaffe of his own. Leaning back in his chair after he had questioned Ehrlichman, he muttered, "What a liar." He thought his microphone was dead, but it was not. Questioned about this by reporters, he said that his words must have been "what a lawyer." Inouye's game with the facts was largely ignored, as was his characterization, before an audience of millions, of a witness whose indictment was imminent. Wilson apologized for his remarks, but his confrontation with Inouye was not ended. The next witness, Haldeman, was also a Wilson client, and Inouye questioned him about charges against Haldeman that arose from an episode in Nixon's campaign for the governorship of California in 1962. On Wednesday, August 1, after Haldeman had concluded his testimony, Wilson returned to the offensive, saying he wanted to offer a motion. "I would like to have, if possible, all the members of the committee present, but particularly Senator Inouye," he said, "because I am going to address my remarks to and about him." Inouye was absent at the time, and Ervin sidestepped the issue by suggesting that Haldeman make his closing statement. When this was over, Wilson resumed: "Senator Inouye has injured my client John Ehrlichman on one occasion and this morning he injured this client of mine in what I think was a blow below the belt and I want to discuss them both."

Baker, sensing another acrimonious fight, pointed out that since the matter involved Inouye personally, and since the senator was not present, it would be inappropriate to take up the matter at that time. He suggested that Wilson offer his motion in writing for committee consideration at a later time. On that note, the committee adjourned for the day. As I made my way to the door, I found myself walking by Wilson. Looking at me with a twinkle in his eye, he said, "They sort of caught me off guard with that comment the other day so I had to make a little comeback." He chuckled to himself as he continued through the crowd.

At the conclusion of Ehrlichman's testimony, I made the following statement:

". . . I am used to courtroom procedure, and this witness has been the subject of moans and groans from the audience, hisses, applause, sustained applause on some occasions, and other demonstrations, and, as far as I know, he is the only witness who has been subjected to all of these things. I think it is unfair to the witness and I don't think it does the work of this committee any good.

"It's not that you, Mr. Ehrlichman, are to be treated any better than any other witness but you shouldn't be treated any worse. It doesn't go to the weight of your testimony or its credibility or whether we believe it or not, but I think it just goes to a matter of common decency and courtesy to which all witnesses are entitled. I think that situation has been rectified now, at least I hope it has, and I just wanted to state that for the last few days' testimony, I have regretted this situation and it is personally embarrassing. Thank you."

Ervin walked out of the room as I began to speak. A few minutes after I finished, Baker called a recess. When we returned to the Caucus Room, Ervin leaned toward me and said, "Fred, I heard what you said about me and I will have to respond to that." He obviously was referring to my statement. Rufus Edmisten walked in, taking his usual position between Ervin and Baker. I moved my chair next to Edmisten and told him, "Rufus, make sure you tell the chairman exactly what I said." He replied, "Yeah, I know you didn't say anything about him." He huddled with Ervin for a moment, and the matter was dropped. I had written my statement in longhand, and I had drafted it so that a critical inference about Ervin could be drawn without my criticizing the chairman directly. In trying to gauge public reaction, I had had to decide just how far an upstart minority counsel could go in challenging a folk hero more than twice his age.

Sizing up the events, I decided that the rules of the game had changed and that I would play by the new rules. So, instead of interrogating Haldeman closely, I threw up one cream-puff question after another. Dash had paraphrased the testimony of Gordon Strachan, formerly Haldeman's top aide, to the effect that Haldeman had told Strachan to destroy documents. In questioning Haldeman, I pointed out that Dash had not accurately characterized Strachan's testimony. Dash inter-

*During a break, Senator Baker, an avid photographer, borrows a camera from a news photographer and takes a shot of the Caucus Room.*

THE NEW YORK TIMES/GEORGE TAMES

jected that he did not pretend to suggest that Strachan had testified that Haldeman told him to destory the files. "The question I put," Dash said, "was that he said he destroyed the tapes and the question put by me to him was did he destroy them on his own initiative." Gurney, seizing on Dash's misstatement, snapped, "What are we talking about, tapes?" Dash responded, "I said files, not tapes." At that moment I started to reenter the discussion, but Baker placed his hand on my arm, without speaking or even looking in my direction. His message was clear—we had made a small point, but it was not worth further argument. Trying to embarrass Dash on a point such as this would be counterproductive. I gave Haldeman every opportunity to make remarks favorable to his position, including statements about the violence that had been conducted against Nixon's presidential campaign in 1972.

Baker questioned Haldeman closely about what he had heard on the White House tapes, the existence of which had been made known at our hearings some weeks earlier. Haldeman had been given access to the tapes by Nixon, and now Haldeman appeared before the committee with the claim of executive privilege, inviting the committee to overrule that privilege. Faced with the choice of recognizing the privilege or listening to statements from the president's chief defender about the content of the tapes, the committee followed the latter approach. On the subject of Nixon's response when Dean told him it would take a million dollars to defend and provide support for the seven original Watergate defendants, Haldeman testified that the president had said there would be no problem in raising that sum, but that "it would be wrong." Baker pressed Haldeman on that point. "Now if a period were to follow 'we can do that' it would be a most damning statement," Baker said. "If, in fact, the tapes clearly show that he said 'but it would be wrong' it is an entirely different context. Now are you sure, Mr. Haldeman, that those tapes in fact say that?" Haldeman replied, "I am absolutely positive." This line of questioning was the basis for a perjury count in the subsequent indictment of Haldeman, a count on which he was later found guilty. When Nixon released the tapes months later, the transcript showed a considerable time period between Nixon's remark that raising the million dollars would pose no problem and his comment that it would be wrong.

Although Baker's line of questioning, and Haldeman's answer, proved to be one of the most serious problems for Haldeman, Baker did not attack Haldeman in the fashion that many reporters and other observers had hoped he would. I heard occasional comments, in fact, that Baker was easing up on the so-called big witnesses. (John Mitchell would not have concurred with those sentiments.) By the time of Ehrlichman's testimony, it was obvious to me that Baker, who had worked hard to support Ervin and to achieve rapport with the chairman, was growing increasingly concerned about the partisan course the proceedings were taking, such as the disruptions in the Caucus Room and the conduct of some members of the committee.

On Saturday, July 28, after Ehrlichman had completed four days of testimony, I called Baker at his home to discuss the situation. It was not his style to develop a strategy in which he and I would operate in tandem. Occasionally I would ask his advice on the best line to pursue with a witness, and he invariably replied to the effect that "You're a lawyer and you have lawyer instincts. You do what you feel you should and I will take up where you leave off." To me, it was apparent at this stage, from his questioning and his demeanor, that although he was seeking to remain on the best possible terms with the chairman, he was not going to engage in what appeared to be a self-destructive course.

The mail we were receiving by then left no doubt that the committee's honeymoon with the nation was over. Many telegrams and letters approved my statement at the end of Ehrlichman's testimony. In an editorial, the *Washington Star-News* stated, "Minority counsel Thompson was on the mark when he later offered the view that Ehrlichman, if he wasn't entitled to better treatment than the other witnesses, was nevertheless entitled to better than he got." The editorial continued, "Once again the committee and its staff displayed their frustration. Senator Weicker rose to new heights of outrage. Majority counsel Dash got himself in trouble, losing some of the precision, composure and sense of fairness that had marked his earlier lines of questioning. A lot of this deterioration can be ascribed to just plain weariness, but not all of it. In my opinion, the Ervin committee had become a little too full of itself, a little too eager to take on and to bring down the two men whom legend had already enshrined as the big bad guys of the Nixon White House. Why, it might be asked, had the committee not been eager to put John Dean through a similar ordeal?"

## The Defenders

Some members of the committee were getting restless. At the session of July 23, Talmadge reiterated his belief that the nation was getting tired of Watergate. "The economy is in bad shape," he said. "Our international relations are suffering, and the people are just plain tired of this business." A week later he suggested that the committee "expedite" the hearings, even if it meant giving up the Senate's August recess, which was then at hand. Baker suggested a ten-minute limitation on questions, with the option to question more than once. Even Ervin had a proposal to shorten the proceedings; he said some insignificant witnesses could be dropped. Ervin's increasing restiveness was apparent at the session of July 30, when Montoya remarked that Ehrlichman had been coached well, so as to give unresponsive answers, and that the chairman should admonish the witness to be more responsive. Ervin ignored Montoya's request. Soon after that, Ervin noted that it would be good to refrain from asking a witness if he thought another witness was telling the truth, which was a favorite questioning gambit of Montoya's. It was agreed to start hearing days thirty minutes earlier, at 9:30 each morning, to cut thirty minutes from the lunch break, and to stay late each day. At a meeting on August 7, Talmadge proposed that the committee break up into subcommittees to speed its progress. "The sooner we finish the better it will be for the country," he said.

If the majority members of the committee detected the sprinkles of criticism that fell on them as the result of their handling of Haldeman and Ehrlichman, they must have felt like some of Noah's friends who didn't make it to the ark after the storm produced by the testimony of Patrick Buchanan, a Nixon speechwriter and one of the most hard-nosed presidential defenders. I first met Buchanan when Dash and I made one of our trips to Fred Buzhardt's office to discuss committee access to the presidential tapes. As I walked down the hall to the restroom, Buchanan greeted me as though we knew each other and said, "Hey Fred, are they going to call me over there to testify?" I replied that I didn't know, although I was aware that he had been questioned by members of the majority staff.

He said that he didn't see how his testimony could possibly be considered relevant, and yet the mere fact that he was called could stigmatize him. Buchanan, whose slicked-down hair gave him a kind of Gatsby appearance, seemed tense. I told him I would look into the situation, and we parted; he gave me the same impression as that of many other younger White House aides I had encountered—defensive and concerned.

I soon learned that the majority staff indeed planned to call Buchanan. The hearing was now into its "dirty tricks" phase, and Buchanan had written a series of political memorandums that the staff members had obtained from the archives. As Buchanan pointed out later, he was "notified" that he was to appear before the committee through the newspapers, which ran articles attributed, as always, to committee sources, that said he was the architect of a campaign of political espionage, or dirty tricks. One of the wire services said Buchanan would be questioned about "blueprints and plans concerning the scandal." A headline in the *Chicago Tribune* read, "Nixon Speech Writer Blamed for Muskie Plot," and the article under that headline began, "Investigators have evidence that Patrick J. Buchanan, one of President Nixon's favorite speech writers, was the secret author of a political sabotage scheme." In the *Baltimore Sun,* under a major front-page headline reading, "Buchanan Linked to 1972 Dirty Tricks," the article started, "Patrick J. Buchanan, Presidential consultant, may emerge as yet another architect of the 1972 dirty tricks strategy, according to Congressional sources."

On one of my regular visits to Dash, I raised hell with him over this latest example of "due process" in action. He said he knew nothing about the leaks but would try to find out. The night before Buchanan was to testify, I was given a two-inch stack of memorandums dating back to 1969; almost all of them had been written by Buchanan. Some had been written by other White House staffers. These would obviously be the basis for his questioning. I went to Dash's office, where a majority staff meeting was in progress, and asked if Buchanan had been shown the memos. Everyone nodded his head affirmatively. I returned to my office that night and read the documents, which were primarily hard-nosed political memos written in confidence by a staff member to his boss. In them, Buchanan appraised the various Democratic candidates and offered suggestions for winning strategies against them, but I could find nothing even bordering on illegality. However, remembering how tense Buchanan had appeared in the Executive Office Building, and gauging the capability for righteous indignation that some committee members had shown, I concluded that Buchanan would probably be eaten alive the following morning. I picked up the phone and reached Buchanan at home through the White House switchboard.

"Pat," I said, "I've got a stack of memos in my lap that you have written. Have you seen them?"

"Yeah," he replied, "they said they had shown me what they were going to use."

"Well," I said, "let's see if they did." I began to read.

"Here's one dated March 3, 1970, from you to the president, where you complain about the institutionalized power of the left concentrated in the foundations that succor the Democratic party and your recommendations about a Republican institute."

"Yeah, I've seen that one."

"Here's a copy of a letter you wrote to [columnist] James J. Kilpatrick on December 11, 1970, referring to press irritation at the lack of press conferences and referring to your view that 'the old man kept the animals at bay with deftness and skill and some gentility' and that the press conferences were clearly a plus."

"No, no," he said, "they didn't show me that."

"What about a memorandum dated March 24, 1971, from you to the president, entitled 'The Muskie Watch' referring to the fact that if Muskie is not cut and bleeding before he goes into New Hampshire he will very likely do massively well there?"

"No," he replied, "I haven't seen that one either."

"You also refer to criticism of Muskie as a 'Democratic

Hamlet with his finger to the wind and his nose in a Gallup poll.'"

"Yeah, I know."

"What about a memorandum dated April 1971, from you to the president, entitled 'The Resurrection of Hubert Humphrey'?"

"I think they showed me that one."

"What about a memo dated June 9, 1971, from you to the president on Kennedy, entitled 'EMK Political Memorandum'?"

"They've got that baby, huh? No, they didn't show it to me."

I was growing more and more angry. The majority staff had obtained all those memos, some of them two and three years old, and had held back on many of them, evidently to surprise him before a television audience, when they hoped he would put on a Richard Moore act and gaze wistfully at the chandeliers while trying to recollect his own words. And this after he had been assured, at the staff interviews, that he had seen all the memos that were to be used. "Pat," I said, "it's pretty obvious to me that they haven't shown you half of these things. Do you want me to go over them with you?"

"Man," he replied, "I'd appreciate it."

So, until late that night, I went over each memo, reading in full those he had not been shown. About an hour into the reading I referred back to his Muskie memo, in which he had written, "We ought to go down to the kennels and turn all the dogs loose on ecology Ed to test his response." I said, "You guys ought to be ashamed of yourselves talking like that."

He laughed. "Boy, you ought to hear the old man when he gets wound up. He makes me sound like a fourth grader." Neither of us realized that the entire nation soon would be treated to a sampling of what "the old man" sounded like when he got wound up.

On we went through the memos, most of which he had not seen since he had written them. Buchanan told me he was sitting on his kitchen floor, sipping Scotch. Most of the time I would read only the first three or four lines, and he would interrupt, saying, "Okay, okay, I've got it," his memory then refreshed. On others I would read the entire memo. Occasionally, as I started to read one he would say, "Jesus! They've got that one, huh?"

Late in the night, as a change of pace, I said, "Here's one dated June 19, 1972, from Ehrlichman to you, congratulating you on the successful cover-up of the break-in."

"What!"

After we both laughed, he took the phone from his ear and I could hear him say, "Honey, you gotta hear this one—you know what he just said?" and he repeated the story. By the time our conversation ended, he was having me go through the memos at a faster pace; he would check them off one at a time and I could hear him breathing into the telephone. He was priming himself for the next day. When I hung up, I wondered if he was going to be such an easy mark.

The following morning Buchanan appeared without counsel at the witness table. A volume of his memorandums had been placed before him. It was obvious from the start that in this match the odds were at least even: Buchanan against the entire committee. Buchanan opened by citing "an apparent campaign orchestrated from within the committee staff to malign my reputation in the public press prior to my appearance." He then cited the newspaper leaks and the fact that it was a direct violation of rule 40 of the committee's rules of procedure. He refuted any insinuations that he knew anything about the break-in, dirty tricks, or anyone who had taken part in either. Furthermore, he went on, although he obviously wanted the weaker Democratic candidate, George McGovern, to win the Democratic nomination, "Republicans were not responsible for the downfall of Senator Muskie. Republicans were not responsible for the nomination of Senator McGovern. It was not Donald Segretti who put together the organization that carried for Senator McGovern the crucial Wisconsin primary."

Gurney interrupted. "Would you pull your mike a little closer?" Gurney was loving it.

*I consult with Senator Gurney during Patrick Buchanan's testimony. After having worked alongside Gurney for months I was shocked later to read of his legal problems that ultimately led to his indictment.*

THE NEW YORK TIMES/GEORGE TAMES

Dash began questioning Buchanan about the memorandums, and Buchanan jumped on him. "The other night when I had my discussion with you and Mr. Lenzner, I asked you candidly at that time if there were any memorandums in your possession which I could look at and study in preparation of a discussion before this committee. You and Mr. Lenzner showed me something like somewhere between four and six memorandums. There are a good deal more than four or six memorandums here. There are dozens of them of tremendous length. If you had shown me these memorandums I would be a good deal more prepared to testify fully about their content."

Perhaps not all of the memos would be referred to, Dash replied. I interjected, trying to muster a look of disbelief. "Mr. Chairman, excuse me. Is my understanding correct, Mr. Buchanan, that you were informed that you would be able to see all the documents you were being quizzed on?"

Buchanan replied that he had repeatedly requested this elementary consideration. Then I stated that it was only fair that a witness who was to be questioned about documents he had prepared himself be allowed to review them, particularly if such a promise had been made. Dash answered that no promise had been made to provide Buchanan with all the memorandums in the possession of the committee, and that the committee's purpose was not accomplished by providing all the memorandums in advance because such a course might produce rehearsed testimony.

I replied, with some heat, that even a criminal defendant, under the Federal Rules of Criminal Procedure, had the right to copies of his own recorded statements in advance of trial. Ervin, who was obviously in a dilemma, agreed that the witness should be given plenty of time to refresh his recollection. Baker commented that perhaps the witness could be permitted to decide if he wanted to proceed or whether he wanted time to refresh his recollection. Finally Buchanan indicated, with apparent reluctance, that we might as well proceed. "Okay," he said, "we'll do the best we can."

Buchanan's best soon made it evident that this witness was not going to live up to his advance billing. Although he stressed the Republican need to take legitimate steps to weaken McGovern's Democratic opponents, he insisted he was no "architect" of a dirty tricks campaign.

Dash resumed the questioning. Did Buchanan really believe it was appropriate to grant programs to friends of the administration and to deny them to unfriendly foundations?

As a general proposition, yes. Democratically oriented foundations had used tax-exempt funds for years for political operations. It is well known, Buchanan said, that the Internal Revenue Service is politically controlled by the Democrats.

Did Buchanan really write a memo saying they should go down to the kennels and turn all the dogs loose on "Ecology Ed"?

"Yes, indeed," Buchanan said with a smile, "but by the use of that exaggerated political metaphor 'going down to the kennels,' I was not referring to King Timahoe" (Nixon's dog).

Dash kept reassuring Buchanan that he was not ascribing improper motives to the witness, but he questioned Buchanan again and again on "how far you would want to go" for the president.

Buchanan's reply was a little general: "I am loyal to the president of the United States; that is correct. I have been loyal to him for eight years. . . ."

"I am not questioning that, Mr. Buchanan."

"What is it that you are questioning, Mr. Dash?"

Dash continued to press for a more specific answer, and finally Buchanan summarized his position: "What tactics would I be willing to use? Anything that is not immoral, unethical, illegal, or unprecedented in previous Democratic campaigns." Even the partisan crowd in the Caucus Room was delighted with the answer, and there was a gale of laughter.

In fact, Dash had never pushed the theory that Buchanan was the architect of the dirty tricks campaign, but someone obviously had. Dash, in a sense, was the victim of his own staff's leaks and of a witness who was both clever and well prepared. Buchanan dealt with every memo mentioned in the questioning as though he had spent all night in a cram session, which in a sense, of course, he had. I made no attempt to conceal my delight. It became increasingly clear that the material, which some members of the majority staff obviously regarded as dynamite, was nothing more than hard-line political comment familiar to every senator on the committee.

After Buchanan left the stand that afternoon, I returned to my office—and for the first time in weeks, I was eager to learn the reaction. Edmisten, who was politically astute, had spent much of the day staring at the floor; I was told that he devoted a lot of time trying to learn who had decided to call Buchanan to the stand. Talmadge reportedly characterized the day's proceedings an "unmitigated disaster," and wondered once more how long the committee planned to continue its hearings. A Democratic senator was quoted in the press as saying, "Buchanan made damned fools out of all of us." And there were other reports that Democrats had called for a tighter rein on the staff and that "we ought to close up shop now."

In fact, of course, the hearings had already accomplished a great deal. The cumulative evidence we had been gathering for weeks had raised questions that could not be more serious or important—the possible criminal culpability of a president, and perhaps the ability of the presidency itself to survive. The dispute between the committee and the White House over the presidential tapes had given rise to a lawsuit that might break new ground in defining a president's power. Through it all there was a sense of unreality. The concept that a group of bungling burglars, trapped in the office of Lawrence O'Brien, whose primary concern at the time was to work off a Democratic party debt of $9 million, could lead to the mortal wounding of a president was the kind of plot that comes out of Hollywood. It certainly could never happen in real life.

Contributing to the feeling of uncertainty and anxiety that was felt by most of those associated with the committee were incidents that occurred periodically. During Magruder's testimony I was motioned outside by one of the Capitol Hill policemen who was on duty in the Caucus Room. He told me somewhat apologetically that he had received a report that my car had been found totally demolished. I informed him that I did not even have a car in Washington.

A few nights later another member of the Capitol Hill police force called me at the office to inform me that he and other officers were at Union Station and that they had arrested a woman who had identified herself as my wife. I told him I had just talked to my wife on the telephone and that she was most definitely in Tennessee.

Later that summer Sarah and the children came to Washington. One afternoon she went to the apartment early and re-

clined across the bed and, because she was expecting me before very long, she neglected to take the precaution of locking
the door—a dead give-away of the fact that she was not used
to life in Washington. She was awakened by the sound of
someone in the living room and because she thought it was
me she did not bother to get up. However, after giving me what
she considered to be enough time to make my presence known,
she looked into the front room, just in time to catch a glimpse
of a strange man leaving through the front door. By the time
she mustered up her courage enough to look out the window
she saw a late-model car speeding away. We reported the
matter to the FBI, but we had a description of neither the man
nor the car, and the man's identity was never determined.

As the August 1973 recess of Congress approached and de-
mands that we wind up our proceedings continued to mount, a
major problem was the testimony of Charles Colson. Colson
was one of the most interesting and complex characters I met
in the entire Watergate investigation. His reputation for toughness and loyalty to Nixon was often summarized by the quota-
tion attributed to him that will certainly appear in his obit-
uary: "I would drive over my own grandmother for the
president."

Colson was a master of the well-placed leak and of White
House infighting. His dedication to Nixon had apparently
moved him closer and closer to the president's innermost
sanctum. To many members of the committee, Colson per-
sonified everything that was evil in the White House, and
although there was no evidence linking him directly to planning the break-in or the cover-up, the general feeling was that
he must be somehow involved.

Whenever Colson's name came up in committee discussions,
committee members made no secret of their distaste for him.
At my first meeting with Baker, Gurney, and Weicker, for
example, I displayed a chart showing the various officials of the
White House and the Nixon reelection committee and their
functions. When Colson's name was mentioned, Weicker said,
"I should have punched the son-of-a-bitch in the mouth years

ago." Weicker told us that Colson had once called Weicker's father in an effort to influence Weicker's vote on a matter before the Senate.

Later, when the committee decided to call Colson as a witness, he and his attorney, David Shapiro, seemed more than eager to have him appear. They had let it be known that Colson had talked to Nixon following the Watergate break-in and that Colson could corroborate Nixon on key matters.

On August 1, 1973, the committee met in executive session to fix a date for Colson's testimony. The forthcoming congressional recess was on everyone's mind, and some Democrats were urging that Colson's appearance be put off. Dash pointed out that Colson's testimony probably would be lengthy and might continue beyond the start of the recess. Ervin said that if we heard Colson before the recess, it might be necessary to call other witnesses we had not scheduled, which would further prolong the hearings. The atmosphere grew tense as it became apparent that some Democrats preferred not to call Colson.

On the Republican side, Sen. Hugh Scott of Pennsylvania, the minority leader, had formally requested that the committee hear Colson's testimony. There was a feeling among both Democrats and Republicans that Colson's testimony might break the tie that then appeared to exist between Dean on the one side and Haldeman and Ehrlichman on the other. I reminded Dash of our assurances to both Colson and Shapiro that Colson would be called before the recess. Shapiro, who was scheduled to leave Washington to try an extended case, became agitated when he discovered that a delay was being contemplated. When the matter was put to a vote, the four Democrats voted not to call Colson. Baker and Gurney voted in favor of calling him, and Weicker, because of his publicly expressed antipathy toward Colson, abstained.

Long before that session, Weicker had agreed to meet Colson and Shapiro for a discussion of Weicker's complaint that Colson had contacted Weicker's father. After Colson and Shapiro arrived in Weicker's office, in the presence of numerous Weicker staff members, Colson tried to explain that

Weicker's anger was based on a misunderstanding. Whereupon Weicker cried out, "You make me sick; just get your ass out of my office," and proceeded to throw Colson out. Within minutes, members of Weicker's staff were distributing written accounts of the confrontation and its finale. It was one of Weicker's best public relations performances, one that Colson himself might have taken pride in a short time earlier.

By the time the committee returned from its recess and reconvened in executive session on September 12, 1973, Colson's situation had changed drastically. Shapiro had informed the committee that Colson was a targeted defendant of the special prosecutor's office and that any testimony by Colson would be prejudicial. Therefore, he said, Colson would now refuse to testify before the committee.

This placed the committee in a quandary because it had been widely reported that Colson would be called as soon as the committee resumed its hearings. "What will we tell the press?" Inouye asked. The committee decided to compel Colson to testify, knowing he would invoke his rights under the Fifth Amendment. And that is what happened, with accompanying page-one publicity.

Even with all the tension, pressure, and partisan infighting that absorbed our days and nights, the weeks of the hearings were not without their lighter moments. Each of us who took part in the sessions came to know the habits and idiosyncrasies of everyone else, and each participant was developing his own distinctive personality.

The experiences of Montoya, for example, seemed to bear out the familiar maxim that intensive public exposure can be a two-edged sword. The senator invariably read his questions from neatly typed 5×8 cards, presumably prepared by his staff, and they soon became the object of humorous comment from staff members and reporters. Montoya apparently did not always hear the discussion that had occurred before it was his turn to question. Even if a matter had been the subject of intense interrogation earlier in the day, if that point was on the

first card in the senator's pile, he would read his question in
full, building suspense in his voice as though he expected the
answer to break the case.

As the hearings continued in ever longer sessions, and as the
participants grew more weary and frustrated, this pattern of
Montoya's questioning became more and more irritating to
Ervin. Occasionally he would turn to his right and, addressing
no one in particular, whisper loudly in exasperation, "Why
does he ask the same damn questions over and over again?
Wasn't he here this morning?"

If, for example, a witness had freely admitted his presence at
a meeting, Montoya would often sternly ask, his voice starting
in bass treble and steadily rising, "Now is it not a fact that you
attended a meeting on January 17?" A staff member standing
behind us would reply for the witness in a stage whisper: "All
right, all right, you've got me, I'll talk, I'll talk, no more, please,
no more."

As Montoya continued his questioning, reporters passed
notes back and forth on the expected dialog:

"Mrs. Harmony, did you ever have a discussion with Gordon
Liddy?"

"No, Senator, I never on any occasion spoke to Gordon
Liddy."

Then Montoya (reading from his next card), "What did you
talk about during these discussions?"

Or this press favorite:

"Mr. Kleindienst, did you go into the Oval Office on September 15, 1972?"

"Yes, Senator, I did, and the president said to me, 'Dick, I'm
tired of this cover-up. I can't stand it any longer. I'm ready to
talk—to tell the whole truth.'"

"I have no further questions, Mr. Chairman."

But for breaking the tension there was no one to match
Ervin. For each humorous comment that he uttered in public
there were at least three or four in private to those of us sitting
around the committee table. For all his fulminations and what

"*. . . then the farmer put the shotgun against his nose and said, 'If she has a miscarriage, will you give her another chance.'*"

I considered occasional lapses from fairness, the chairman was a completely disarming person much of the time.

When Ervin thought of a good story—and his stock appeared to be limitless—he would place his hand over the microphone, his eyes alight with mischief, turn to his right, and regale his companions.

Once, during Mitchell's testimony, the witness was questioned about his hindsight, and asked what he would do if he had the opportunity to relive the Watergate episode. Ervin leaned over to Baker and said that reminded him of a North Carolina farmer whose daughter had fallen under the evil influence of the town charlatan, and had become pregnant. The farmer, shotgun in hand, called on the man and shoved the gun in the villain's face: "You have defiled my daughter and now I'm going to shoot you for it." The charlatan replied, "Now hold on a minute. I'm a rich man. If your daughter has a girl child I will give you a thousand dollars. If she has a boy child I'll give you two thousand." Whereupon the farmer put the shotgun against the man's nose and said, "And if she has a miscarriage, will you give her another chance?" He was shaking with laughter by the time he finished.

# Chapter VI · The FBI

During John Dean's interrogation by Sam Dash prior to his appearance before the Watergate committee, I got word that Dean had turned over several documents that the minority staff had not seen. Dash confirmed the report. He told me that the material dealt with scandalous accusations against certain persons, most of them politicians, that had nothing to do with our inquiry. Under those circumstances, I told Dash, I did not want to see the documents, and it was agreed that Dash would keep them sealed and locked in his safe.

Some time later, however, rumors began circulating that the information in Dash's safe had been turned over to Dean by William C. Sullivan, who was assistant to J. Edgar Hoover, director of the Federal Bureau of Investigation, before Sullivan's retirement in 1971, and that it dealt with improper use of the FBI on the part of administrations prior to Nixon's. If this was true, it seemed to me, the material was indeed relevant to our inquiry. If our goal was to study American political practices in order to recommend legislation that would correct abuses, surely we should examine past activities and compare them with the abuses of Nixon's White House. There was a large body of opinion that the Nixon transgressions represented nothing more than "politics as usual"; the contrary view was that it went far beyond anything previously known, both in scope and in kind. I believed the truth lay somewhere in between. Although it would be impossible for our committee to conduct a full-scale investigation of the misconduct of prior administrations, I believed that the committee could not ignore whatever information on past practices had been made available to us.

On August 15, 1973, William Safire, the conservative columnist of *The New York Times,* referred in a column to the rumors about prior abuses of the FBI. He criticized the committee for not exploring these matters, and he quoted a conversation he had had with me a few days earlier. He expressed particular concern that I, as minority counsel, had stated that I was not aware of the truth of the rumors because I had decided not to examine the documents in Dash's safe.

What I did not tell Safire in our chat was that I had decided that I would only be inviting trouble if I obtained copies of documents that contained derogatory comments of a personal nature about Democratic officials. In my view at the time these matters were not only outside the purview of our committee, but the likelihood was high that such material would be leaked to the press and that I would be blamed. Nevertheless, the pressure was building, and I decided that the time had come to look at the material. I notified Dash.

Rufus Edmisten delivered the documents to my office and left before I read them. In this case, as in so many others, it developed that the speculation in the press was accurate: the papers were indeed the so-called Sullivan memos, one of five pages and another of two. But they contained not just information of a solely personal nature, as I had been led to believe; they cited a number of instances in which the FBI had been used for improper political purposes, primarily under the Johnson administration.

I immediately went to Dash, who said apologetically that he had not examined the documents either, that his information on their content had come from Edmisten, to whom he had entrusted them for safekeeping. I never had the time to trace the staff members who made the decision to cache the Sullivan papers.

Sullivan's memos cited episodes in which the FBI was used to spy on and provide derogatory information about political opponents of Democratic presidents. More important, they made clear a willingness on the part of the FBI to provide the agency's services to any occupant of the White House.

Following is Sullivan's five-page document, which I have excerpted to eliminate some unpublished names and scandalous material about certain individuals:

---

## TOP SECRET

### Preface

First I will make a general statement relative to the FBI and politics and various administrations.

The FBI under Mr. Hoover always tried to develop and maintain a very close unilateral relationship with Presidents and their key Administration officials. Once established the Attorney-Generals were ignored. Different Senators, Congressmen, Cabinet Officers, etc. were carefully and systematically cultivated. The cultivation included both Democrats and Republicans but it was done with such skill and finesse that each one usually thought he was alone getting the special and helpful treatment. On some occasions this activity extended to Governors either because they could be helpful directly or because of their connections which could indirectly be of value. In the main the concentration was on the federal plane here in Washington. To repeat all this was done with great astuteness and adroitness and it was not until recent years that any bungling occurred.

It goes without saying that the above relationships were based on reciprocity. It had to be a two-way street. The FBI gave out valuable information to the kinds of office holders mentioned above in exchange for their support. . . .

With relatively few exceptions no permanent records were kept of this political activity where FBI response was involved. However, written records would be kept of the request be it from a President or a person down the ladder. Such sensitive [material] would be usually kept in special files in Mr. Hoover's office. Action by the FBI would be verbal. Where necessary to write out anything it was done years ago on a "pink memo" which was later destroyed and later by preparing a "Do Not File" memo also later destroyed.

To my memory the two Administrations which used the FBI most for political purposes were Mr. Roosevelt's and Mr. Johnson's. Complete and willing cooperation was given to both. For example, Mr. Roosevelt requested us to look into the backgrounds of those who opposed his Lend-Lease Bill and other similar activity which politically was contrary to President Roosevelt's views. Mrs. Roosevelt would also make some unusual requests. The contrary was also true in that the Roosevelts would indicate to FBI they were not interested in FBI pushing certain investigations too far if the subjects were ones the Roosevelts did not want derogatory information developed on for they liked them or wanted to avail themselves of their services. [Two examples were listed here of individuals under investigation. One was a high-ranking official reported to be a homosexual.]

President Johnson, however, far exceeded the Roosevelts in his use of the FBI for political purposes and to this I will now turn.

The relationship between President Johnson and Mr. Hoover had been close officially and socially for some years. This may have facilitated somewhat the use of the FBI by President Johnson. They had been neighbors. With President Johnson as a Senator and later Vice-President, the relationship became ever more close. (Incidentally President Johnson used to call the Director from time to time and kept repeating one question: "Did you have a telephone tap on me when I was in the Senate?" He was always told we did not, which was the truth, but he never seemed to believe it.)

RE: *Mrs. Claire Chennault and Embassy of South Vietnam*

President Johnson requested FBI put a physical surveillance on Mrs. Chennault for the purpose of developing political information which could be used against Mr. Nixon. On November 7, 1968 Bromley Smith of the White House called the FBI and said that he had just conversed with President Johnson who now wanted the physical surveillance discontinued but the wiretap on the Embassy should be maintained. Mr. Smith said: ". . . the President was of the opinion that the intelligence obtained by the FBI in this operation was of the highest order. He stated that the facts furnished by the FBI had been exactly what had been needed by the White House and that he and the President were very grateful."

RE: *Democrat National Convention Atlantic City, N.J. 1964*

President Johnson requested the FBI set up a special squad at the Convention to be of assistance to him in various ways. The "cover" would be that it was a security squad to guard against militants, etc. Nothing of this scope had ever been done before or since to my memory. Included in the assistance rendered was the development of political information useful to President Johnson. On September 10, 1964, Walter Jenkins, Special Assistant to President Johnson at that time, called the FBI and talked to Mr. Hoover. Mr. Jenkins said "the President wanted him to call, and the President may have mentioned this himself, but he was not sure and that was that he, the President, thought the job the Bureau had done at Atlantic City was one of the finest he had ever seen."

RE: *Democrat Convention 1968*

John Criswell, National Treasurer, Democratic Party, called the FBI and said he had dinner with Marvin Watson, Postmaster General, and Watson had told him of the great services performed by the FBI during the last Democratic Convention in Atlantic City, New Jersey. He asked if the same service could be performed at the Democratic Convention in Chicago. Some assistance was given by the Chicago FBI office but it was not at all of the nature and scope of the services rendered Johnson at Atlantic City.

RE: *Walter W. Jenkins*

President Johnson called the FBI on October 27, 1964 to give instructions that [one of the individuals involved with Jenkins be pinned down as to whether he knew two Republican National Committee Members]. President Johnson also said that the FBI should bring pressure to bear on the Park

Policeman who had lied about Jenkins attempting to solicit him in LaFayette Park on the night of October 7, 1964. The FBI in keeping with Johnson's wishes had already asked Bill Moyers to have Stewart Udall, Secretary of the Department of Interior, bring pressure on the Park Policeman with no results. President Johnson next discussed in some length on the "unfortunate publicity" about the flowers which Mr. Hoover had sent to Mr. Jenkins.

RE: *Walter Jenkins*

Abe Fortas, then on the Supreme Court, called the FBI on October 19, 1964 to say that he had learned that Jenkins is suffering from a very serious disease which causes disintegration of the brain. Fortas said that only Jenkins' doctor, Fortas and the President knew of this so hold the information tight. Later Fortas and an FBI official together visited Jenkins' doctor to get him to make a public statement to this effect but the doctor refused saying his examination showed no brain injury or disease.

RE: *Mrs. Claire Chennault Embassy of South Vietnam*

On November 4, 1968 Bromley Smith of the White House called the FBI on the instructions of President Johnson who wanted all messages sent from the FBI to the White House on the above matter (see Item 1) to be completely protected and secured. Smith said that "this situation may very well blow the roof off of the political race yet."

RE: *Senator Barry Goldwater*

President Johnson asked that the FBI look into members of Senator Goldwater's staff [for possible derogatory information].

RE: *George Reedy*

On October 20, 1964 President Johnson called the FBI and said the Republicans might try to criticize George Reedy for his socialist activities while at the U. of Chicago. President Johnson asked the FBI to obtain from Reedy a list of outstanding people he knew in college that would identify him as an anticommunist.

RE:  *Walter Jenkins*

President Johnson called the FBI on October 20, 1964 and instructed that the FBI report on Jenkins should contain at least four things: (1) the fact that Jenkins had engaged in no other incidents of homosexuality (he was told that Jenkins had admitted engaging in a homosexual act while a child. The President replied that this did not amount to anything); (2) that of the hundreds of people interviewed no one spoke derogatorily of Jenkins; (3) that Jenkins had been a devoted Government servant in peace and in war; (4) that the FBI investigation had failed to show any breach of security whatsoever. (This latter point was of grave concern to some men in the FBI. Jenkins could have seriously compromised our national security for he had access to the most sensitive secrets. Nothing could be proven one way or the other)

---

I was struck, particularly, by Sullivan's assertion that FBI information was available to selected leaders of both parties. It was also apparent that this kind of activity could be extraordinarily devious and complex. For example, in a section of the memo that I have deleted, Sullivan discusses a tactic in which President Johnson would ask the FBI for derogatory information about Democratic senators who were opposing him. These data would be passed to a Republican senator who would use it to attack Johnson's Democratic critic.

Sullivan's second document, "Re:  President Johnson Politics and the FBI," follows:

---

## SECRET

### RE: *WATERGATE*

In light of the recent "Hearings" it could be that the coming specific probing of the Watergate Affairs may turn out to be more troublesome than anticipated.

Should "worse come to worse" keep in mind that I would be willing to testify in behalf of the Administration and draw a very clear contrast between the past Administration we discussed and the present one. Presenting the facts as I experienced and knew them would put the current Administration in a very favorable light within the context where the dispute now rages. Some material, of course, would have to be declassified if the entire truth is to be set forth.

RE: *President Johnson, Politics and the FBI*

At President Johnson's request on November 12, 1968, the FBI was requested to check all outgoing telephone calls made by the then Vice Presidential candidate Mr. Spiro Agnew on the date of November 2, 1968 at the time he was in Albuquerque, New Mexico. This was done.

[Five of Agnew's phone calls were listed. Evidently none of them were of any significance.]

President Johnson called at 4:00 P.M. November 13, 1968 to ask about the progress FBI was making in the matter. He was given all the information listed above plus additional details. President Johnson then instructed that a check be made to determine if the fifth call could have been to Mrs. Chennault. This was done.

President Johnson then instructed that the FBI check to see if there had been any phone calls from Mrs. Chennault to New Mexico, Texas or Los Angeles on the date of November 2, 1968. This was done with negative results. . . .

On February 18, 1966 Marvin Watson called from the White House to say that President Johnson wants the FBI to cover the TV presentation of the Senate Foreign Relations Committee Hearings. Watson said the President is watching these hearings and feels his policies are losing considerable ground. Johnson further felt that Senator Fulbright and a number of other senators on this committee are receiving information from communists as well as other subversives. (Note: there was no evidence of this, additionally, while FBI agents are versatile, they are not authorities on the complexities of foreign policy etc. hence the request was absurd apart from its political aspects.)

It is to be also noted that during a riot in New York President Johnson called and said he has reason to believe some Republicans had instigated the riot to embarrass him and asked the FBI look into it. When we did and found nothing as we expected Johnson came back with the question: Wasn't there at least one or two Republicans involved. Again the answer had to be no.

---

A variety of questions occurred to me as I read the Sullivan documents. Most important, perhaps, were these two: Why had Sullivan given this information to Dean? And how much of it was based on Sullivan's personal knowledge? Don Sanders was the logical person on our staff to pursue the matter; he had been an FBI agent for several years and he was, above all, an FBI loyalist. Sanders was astounded by what he read. He obviously had never heard of the activities described in the documents.

Sanders and I discussed our approach to the matter. We knew that the Democrats would take the position that the Sullivan memos fell outside "the scope of our mandate," since they did not pertain to the 1972 election. Moreover, neither of us wanted to harm the FBI for what might appear to be an effort to gain political advantage. But we agreed that, at a minimum, we had to determine the truth of Sullivan's allegations. Such an inquiry would provide perspective on the abuses so apparent in the 1972 campaign, including the activities of Patrick Gray, the Bureau's director in 1972. It might also be of long-term help to the FBI if such political activities were exposed before they became an accepted part of the working operations of every White House administration. In addition, we were both unhappy about what appeared to be a cover-up of this matter, at a time when the committee was supposed to be investigating wrongdoing on the part of both political parties.

Sanders and I agreed that he would interview Sullivan and any other present or former FBI employee with knowledge of the material in the Sullivan memos. We consulted Senator Baker, who agreed with our plan.

On August 18, 1973, Sanders interviewed Sullivan, a thirty-year veteran of FBI service who became assistant director of the Bureau's domestic intelligence division in 1961 and assistant to the director in July, 1970, a post he held until his retirement the following year. Sullivan testified that he had been summoned to the White House by John Dean on February 22, 1973. That was just about the time that the Watergate committee was being formed, and Dean wanted Sullivan to provide him with examples of prior political use of the FBI. Dean obviously wanted the information to counteract accusations that the Nixon administration had undertaken similar political activity. Dean also wanted Sullivan to supply the names of persons who had been wiretapped by the FBI in its investigation of national security leaks.

Sullivan said he met again with Dean on March 1, 1973. The witness said he had originally been wary of Dean, but had agreed to cooperate after being assured by the White House counsel that he was acting on the orders of John Ehrlichman. In addition to the material contained in the two memos, Sullivan said, he gave Dean additional information, reportedly dealing with the assistance given by the FBI to Sen. Joseph McCarthy during McCarthy's prominence as a Communist investigator.

One of the documents that Sullivan gave to Dean was a "strategy memo" in which he proposed a plan to handle the Watergate situation from a political point of view. Dean was upset, Sullivan recalled, when he learned that Sullivan had used a secretary to type the memorandum. He said he later provided Dean with the two memos the committee had in its possession.

Sanders questioned Sullivan in detail, item by item, on every substantive allegation in the two memos. The witness did not have personal knowledge or recollection of every item. Some of the material had been mailed to him anonymously, and he said he did not know who had sent it to him or why. But some of the material was based on Sullivan's own knowledge. For example, he recalled having seen "do not file" memos relating to the allegation that President Johnson had given Republican senators FBI information regarding Johnson's Democratic opponents in the Senate. According to Sullivan, this type of memo did not go into the permanent files, but would be circulated among key FBI officials on a "need-to-know" basis and then destroyed.

On the allegation that President Roosevelt asked the FBI to investigate persons opposed to his Lend-Lease Bill, Sullivan said that at the time he was a supervisor at FBI headquarters and that he recalled that a physical surveillance, a telephone tap, and a microphone surveillance (a bug, in common parlance) had been placed on one of the opponents. Sullivan asked that he not be required to disclose the identity of Roosevelt's target; Sanders agreed.

Sullivan had personal recollection of other allegations involving President and Mrs. Roosevelt. He remembered the two examples cited in his memo in which the president and his wife indicated to the FBI that certain investigations concerning their friends should not be carried too far. In the case of the official who was alleged to be a homosexual, Sullivan said he was told at the time that Francis Biddle, then the attorney general, had told Roosevelt that the FBI had the facts. Roosevelt listened without responding, Sullivan said, and Biddle then repeated the information. Whereupon Roosevelt supposedly said, "Well, he's not doing it on government time, is he?"

Sullivan said he also had personal knowledge of the physical surveillance placed in 1968 on Claire Chennault, a prominent Nixon supporter, to develop political information that could be used against Nixon. And he said he knew personally of the pressure brought on the FBI by President Johnson in connection with the homosexual episode involving Walter Jenkins, a top Johnson aide, and of Johnson's directions that the FBI check members of Sen. Barry Goldwater's staff. And Sullivan said he recalled having seen a 1968 memo that, pursuant to a request from Johnson, instructed the Bureau's domestic intelligence division to check all outgoing phone calls of Spiro Agnew, then vice-presidential nominee, while Agnew was in Albuquerque.

All the other information in the two memos, Sullivan said, was based either on hearsay or on anonymous communications that he had received over a period of years.

Sullivan could shed no light, from his own knowledge, on a report that had been widely circulated, but never proved: that Johnson asked the FBI to set up a special squad at the 1964 Democratic National Convention in Atlantic City, N.J., to perform political chores, and that Martin Luther King and others had been wiretapped in the course of that activity. Sullivan said he had always assumed that no written orders were issued in that matter.

At the end of the long interview, Sullivan said he might have a problem if he were asked to testify about the memos because some of the matters had been classified by the FBI as involving "national security." Sanders said he was sure the committee would not require the airing of bona fide national security matters, but that purely political activities were in a different category. On the basis of the interview, Sanders and I agreed that Sullivan indeed had knowledge of the activities cited in his memos and that other former FBI employees, particularly those with possible knowledge of the surveillance of the 1964 Democratic convention, should be interviewed at once.

In the following week Sanders interviewed five former top FBI officials. The first four could give no help, but the fifth—questioned on August 24—was most enlightening. The witness was a former agent, with twenty-four years of service with the FBI. He said he was part of the team that the FBI sent to Atlantic City and that he was willing to describe in detail how the Bureau had bugged the hotel room of Martin Luther King. Although the former agent was reluctant to embarrass the FBI, he said he believed that questions of ethics and morality were involved, and that the primary problem raised by Watergate was one of misguided loyalty. Therefore, he told Sanders, if a member of the Democratic staff was also present, he would be willing to talk with us. Sanders called on David Dorsen of the majority staff and Dick Schultz, also a former FBI agent, of the minority staff. Our witness—he will not be identified here—gave the following testimony:

There was concern in the FBI that subversive groups might attempt to disrupt the 1964 Democratic convention. On August 21, 1964, he received a call from one of J. Edgar Hoover's assistants, who said that the White House had requested "special assistance" from the Bureau in connection with the convention. The operation was to be independent of the Secret Service. One of its objectives would be to infiltrate dissident factions at Atlantic City and to advise Walter Jenkins of Johnson's staff of developments; the stated purpose was to head off any potential disorder. Certain persons and delegations were of special interest, among them Victoria Gray, a national committeewoman, and Edwin King, a national committeeman. The Bureau also asked its team to verify the hotel rooms in Atlantic City where Martin Luther King and Jessie Farmer would be staying. According to our witness, the Bureau told the team members that this was the first FBI operation of its kind, and that the Bureau was looking for imaginative ideas in carrying it out. The witness said he had confirmed that King and Farmer would be staying at the Claridge Hotel; he was then requested by a Hoover aide to evaluate the feasibility of establishing surveillance through wiretapping and microphones.

The witness said he rented Room 1821 at the Claridge and arranged with the hotel to set aside for King rooms 1901, 1902, and 1923, which were directly above 1821. The witness also checked on the housing arrangements for several other black leaders with the idea of setting up possible technical surveillance. The following day, he said, two agents from the Newark office arrived to install the tap and the bug; with the help of the hotel's management, they were given the keys to King's rooms. A day later, Sunday, August 23, additional top FBI personnel involved were told by a Hoover assistant that the president was insistent that he not be embarrassed by disturbances at the convention.

In addition to its own force of agents, the FBI had a number of informants at the convention. The team was given a phone number in Washington that would be manned by FBI agents; for identification, those calling the number were to say, "This is Elmer." One black agent posed as a news photographer. Another had credentials as an NBC correspondent; he interviewed key members of various convention factions. When the operation was at its peak, thirty agents were involved. A direct telephone line, bypassing the White House switchboard, connected FBI headquarters at the Claridge with President Johnson in Washington. Room 1821 in the Claridge was used to monitor the installations in King's rooms and in a storefront headquarters at 2414 Atlantic Avenue that had been rented by the Congress for Racial Equality. A wiretap and a microphone were installed at the storefront, which became the headquarters for several groups.

Our witness remembered overhearing conversations in which one of Hoover's top aides summarized the information obtained from the tap and the bug to both President Johnson and Hoover. In one conversation with Johnson, the witness overheard discussions about the seating of delegates or delegations, about possibilities for the vice-presidential nomination, and about the identities of members of Congress seen entering or leaving King's quarters. The activities of Robert Kennedy were of particular interest, including his contacts with King. The White House wanted to know who was seeking the support of black leaders in connection with maneuvers surrounding the seating of the Mississippi and Alabama delegations. From the witness's testimony, it appeared that the concern about potential violence or disruption was less important than practical political considerations. The September 7, 1964 issue of *Newsweek* stated the political problem:

But behind the scenes, the drama was far more subtle, a heady blend of principle and pragmatism unfolding in smoke-filled rooms, corridor conferences and untold telephone calls. Before the week was out, it involved a constellation of party leaders—all the way up to LBJ. In a year of unprecedented Negro ferment and ominous talk of white backlash, the Democrats knew they were in for trouble over the pesky problem of credentials long before they arrived in Atlantic City. The party loyalty of the 36-vote delegation from Alabama—where Governor George Wallace had legislated a slate of unpledged Democratic electors—was sure to be challenged. The Mississippi situation was even more explosive. For weeks, northern liberals had been canvassing nationwide support for seating a full delegation for the predominantly Negro Freedom Democratic Party. To disregard the Negroes' demand would be to repudiate the moral drive of the Negro revolution; to satisfy that would mean a floor fight almost certain to trigger a Southerners' walk-out.

To get the full picture of the situation in Atlantic City, however, we needed to interview one more person—Cartha (Deke) DeLoach. He had immediately preceded Sullivan as Hoover's assistant; from our interviews we knew that he had been in Atlantic City and that he perhaps had been in charge of the Bureau's activities at the convention.

When Senator Baker and Sanders interviewed DeLoach on October 3, 1973, he confirmed that he had been aware of the physical surveillance placed on Anna Chennault in 1968 by the FBI, acting under instructions from a top aide to President Johnson. He had been told, DeLoach said, that this was a matter of the "gravest national security." He also recalled a White House instruction in 1968 that directed the FBI to check all long-distance phone records of Spiro Agnew. DeLoach said he had refused to do this, and that President Johnson had called him and upbraided him for his stand. DeLoach said he had advised Hoover, and that Hoover had concurred with his refusal. But shortly afterward, DeLoach said, Hoover directed DeLoach to have the FBI in Albuquerque run a check on Agnew's calls; Johnson had evidently spoken directly to Hoover. DeLoach also recalled that Johnson had contacted the FBI personally in regard to the investigation of Walter Jenkins following the reported homosexual episode; the president, DeLoach said, gave his ideas of what should be included in the FBI report on the matter.

Then Sanders turned to the 1964 Democratic convention. DeLoach confirmed that he had, in fact, taken a number of FBI supervisors and agents to the convention, in accordance with White House instructions, for the purpose of keeping abreast of any "potential violence." But DeLoach told us a story completely different from the one we had heard from the former agent on the subject of who was responsible for the electronic surveillance at the convention. According to DeLoach, the installation was carried out under the authority of Attorney General Robert Kennedy as part of a continuing surveillance of an individual believed to be under the influence of the Communist Party. DeLoach denied that President Johnson had had any knowledge of this installation. The witness declined identifying the person under surveillance, but there was little doubt in our minds that he was referring to Martin Luther King.

DeLoach also denied that he had received any wiretapping information of a purely political nature. He said he had never spoken with President Johnson personally while he was in Atlantic City, by telephone or otherwise, and he denied the existence of a direct phone line from the FBI to the president.

We thus had additional proof that the Johnson-versus-Kennedy factionalism, of which so much was written in the early 1960s, was still with us in the summer of 1973. Here we had the statements of two high-ranking FBI officials, both of whom had been present at the 1964 convention. One said that information from taps and bugs was funneled directly to President Johnson and that Johnson was interested, among other things, in the activities of Robert Kennedy. And the other said that Kennedy had authorized a tap and that Johnson knew nothing about it.

In addition, all those interviewed stressed "potential violence" as the main reason for the surveillance. If that was the primary reason, it was also apparent that political strategy was a major consideration. To check the testimony of the former agent who said that purely political information was being phoned directly to Johnson, we subpoenaed the logs of some of the agents who were present during the surveillance. These confirmed the nature of the information that was sought, and they gave strong support to the contention that information was given directly to President Johnson.

One such log, dated August 21, 1964, contained several names, including DeLoach's. Much of it was illegible, but on the bottom of the first page was the notation, "Infiltrate warring factions—report to Walter Jenkins." On the second page was written, "Tech? on Chairman of delegation Aaron Henry." (Henry was a leader in the Freedom Democratic Party of Mississippi.) A third notation was, "10:48 A.M. Bob Wick [Wick was DeLoach's principal assistant], National Committeewoman, Mrs. Victoria Gray, National Committeeman Reverend Edwin King, Chairman of delegation, Mr. Aaron Henry, Vice Chairman of delegation Mrs. Fannie Lou Hammer, Secretary, Mrs. Annie Devine."

On another page, under the heading "Walter Jenkins 1095 Deauville Motel," were the words, "install mike in store."

There were no dates at the top of the pages of most of the logs. One page had the note, "MLK to appear before the credentials committee—and plans to leave immediately on crutches."

On another page, this one dated August 24, 1964, was the comment, "Lee White talked to King this morning on phone: King advised that a compromise might avoid a floor fight and prevent a breakage of [illegible]. . . . Someone inside told Bob Moses [another leader in the Mississippi faction]—caucused all night 30 to 35 people all members of Mrs. Hammer, Aaron Henry." Beside Mrs. Hammer's name was the nota-

A scene the public rarely got to see: one of the many informal committee meetings.

THE NEW YORK TIMES/GEORGE TAMES

tion, "called home." At the bottom of the page were the words "some of the members of the credentials committee friendly to [illegible]."

On the following page were the words, "after Rauh [Joseph Rauh was the lawyer for the Freedom Democratic Party] and his group met with King—he went to subcommittee [illegible] their proposals—rejected."

All these remarks obviously related to the political strategy of the black groups at the convention. None of the notations on the logs we saw made any reference to potential violence.

Baker called a meeting of the Republican senators on the committee. He put the question to Gurney and Weicker: "Do we want to call Sullivan as a public witness?" Weicker was adamantly opposed. He said it would look like an attempt to justify some of the actions of the Nixon administration. Gurney reluctantly agreed. He didn't want to further tarnish the image of the FBI. He also felt, as I think we all did, that the press would downplay the story and treat it as a Republican attempt to take the heat off of Nixon. The fact that FDR and LBJ had used the FBI for political purposes might be a significant story at another time, but not while Nixon was on the ropes.

Later, when we were writing the committee report, the information that we on the minority staff developed met the fate that we expected. The staff of the Democratic majority, and a majority of the committee members, contended that we had no jurisdiction to investigate these matters and that it should not be part of the committee report. They rejected the view that the information shed considerable light on the FBI's role in this country and raised the possibility of abuse of governmental agencies by any administration. Baker insisted that the material at least be turned over to the congressional committees that oversee the FBI, and the Watergate committee agreed.

Aside from some subsequent leaks to the press on the information we obtained, that was the last we heard of the matter.

# Chapter VII · The CIA Connection

While the main thrust of the Watergate investigation continued, Senator Baker undertook his own inquiry into what may ultimately prove to be one of the more significant areas of the entire Watergate episode—the role of the CIA. Without question, it was the most mystifying.

Baker's inquiry brought into play some of the most powerful forces in Washington—the CIA, the heads of powerful Senate and House committees, and the press. It set off a continuing, unpublicized power struggle that caused one of the very few breakdowns of "senatorial courtesy" that I observed while working for the committee. It also provided insight into the importance of how the press covers a story; into the way the press can be "used," without sinister motivations but through old ties and friendships; and in this instance, into the skepticism of the "Watergate press" toward the motives of those on the committee who did not make the White House the sole target of their labors.

From the beginning of our work, Baker was not satisfied with the explanation of the CIA's involvement in the Watergate matter. From the hearings, we knew that the CIA had furnished Howard Hunt, a former agent and White House consultant, with a wig, a camera, and other equipment, some of which were used in the burglary of the office of Daniel Ellsberg's psychiatrist, Dr. Fielding. The CIA had also produced a psychological profile on Ellsberg. Hunt had first disclosed these matters to the Watergate grand jury on May 2, 1973. Later that month Lt. Gen. Vernon Walters, deputy director of the CIA, appeared before the Senate Armed Services Commit-

tee, which oversees the CIA, and confirmed these facts. All this
CIA activity mystified Baker, who was also puzzled by the
fact that James McCord, after his arrest at the Watergate
building, continued to write letters to CIA officials and apparently remained in close contact with them.

Richard Helms, the former director of central intelligence,
Robert Cushman, the former deputy director, and Walters all
testified to the Watergate committee, in effect, that they had
been duped into providing the White House with assistance in
unlawful and improper activities. Further, they said the Agency
had courageously resisted pressure by Haldeman and Ehrlichman after the Watergate break-in when those White House
aides had attempted to include the CIA in the cover-up. Nevertheless, before long additional CIA involvement in the Watergate matter began to stick out of the investigation like quills on
a porcupine.

Both Howard Hunt and James McCord had been CIA employees. All but one of the Cuban-Americans involved had CIA
backgrounds. CIA officials had asserted repeatedly that the
Agency had cut its ties with all the Watergate burglars before
the break-in; but in my questioning of Helms I elicited from
him the fact that one of them, Eugenio Martinez, was still on a
CIA retainer when the break-in occurred.

Later in 1973, interesting magazine articles about the CIA
began to appear. On September 14, Miles Copeland, a former
CIA agent, suggested in an article in the *National Review* that
McCord might have been given what the writer called a "non-
order" to sabotage the Watergate burglars' operation; that is,
that the desires of the CIA hierarchy were made known to
McCord without a specific order. David Young, one of the
directors of the "plumbers" (a White House task force originally formed to plug national security leaks), who never testified in public, told us that the White House, and especially
Secretary of State Henry Kissinger, was dissatisfied with the
nation's entire intelligence-gathering community. According to
Young, during the Vietnam war Kissinger sometimes would

write "this is a piece of crap" across a CIA estimate and send it back.

It must have been clear to the CIA that the White House was setting up its own intelligence capability when it created the plumbers and hired Jack Caulfield, a White House undercover agent and CRP employee; Tony Ulasewicz, a New York gumshoe; and others. In the eyes of the CIA, the future of the Agency could have been in doubt. From our point of view, it seemed beyond comprehension that the CIA, with its existence in apparent jeopardy and so many of its alumni involved in White House operations, would not at least attempt to monitor the activities of the plumbers and the other White House intelligence operatives.

In November of 1973, Andrew St. George wrote in *Harper's* magazine that Martinez had reported to his CIA superiors on the planning of the Watergate break-in and that Helms himself had been informed of the break-in planning.

As a result of all these developments, on November 8, 1973, Senator Baker wrote to William Colby, then the CIA director, and posed a set of questions. One of them was, "On or after June 17, 1972, did any of the individuals associated with these break-ins in any way communicate with any individual associated with the CIA to discuss the Watergate break-ins or the Ellsberg psychiatric office break-in, other than Mr. McCord who wrote letters to the CIA which are a part of the Watergate hearing record?"

Nearly a month later, the CIA responded. "On July 10, 1972 [less than a month after the break-in], an officer of a commercial concern communicated to an employee of the CIA information which had come to his attention concerning the Watergate five." The letter went on to say that the relationship with this informant was classified and the information was basically hearsay, so no further action was taken.

Baker had thus dug out the first chunk of what turned out to be a mountain of inexplicable CIA entanglement with the Watergate matter. The senator demanded details of the CIA's information. The CIA grudgingly acquiesced—and thus opened itself to the most profound analysis the Agency had undergone, prior to the CIA inquiries that were initiated early in 1975.

The CIA produced for Senator Baker what it referred to as "Volume 4," which consisted primarily of internal memorandums collected after the Watergate break-in. It contained a memorandum dated July 10, 1972, which, we later learned, had been hand delivered to Helms because of its sensitivity. The memorandum disclosed that Robert Bennett, president of Mullen & Company, a public relations firm in Washington, had been debriefed by Mullen's CIA case officer, the official to whom a CIA operative reports, shortly after the Watergate break-in. Mullen & Company had long been suspected in Washington as having CIA connections, but the fact that its president, a former Nixon administration employee in the Department of Transportation, was reporting on information concerning the break-in was intriguing.

The memo outlined Bennett's plan to stifle any revelation of the CIA's relationship with Mullen & Company and to keep both the CIA and the company as far removed as possible from Watergate. Bennett said he had established a back-door entry to Edward Bennett Williams, counsel to the Democratic National Committee, to block revelations of the Mullen-CIA connection; he said he was putting pressure on Charles Colson through the news media to divert attention from the CIA and that he was feeding stories to Bob Woodward of the *Washington Post,* who was "suitably grateful," according to the memo. Bennett said Woodward was protecting Mullen & Company and Bennett.

Baker arranged for an interview with Bob Bennett. Bennett was the son of Sen. Wallace Bennett, the respected senior senator from Utah, who was serving his last term. Senatorial courtesy being what it is, Baker arranged the interview so that Senator Bennett could be present. Senator Baker's informal interview was closely followed by a staff interview of Robert Bennett under oath. On both occasions the story was the same. Although he had been "puffing" somewhat, the statements set forth in the memo were basically the same as what he had related to the CIA case officer. For some time Mullen & Company had furnished "cover" for various CIA operatives abroad. However, Bennett said he knew nothing about the Watergate break-in before it happened and was only interested in seeing that his company's arrangement with the CIA was not revealed.

However, we discovered from Bennett that he had acted as an intermediary between Howard Hunt and Gordon Liddy after the Watergate break-in and had delivered messages between them. Also, when the young political spy Tom Gregory, who had been recruited by Hunt, had second thoughts about some of Hunt's and Liddy's plans to bug Democratic contenders' offices he went to Bennett and told him he was quitting. This was on June 16, 1972, the day before the final Watergate break-in.

As we dug deeper we discovered what had been not only a close relationship between the Agency and Hunt and Bennett but a surprising degree of cooperation between the Agency (through Bennett) and Howard Hughes. We discovered that Hughes Tool Company, a Howard Hughes corporation, was Mullen & Company's major account and that the Agency contemplated utilizing the Mullen-Hughes Tool relationship for cover arrangements in South America and to gather information on Hughes' former top aide, Robert Mahue. Hughes had fired Mahue, sparking a bitter court fight.

The interrelationships became even more complex when we interviewed Howard Hunt again. Hunt had previously told us that in 1964, while he was with the CIA's Domestic Operations Division, he had done a bit of spying on the Goldwater campaign. This was done at the behest of an aide to President Johnson. This time Hunt told us that he had been approached by Bennett with an inquiry from the "Hughes people" as to the cost of bugging the home of Clifford Irving at the time he was writing the spurious Howard Hughes biography. Hunt got an estimate from James McCord and reported back to Bennett. Bennett in turn reported to the Hughes people, who considered the endeavor too costly. Hunt revealed other Bennett activities we had not known before. It was Bennett, he said, who suggested to Hunt that Hank Greenspun, publisher of the *Las Vegas Sun,* had material in his safe that would be of interest to both Hughes and the Committee for the Re-election of the President.

Hunt and Liddy went so far as to discuss a possible burglary of Greenspun's office with some of the Hughes people. Also, Bennett had arranged a Hunt interview with Clifton Demotte, who Bennett said possessed damaging information about Sen. Edward Kennedy and the episode at Chappaquiddick. Furthermore, Bennett coordinated the release of ITT lobbyist Dita Beard's statement from Denver, after Bennett learned of her whereabouts from a Hughes Tool Company executive. It was at the interview of Dita Beard at the hospital in Denver that Hunt wore his famous red wig. Up until our interview with Hunt, Charles Colson had gotten almost exclusive credit for the Demotte and Dita Beard capers.

What this meant was that (1) while Hunt was at the White House on Charles Colson's payroll, Bennett was, at least, suggesting and coordinating many of Hunt's activities; (2) Bennett obviously enjoyed a close and confidential relationship with some of Howard Hughes' top people at a time when they were furnishing cover for the CIA; and (3) Bennett was acting as a go-between between Hunt and Liddy immediately after the Watergate break-in, and during all of these activities he was undoubtedly reporting periodically to the CIA case officer. After the break-in he was providing detailed information concerning Watergate to the CIA—information that was not being forwarded to the FBI, which was investigating the case. In addition, Bennett acknowledged that he had not told the Watergate grand jury everything he knew, a fact that took on greater significance when we learned that the CIA had paid half his attorney's fees in connection with his grand jury appearance.

We now had a clear indication that the CIA had kept close check on the Watergate situation immediately after the break-in through at least one well-placed informant. At this point Baker and I discussed questions that were to recur often in the next few months: if the CIA is giving us this information at this late date, what else does it have that it is unwilling to give us? What other reports had Bennett made to the Agency? What had he reported *before* the break-in? An examination of the documents in Volume 4 indicated that the CIA had been less than candid in relating its knowledge of the Watergate affair to the appropriate authorities, including our committee. There had to be more.

Early in January 1974, when I returned from my Christmas holidays, I found that Senator Baker had decided to set up a task force to explore this whole question. It was to consist of Howard Liebengood, Michael Madigan, and me. From then until early March, the CIA investigation occupied most of the time of the three of us; in addition, I had to try to keep abreast of the majority staff and the never-ending series of interviews it was conducting in other areas of the case.

On January 9, 1974, Liebengood and Madigan interviewed Victor Marchetti, a former CIA agent who has since published *The CIA and the Cult of Intelligence,* a book that the CIA fought in court, winning the deletion of dozens of passages. Almost in passing in his interview, Marchetti said he suspected that the CIA might have had a central taping system.

After Baker and our task force began to request CIA documentation with increasing frequency, the Agency assigned Agent X* to work with us. A good-looking, well-groomed man in his early forties, X had been with the CIA since college. He had experience in public relations and gave the impression of being wholly cooperative. It was clear to us that X's job was to keep Baker happy—up to a point. Soon after the Marchetti interview, Liebengood, Madigan, and I were having one of our periodic sessions with X in my office. Liebengood asked if it was true that the CIA had a central taping system. X muttered somewhat nervously that he didn't believe so; if one existed in

---

* The identity of Agent X, like that of most CIA personnel we dealt with, has been "classified" by the Agency.

the past, he said, it was no longer in operation. Two days later, in a conversation with CIA Director William Colby, Baker brought up the matter of tapes. Colby volunteered the fact that the Agency had had such a taping system in the past. Baker asked for all relevant tapes and Colby agreed to provide them.

This scrap of information opened up a lot of new possibilities; the analogy to the White House and its taping system did not have to be drawn. But our hopes were deflated when Colby advised Baker that he had discovered that the CIA destroyed its tapes on January 18, 1973. That the Agency had gotten rid of such material in the midst of the trial of the Watergate burglars struck us as enormously significant, particularly because Sen. Mike Mansfield, the Senate majority leader, had written to all government agencies requesting that all evidentiary materials be retained.

This disclosure caused us to intensify our investigation. We demanded that all CIA personnel in charge of the taping system be produced for interrogation. The Agency employees who came forward included security technicians, the former secretary to Helms, the secretary to Cushman, and others. As we expected, their stories were consistent: the tapes were destroyed in the ordinary course of business and not because they contained any damaging information. From Helms' secretary, a middle-aged woman who combined charm and toughness, we obtained one important admission—that among the telephone conversations the CIA had recorded were some involving Nixon, Haldeman, Ehrlichman, and other White House officials.

We next turned to Eugenio Martinez, who had met with his CIA case officer in Florida while he was associated with Hunt and Liddy in such enterprises as the break-in of Ellsberg's psychiatrist's office and the Watergate burglary. According to rumors that had come our way, Martinez had outlined details of the Watergate burglary to his case officer; and Rinaldo Pico, one of the participants in the first Watergate break-in, had told us that he believed Martinez was reporting to someone on the group's activities. In addition, of course, we were aware that

Martinez was still on a CIA retainer of at least $100 a month at the time of the Watergate break-in.

In response to our demand for all case-officer contact reports, CIA correspondence, and other data relating to the debriefing of Martinez, we received only "abridged" reports, and these appeared to be given with great reluctance. Even this material, however, was eye-opening. It was apparent from the documents that in November 1971, a month after he took part in the Fielding break-in, Martinez mentioned his association with Hunt to his case officer who, in turn, took Martinez to the CIA's chief of station in Miami.

We immediately requested that the chief of station be brought from Florida for an interview. The chief, a heavyset man who appeared rather nervous, told us that in March 1972, Martinez had asked him if he "really knew all about the Agency activities in the Miami area." Martinez had dropped hints about Hunt's activities, the chief said, which had concerned him so much that he wrote a letter to CIA headquarters inquiring about Hunt's status. The answer, we were told, was that the chief should "cool it" and not concern himself with Hunt's affairs. Angered and perplexed, the chief said, he had Martinez prepare a "cover story," in Spanish, in which Martinez omitted many of the suspicions he had voiced earlier to the chief. The cover story remained in the chief's file until after the Watergate break-in; this account confirmed reports we had received from several sources that it was standard CIA practice to keep cover stories and doctored records on file for display to curious congressmen and their staffs.

In our opinion, Martinez, a loyal CIA operative with a record of many undercover missions for the Agency, would have advised his case officer fully of Hunt's activities unless he knew the Agency was already aware of them. We discovered that Martinez had had two case officers. The first one, according to the Agency, was on an "African safari" at the time of the Watergate break-in, an assertion that we greeted with loud guffaws. The second one, the man in charge of Martinez at the time of the break-in, was rushed within days of the break-in to CIA headquarters, where he is still assigned.

As for Martinez himself, he loyally clung to his cover story. When we interviewed him in my office on December 10, 1973, he struck all of us as a highly intelligent, highly motivated person. Questioned about his loyalties to the CIA and to Hunt, and asked whether he had not always kept the Agency informed of all his activities, he would either answer evasively or deny any CIA involvement in Watergate matters.

In speaking of the CIA, he said, "You must understand these people are not our enemies, these people are our friends. They are friends to your country. What they do is good for your country. They are fighting our enemies." I agreed that the CIA was not our enemy.

Finally, I asked him, "Mr. Martinez, if in fact you were a CIA plant on the Watergate team and were reporting back to the Agency, would you tell us?" He broke into a broad smile, looked around the room, and laughed. He never answered the question; no answer was necessary.

At about the same time that we were reexamining Martinez's role in the case, we were checking into a report about another familiar, equally complex figure—Charles Colson, who had pleaded the Fifth Amendment before our committee near the end of our public hearings.

Robert Bennett's memo to his case officer—the one written on July 10, 1972—contained a reference to Colson. Our reading of the memo indicated that Bennett was seeking to direct attention to Colson and to implicate him in the Watergate affair, even though the memo acknowledged that Bennett had no proof of such involvement. In investigating Bennett's background we learned that Bennett's closest involvement with Howard Hunt took place while Hunt was on Colson's payroll at the White House.

In our pursuit of the leads provided by Bennett's memo and his interview, we decided, with Baker's approval, to interview Colson. At my request he agreed to drop by Baker's home. I had not seen him in months—not since the early stages of the investigation, at an interview that took place long before we discovered the Bennett memorandum. At that interview Colson, one of the so-called hatchet men in the Nixon White House, had appeared to be meek and honestly bewildered by some of the pointed questions that we had leveled at him.

At Baker's house, Colson looked nervous. It was a cold day, but I thought I could detect a few beads of perspiration on his forehead. Asked by Baker if he knew Bob Bennett, Colson replied that he had known Bennett for some time and considered him a good friend. From the memorandum, it was obvious that Bennett's opinion was quite different.

Did Colson know of any information in Bennett's possession that would implicate Colson in the Watergate break-in? "Absolutely not," he replied. Did he know of any reason why Bennett or the CIA would seek to involve him? "None whatsoever," he said. When Baker finished his reading of the portions of the Bennett memo pertaining to Colson, Colson said "Jesus Christ!" and then sat for a moment in stunned silence. That ended the brief encounter, but Colson had no intention of allowing the matter to rest there.

A few days later, after thinking things over, Colson called me. Putting together the facts—that Mullen & Company was a CIA front, that Hunt had apparently been maintaining his links with the CIA through Bennett while working under Colson, and that Hunt and Bennett had been working together on matters that Colson had not previously been aware of—Colson concluded that Hunt was still a CIA employee while working at the White House and that Colson, perhaps because of his reputation as a tough guy, had been selected as the "patsy." Colson's theory was one that we had discussed earlier among ourselves, but had dismissed it as too farfetched. Nevertheless, as the CIA story continued to unfold, we excluded no possibilities. I could not decide if Colson's belief was genuine or if he was seeing the same man I had chatted with on the telephone. I continued to hear from him.

Colson continued to call me occasionally, usually to give me a piece of information he had picked up or to elaborate on his theory. Although I was aware of Colson's reputation and thus somewhat skeptical of his motivation, I never discerned in our conversations any of the ruthlessness that was said to be his trademark. His tone was moderate, almost totally devoid of profanity, and I was not completely surprised later to read that he had undergone a conversion to evangelic Christianity. Watching him discuss his conversion on television one day, I was seeing the same man I had been chatting with on the telephone. I continued to hear from him.

Our CIA inquiry, meanwhile, continued to expand. One phase of it focused on the Agency's role in supplying Hunt with all the paraphernalia he assembled for the Fielding burglary, the Dita Beard interview, the Demotte interview, and possibly other escapades—a wig, a voice-alteration device, a heel lift that caused a limp, false glasses, a phony driver's license and identification card, a camera hidden in a tobacco pouch, and a tape recorder disguised in a typewriter case. The CIA had consistently maintained that it had no idea what Hunt was doing with all this equipment. We interrogated a number of employees of the Agency's Technical Services Division, the unit that had supplied the material to Hunt. A stream of technicians appeared in our interview room, each one accompanied by Agent X and a CIA lawyer. From these interviews, a new pattern began to take shape: witnesses acknowledged that the CIA had developed film for Hunt and Liddy and they agreed "in retrospect" that these were indeed pictures "casing" Dr. Fielding's office for the plumbers. Not only was the film developed by CIA technicians, we were told, but the material was also reviewed by CIA supervisory personnel before it was returned to Hunt. The deputy chief of the Technical Services Division, in his interview with us, conceded that he had found the photographs "intriguing"; he also acknowledged that he had ordered one of the photos enlarged, and that the blow-up disclosed the name of Dr. Fielding in the parking lot next to his office. And the CIA official who reviewed these photos said he had immediately reported their content to his superiors.

It would have required little sophistication for the Agency to conclude that Hunt and Liddy were casing the office of a "Dr. Fielding." Couple this information with the fact that the CIA was compiling a psychological profile of Daniel Ellsberg, that the Agency's file on Ellsberg surely contained the name of Fielding as Ellsberg's psychiatrist, and the conclusion is obvious: the CIA, while providing technical assistance to Hunt and Liddy, had to be aware that Hunt and Liddy were casing the office of Ellsberg's psychiatrist.

The CIA's dissembling about aid to Hunt was not limited to the Fielding break-in. Our inquiry made it equally obvious that a memorandum prepared for the record by Lt. Gen. Vernon Walters, Cushman's successor as CIA deputy director, dated July 28, 1972, in which Walters said the CIA had had no contact with Hunt after August 31, 1971, was patently false. Secret CIA materials that we were eliciting showed that Hunt had contacted the Agency's external employment assistance branch and had approached CIA personnel still on active duty in connection with several operations, including one request for persons skilled in lock-picking, electronic sweeping, and "entry operations."

As our investigation progressed, we found ourselves stepping on more and more sacred toes within the Agency. Helms, the former CIA director, testified before the Senate Armed Services Committee on May 17, 1973, that he had not been aware that Hunt was involved in the CIA's project to prepare a psychological profile on Daniel Ellsberg. Yet the psychiatrist primarily responsible for that profile told us that he had been advised that Helms had been informed of Hunt's participation; in fact, the psychiatrist said, he had insisted that Helms be advised because the psychiatrist was himself concerned about Hunt's involvement.

Liebengood and Madigan were working eighteen hours a day on the CIA project, preparing and conducting interviews and preparing requests for documents based on the new information we were receiving. It occurred to us that we three minority staff members might have seen more CIA agents, reviewed more classified Agency material, and delved deeper into CIA affairs than any outsiders in the history of the Agency —including the committees of the House and Senate that were responsible for overseeing the CIA. As was true in the main Watergate investigation, we were getting our most productive information from relatively low-level CIA employees. In our opinion, they had not been advised of the big picture of any CIA activity, including this one. Unaware of what full disclosure of the Agency's role might signify, they gave us straightforward rather than defensive answers.

We knew that the only reason we were able to interview so many witnesses and have access to so many documents was the CIA's concern about Senator Baker's position on the Watergate committee. Even so, friction was beginning to develop. It became apparent that the CIA hierarchy, which was kept informed of all the testimony we were receiving, realized that we were drawing conclusions. As more and more information came to us, Agent X, whom we were constantly pressing to produce more documents and more witnesses, grew increasingly concerned. I was somewhat sympathetic toward X. He was in the impossible position of keeping both us and his superiors happy. And he was trying to protect the Agency, an organization he had been with for twenty years.

In fact, Baker was very much concerned that his actions might be construed as being "anti-CIA," a concern that I shared. He considered a strong CIA to be of vital importance. However, as we were discovering firsthand, the CIA had become so autonomous that in effect it was accountable to no one. It seemed to be completely outside our system of checks and balances. So we continued to press—and press hard. Periodically Agent X and I would engage in conversations that would end in shouting matches over the CIA's response, or lack of it, to our requests.

We discovered, for example, that the CIA had a file on a "Mr. Edward," a code name for Hunt, that detailed all Agency contacts with Hunt. We demanded the file; the CIA declined to produce it. We were unable to get the unabridged reports of

Martinez's case officer, which we suspected would show the extent of the CIA's knowledge of Hunt's activities while he was planning the Watergate break-in.

Furthermore, we were told that the Martinez case officer who supposedly had been on the African safari had moved on to Asia and was still unavailable to us. The "African safari," and all that it implied to us about the CIA's attitude of non-cooperation became a symbol. In seeking the appearance of an important witness, frequently we would comment that he too was probably on safari in Africa. X did not consider this amusing, but it gave us some leverage.

It became a kind of psychological warfare: how much would the Agency let us have to get us off its back and still not give away the whole ranch? I, frankly, was amazed that we had been able to get as far as we had. In my opinion, we had already determined that the CIA was aware of the activities of the Watergate burglars prior to the break-in and that it perhaps knew more than that. This was apparent not only from the facts we had uncovered, but also from the Agency's tactic of shutting the door in our faces whenever we seemed to be penetrating too deeply into certain areas. The "Mr. Edward" file and the Martinez case-officer reports were not the only documents denied to us; Liebengood and Madigan had determined the existence of a five-inch reel of tape labeled "McCord incident 6-19-72." This was a tape recording made by the CIA Office of Security two days after the Watergate break-in. That it was related to the burglary was obvious, but although we were shown a purported transcript, we were never allowed to hear the tape.

Our investigation also determined that the Agency had a "Watergate" file, something the CIA had denied. Agent X insisted that the file had been "disassembled" and could not be put back together again. From secret CIA documents we also learned that Paul O'Brien, who had served as counsel to the Committee to Re-elect the President after the Watergate break-in, was a former CIA operative. In my mind, the question was becoming one of whether the CIA had been a participant in or a benign observer of the break-in, or, in view of the bungling of the burglary and the mysterious circumstances surrounding it, whether CIA operatives had perhaps sabotaged the break-in to weaken the White House and strengthen the Agency in its struggle for survival. Another consideration, of almost equal importance, was the extent to which perjury might have been committed by CIA officials before various congressional committees.

So we kept pressing. Baker, who was constantly informed of our work but left nearly all the details to us, requested CIA logs and other materials that might shed light on material in the Agency's destroyed tapes; Madigan and Liebengood continued with their requests based on the revelations from the interviews. Throughout the process, our interviews were conducted in utmost secrecy; I had agreed with Dash to permit one majority staff member, chosen mutually, to sit in on the interviews, with an absolute no-leak understanding. The majority member, James Hamilton, lived up to the bargain completely. I stressed constantly that any leak of the material we were receiving would give the CIA an irrefutable argument to terminate our investigation. Most of the time the press was not even aware that CIA interviews were being conducted; the identity of those interviewed was never made public. It was a remarkable event in Washington: a no-leak inquiry.

On February 19, 1974, the CIA evidently determined it was time to halt our efforts. Agent X drafted a statement for the signature of William Colby, the CIA director; it stated that the CIA had produced all the Watergate-related information in its possession for our committee and for all the congressional committees with CIA oversight. We learned later that this came to the attention of a low-level CIA personnel security officer; he told his superiors that he could not subscribe to such a statement. Apparently fearing a rebellion from within, the CIA made a startling disclosure.

On Saturday, February 23, Baker, Liebengood, Madigan, and I were sitting in my office discussing the week's events and waiting for the former deputy director of Clandestine Services to arrive for his interview. He had been the one who had instructed the CIA Miami chief of station to "cool it" with regard to inquiring into Hunt's activities in the Miami area, even though Hunt was in direct contact with Martinez, a CIA operative. We wanted to know why.

There was a knock at the door. Agent X walked into the room looking even more intense than usual. He wanted to see Senator Baker alone. They stepped into Dash's office, which was empty. After a few minutes Baker walked back into my office, closed the door, and said, "Take a look at this," as he laid several sheets on my desk. It was a CIA memo. The memo had been prepared by the dissident personnel security officer, although the document contained no clue as to its author. It disclosed that, in June 1972, the CIA had information that one of its paid operatives, Lee R. Pennington, Jr., had entered the house of James McCord shortly after the Watergate break-in and had destroyed documents that "might show a link between McCord and the CIA." It disclosed further that when the FBI asked the CIA about a "Pennington" in CIA employ, the Agency provided information about another Pennington, not the man they knew the FBI was interested in. To our amazement, the memorandum also listed the names of the CIA officials who had been shielding this information. Liebengood, Madigan, and I now realized that the CIA might have its own John Dean who was forcing the disclosure of these new facts. We immediately scheduled interviews for all the persons mentioned in the memorandum.

The CIA employee who refused to go along with the memo, whom I'll call Security Officer No. 1, was as unlikely a prospect for the role as Dean himself. A short man with a crew cut, who appeared almost cheerful, he reminded me of everyone's favorite college professor. When we began to question him, he nonchalantly flipped across the table another memorandum he had prepared and said, "You might want to take a look at this first."

The memo told of a concerted effort within the CIA to cover up the Pennington matter and to separate the Pennington materials from other CIA files, for possible destruction. It said that Security Officer No. 1 had told his superior that "up to this time we've never removed, tampered with, obliterated, destroyed, or done anything to any Watergate documents" and that the CIA "could do without its own L. Patrick Gray." Because of the actions of their superiors, Officer No. 1 and a fellow security officer had made separate copies of all Pennington-related materials to prevent their destruction.

We gathered more and more information on the Pennington matter. From our interviews with other witnesses, it appeared that Pennington was working out of the CIA's Security Research Staff, the same unit that McCord had worked for. Our investigation led us to the tentative conclusion that the Agency was concerned not merely with the revelations that documents had been burned in McCord's home, but more important, that Pennington himself could have been a "domestic agent," in violation of the CIA charter, which prohibits domestic activity by the Agency. We considered the possibility that the Security Research Staff was at the heart of the CIA's domestic operations, an activity that had been rumored for years, but never proved. The disclosure of Pennington's work could uncover the entire domestic operation.

We puzzled over this question. Since it was common knowledge that McCord had been a CIA employee, why should the Agency be concerned about the finding of CIA-related documents in his home? The only answer that occurred to us was that a CIA relationship with McCord still existed at the time of the break-in at the Watergate. Again, as we got close to the answer, another stone wall arose in front of us. Pennington, who had been summoned to my office that same Saturday night and questioned by Senator Baker personally, testified that he had not visited the McCord home to destroy CIA-related documents, but that he had seen Mrs. McCord destroy a few documents. Later, we learned that the burning of the "few" documents produced so much smoke damage in the McCord living room that the room had to be repainted. Pennington also told us that he merely performed odd jobs for the CIA, picking up copies of public testimony before congressional committees and "things like that."

Meanwhile, our interrogation of Security Officer No. 1 began to give us an inside picture of what went on at the Agency immediately after the break-in. Helms had testified that the Agency had conducted no thorough investigation of its own, even though a number of its former employees were involved. No. 1 told us, on the other hand, that the Agency conducted a vigorous internal investigation that began almost immediately after the break-in became known. This testimony was verified in our interviews with Security Research Staff officers.

Why then, had Helms misrepresented the CIA investigation? Why should the Agency seek to hide its concern? Was the CIA trying to determine the role of its former agents or was it worried that its own participation in the Watergate plot might be exposed? We discovered that the executive officer to the CIA's director of security had been given a special assignment by William Colby, then executive director-comptroller of the CIA and now its director, to conduct a secret investigation of the Watergate matter. The executive officer was instructed to keep no copies of his findings and to make no records; he typed his own reports and used no secretary.

We also pondered the Agency's motives in providing the information we had. Were they attempting to come clean? (On more than one occasion, Baker expressed faith in Colby.) Was the material less explosive than it seemed to us? Had we won the Agency's respect, and were its leaders fearful of the consequences of an outright refusal to provide us material? Would the CIA subsequently leak a damaging bit of information after turning it over to us and use that development as an excuse to end our investigation? Or did the CIA believe we would decide we had seen the most damaging information and that we would shut off the investigation ourselves?

We saw memorandums, unrelated to Watergate, showing that the Agency had bypassed J. Edgar Hoover on one occasion, and had gone directly to Attorney General John Mitchell to urge a very sensitive clandestine operation. We considered this red-hot material. Why were they showing it to us?

Was it designed to take some of the heat off the CIA and place it on the FBI? Such interagency finger-pointing was not uncommon. Not long afterward a reporter told me that the FBI had leaked the "Pennington" information to him, pointing out that the CIA had misled the FBI as to the true identity of Lee Pennington. It was the old game of self-protection.

We were also shown CIA cable traffic compiled shortly after the Watergate break-in, material that we were furnished a bit at a time. It disclosed, among other things, that a Democratic state chairman had pressed a Secret Service agent for information on McCord on June 17, 1972, the day of the break-in. Who was the state chairman, and how did he learn so quickly of McCord's involvement in the break-in? We never found out. We did discover, however, that the CIA advised the Secret Service agent that it was concerned about McCord's emotional stability prior to his retirement from the CIA.

Another of our tentative conclusions was that the CIA had given us the Pennington material because it feared that Officer No. 1 was likely to make it public and the Agency wanted the credit for releasing it. Always, there were more questions than answers—questions that related to the nature of the CIA and its future—as we kept penetrating into the never-never land of an agency that had been so mysterious for so many years, an agency whose workings had been utterly unknown to us a few months earlier.

One thing we did know: Senator Baker was the reason we had been able to get anywhere. In the eyes of Agent X, I represented Baker. The senator was constantly painting the broad picture for us, mapping the route we had to travel, and permitting the staff to work out the details. I knew Baker would support me as long as I stayed within the bounds of my assignment; and Agent X knew this too, even as he continually bobbed, weaved, stalled, and tried to compromise.

It became clear to us that deception was at the root of the CIA's very existence and survival. Deception took a variety of forms, but it appeared every time we made a minor or major breakthrough. Liebengood and Madigan, for example, questioned X repeatedly about the existence of a master Watergate file within the CIA. Definitely not, X responded, and, at our demand, he put the answer in writing. But he retained the document in his own file, insisting that the material was too sensitive to leave in our possession. Liebengood, Madigan, and I all specifically recall seeing X's negative answer in his file. Later, No. 1 told us there was indeed such a Watergate file, that it was maintained by the Agency's Office of Security and was in the possession of the CIA inspector general. When we so advised Baker and told him we could not work effectively without the files, Baker insisted to the Agency that the files be left with us. X complied; but the next night when we went over the material, we discovered that the page containing his "no Watergate file" response was missing.

We also discovered that the Agency had a "Pennington file" containing memorandums and other documents involving this operative, including his domestic activities. But when we pressed X on this point, he said he could not turn the file over to us because it was "incomplete." The file now had "gaps" in it during certain relevant time periods.

In another of my impassioned arguments with X, I cited the transcript of a conversation between Hunt and Cushman, then the CIA's deputy director, on July 22, 1971. When Cushman testified before the Watergate committee on August 2, 1973, he presented a transcript of his conversation with Hunt on the date in 1971, in which Hunt had asked CIA assistance. Months later, in February 1974, after Baker insisted on hearing the original tape, the CIA reported that it had turned up a "more complete" transcript, which had been located only the day before Baker was to listen to it. It developed that the transcript given to the committee had somehow omitted an uncomplimentary reference to Nixon. The Agency, aware that Baker would detect the omission, took great pains to persuade Baker that, although it had searched for the original transcript in Cushman's safe after Cushman left the CIA in December 1971, the original had not been found until a second search was made. As a result, the CIA explained, an abbreviated transcript had been offered to the Watergate committee. It was not necessary to add that the abbreviated version would cause the CIA fewer problems with the White House.

That was not the only Cushman conversation in which a transcript turned up late. One day X came to my office and said he had to see Baker immediately. In the senator's office he handed Baker the transcript of a portion of a conversation between Cushman and Ehrlichman. The CIA had consistently maintained that it had provided technical support to Hunt in 1971 because Ehrlichman had insisted on it, but it had no documentary evidence. Now it appeared that Cushman had taped his conversation with Ehrlichman, and the transcript supported the CIA version; it quoted Ehrlichman as saying that Hunt was working for the president and that the CIA should give Hunt "carte blanche." The transcript, amazingly, had turned up in a third search of that Cushman safe. Asked why Cushman had not told us previously that such a tape existed, Agent X said that Cushman's secretary, without Cushman's knowledge, had monitored his call from Ehrlichman and had typed the transcript. We interviewed the secretary, who verified the episode. It was, of course, the only explanation that would exculpate Cushman from a charge of withholding this important information from the committee. We were being asked to believe that the number 2 man in the Central Intelligence Agency was unaware that his secretary was monitoring and transcribing his most private, sensitive conversations. We made no secret of our disbelief of the CIA explanation; more significantly, perhaps, we had pressed the Agency to the point where it felt the necessity to produce the transcript to shore up its defense, even with an incredible story of how the document came to its attention.

Agency action that I considered to be a setup occurred shortly thereafter. A reporter for *The New York Times* called me and asked for a copy of the Cushman-Ehrlichman transcript. When I asked him who told him that there was such a document he told me it was the CIA and that they told him that if he called me I would probably give it to him. Not only was the Agency trying to get a favorable story out, but they were trying to entice me into divulging what was at that time classified material. Highly annoyed, I voiced my displeasure to Agent X in no uncertain terms. He didn't know what to say. It was obvious that he had not been made privy to this bit of Agency strategy.

Most of the interviews were being conducted in my office. Each day before the interviews began a team of CIA technicians would enter my office and methodically "sweep" the office to check for any electronic listening devices. I watched very closely as the technicians moved around the room checking each piece of furniture as well as the telephones. Not only was it fascinating to me to see how a sweeping operation was conducted, but I wanted to make sure that they didn't accidentally leave any of their spare equipment—such as a listening device.

During this period Colson continued to call me. I did not feel completely comfortable talking to a potential Watergate defendant on a regular basis, even though the majority staff had engaged in the same sort of unilateral contact with witnesses. However, we were seeking information from any available source, and Colson's ability to gather material never ceased to astound me.

Like an investigative reporter who had been in Washington for twenty years, Colson appeared to have "sources" in almost every federal agency. A few days after the CIA gave us the information about Pennington, for example, Colson called me and asked what I thought of the Pennington matter. I was flabbergasted; as far as I knew the only non-CIA personnel privy to this information were Baker, Liebengood, Madigan, and I. Not even Ervin or Dash had been advised at the time.

Colson did not mention the source of his information and did not press me for details; he gave the impression that he knew them all. He merely wanted my opinion of their significance. I said I considered the information extremely significant, but that it was most important that the story not be leaked to the news media, an action that would cause the CIA to cut us off from all further inquiries. Colson agreed.

A few days later Colson called to give me the name of a woman who worked for the CIA. He said he had information that the Agency had funded some of the plumbers' activities and that this woman had handled the money. The name was new to me. In my next meeting with Agent X I told him to add her name to our witness list. He looked up from his note pad quizzically, obviously wondering where I had obtained the name. But he put it down without a word and said she would be produced.

The witness suggested by Colson, a well-groomed, middle-aged woman, told us she was secretary to the chief of the CIA's Narcotics Control Group. Yes, she said, the group had funded some of Egil Krogh's activities when Krogh headed the plumbers in the White House; however, she went on, this was part of the Agency's program on foreign narcotics control and, to her knowledge, had nothing to do with any domestic activity. Why were the funds provided by the CIA, rather than by some other, seemingly more appropriate, government agency? The witness did not know. We sought interviews with her superiors, but they were never made available to us, and our questions never got answered.

On one occasion Colson called and told me that he had learned that the CIA had contracted with Howard Hughes to build a ship called the *Glomar* for deep-sea mining. Although it was another CIA-Hughes link it seemed of little importance and I promptly forgot about it. Over a year later, in March of 1975, I was driving home from my office in Nashville late one night and was astounded to hear a news bulletin that it had just been learned that in 1968 the CIA had contracted with Howard Hughes for $350 million to build the *Glomar Explorer* and that the Agency had used the ship for the purpose of recovering a sunken Russian submarine in the Pacific. It had been a highly classified top CIA secret for seven years.

As late as March 1974, I was surprised to discover that

Colson still apparently had access to Nixon. He called me at home on Sunday, March 3, and implied strongly that he had taken his suspicions about the CIA directly to the president. From some of the things that Colson told me, I concluded that he had access to some White House records, including certain CIA materials, that he thought might help his case. I never understood how or why the White House had obtained this material from the CIA. But it appeared that Nixon had ordered that Colson, the loyalist, was to have access to whatever he wanted and that the order had met with less than universal approval among the top White House aides.

As our inquiry went on, we detected the outlines of a CIA counterattack. To undercut Baker and our investigation, the Agency went to work simultaneously with the congressional committees that oversee its activities and with the press. The object appeared to be to sell the theory that Baker's pursuit of the CIA was really an attempt to protect the White House; if the public bought that idea, Baker could be discredited. The enormous invisible power of the CIA was being applied, and we had only begun to experience it.

Time and time again, when we came into possession of significant information and asked for additional data or supporting documents, the CIA would say the requested material had been given to the congressional committees with CIA oversight responsibilities. It was obvious to us that the Agency was using these as a form of protection against us. The relationship between the CIA and these oversight committees of the Senate and the House has been documented over the years by numerous experts. All of them conclude, as we did, that there is in fact no effective oversight of the CIA, no monitoring of the Agency's vast worldwide operations. The CIA budget is secret, so secret that not even the oversight committees know how much the CIA spends or where its money goes. The CIA hierarchy had developed close relationships with three key members of Congress—Lucien Nedzi, Democrat of Michigan, chairman of the House Armed Services Subcommittee, which oversees the CIA; John Stennis, Democrat of Mississippi, chair-

*A public moment for members of the Minority staff, who did their superb work out of the limelight. Seated, from left to right: Michael Madigan, me, and Don Sanders; standing, from left to right: Dick Schultz, Joan Cole, Howard Liebengood, Brenda Roberson, and Gail Oliver.*

THE NEW YORK TIMES/MIKE LIEN

man of the Senate Armed Services Committee; and Stuart Symington, Democrat of Missouri, acting chairman of the Senate Armed Services Committee. These respected lawmakers relied on the assurances of their friends in the CIA hierarchy that the Agency's activities were proper and lawful. Apparently, not until early in 1975, when the Senate and House formed special committees to examine the entire intelligence community, had there been any systematic effort to do more than accept the word of CIA officials on the nature of the Agency's operations.

At the same time that we were looking into the circumstance

surrounding the CIA destruction of its tapes on February 21, 1973, I read in the *Washington Star* that Representative Nedzi said the CIA had given him a voluminous report, leading him to announce that the Agency was blameless in the incident and that somebody—obviously Baker—was trying to "blow smoke" about the Agency's involvement in Watergate. Nedzi acknowledged later that he had not even read the CIA's report when he gave the Agency its clean bill of health. Agent X told us that we had been given everything the CIA had on the destruction of the tapes, but we did not have the "voluminous report." Once again, Nedzi was relying on assurances from his friends at the CIA rather than on his own inquiries.

Shortly afterward, when we had turned up the Pennington memorandum, we learned that the same information had gone directly to Nedzi and the other oversight committees. When we pressed the Agency about the Pennington file with its curious gaps, we were told that it had been made available only to Nedzi's subcommittee, and that it would not be given to us. From time to time, as pressure began to mount on the CIA as a result of our work, Nedzi would hold a few days of secret hearings—as he did when the Pennington matter came to light—and emerge just long enough to announce that all was still well with the CIA.

The Agency was calling in all its chips from its friends on the oversight committees. Rumors began to fly. One of the more bizarre was that Gen. Alexander Haig, then White House chief of staff, had persuaded Baker to make a speech attacking Richard Helms on the Senate floor. All this, of course, was aimed at neutralizing Baker and getting him to call off his investigation.

The Agency was making great progress in its campaign to isolate our little team from that respectable body of senators and House members charged with supervising CIA activities. At no time did it manifest itself more acutely than at our crucial interview with Richard Helms.

Helms, by then the ambassador to Iran, had been summoned home by the State Department, pursuant to our request, for an interview. Senator Symington asked Baker that he be informed of the time and place of the interview as soon as it was determined; it was apparent that Symington wanted to be present. Baker agreed, and the date was subsequently set for Friday, March 8, 1974.

Baker, Liebengood, Madigan, and I waited in the committee's windowless interview room. Because of the importance of the witness, Ervin and Dash were also on hand; they had no idea of what we had in mind, other than a slight suspicion that we were seeking to use Helms and the CIA in some way in an effort to exonerate the White House.

At approximately 10:00 A.M. Helms and Symington walked through the door. We all shook hands, but it appeared that their friendliness toward Baker and the members of the minority staff was a bit forced. After some small talk, Baker briefly outlined the major areas of our concern and expressed the hope that Helms could illuminate certain matters for us, particularly with regard to the destruction of the CIA tapes. He made no accusation against Helms; indeed, Baker thanked the witness in advance for the cooperation he knew we would receive. Nevertheless, it was obvious that Helms had not been brought all the way from Iran for a mere reiteration of his statement before the Watergate committee that the CIA had had no Watergate involvement whatever.

Senator Baker began the interrogation. Asked why the CIA tapes had been destroyed, Helms replied that he was leaving his position as director at the time and that it was simply a matter of good housekeeping. Then Baker went directly to one of the critical questions:

"Did any of the destroyed tapes contain conversations with the president?"

Helms' eyes flashed. "No!" he said adamantly.

"Did they contain any conversations with Haldeman?"

"No," Helms said in an even louder voice.

The performance was in many ways similar to the one he gave in public session before the Watergate committee. On that occasion he practically shouted his assertion that the CIA had no Watergate involvement and looked around confidently, asking if the press had heard what he said. This time, though, he seemed more tense, not quite so confident.

"What about conversations with Ehrlichman?" Baker's tone of voice was still even.

"No!" Now Helms was practically shouting, but his technique was not working. He did not know that his former personal secretary had told us that some of the transcripts of the destroyed tapes did in fact contain conversations with Nixon, Haldeman, and Ehrlichman, although she could not remember the subject matter.

Finally Helms said, "Wait a minute. I want to tell you, Senator, that I don't appreciate the tone of some of these questions."

Baker, who is usually slow to anger, responded with equal force. "Mr. Ambassador, I don't appreciate a lot of the things that have been going on around here for the last several days. I have heard rumors that I'm doing a hatchet job on the CIA; that Haig persuaded me to make a speech against you. I'd like to know the source of some of these stories myself."

Symington's demeanor had changed. His detached unfriendliness had become a scowl. His personal friendship with Helms was well known, although it was his committee's responsibility to oversee the agency that Helms had directed. The transcripts of Helms' appearances before the Senate Armed Services Committee were full of Symington's praise for his friend.

Interrupting Baker, Symington said that, because of his close friendship with Helms, whom he considered a great American, and because of some of the things that he had heard were going on in our investigation, he had accompanied Helms to "see what Mr. Thompson wants." It was evident to me that Agent X and Symington had been discussing my "sinister motivations."

"It's not Thompson, it's me," Baker replied immediately.

Symington appeared taken aback. He referred again to unsettling things he had heard, without mentioning their source. Then, in a more conciliatory manner, Symington said he would like to know just one thing. "Of course," Baker said. Symington wanted to know if I had ever made the statement that Ambassador Helms would be indicted.

I was flabbergasted. It would have been a preposterous comment for me to make, even if I believed it to be true.

"Senator Symington," I said, "I have never made that statement to anyone. And, with regard to whether we are trying to take unfair advantage of the CIA [the idea that we could take advantage of possibly the most powerful agency in the country was so ludicrous that the remark almost stuck in my throat as I said it], I think you ought to know a few of the things we have been dealing with."

I described the mysterious relations that Martinez had had with the Agency before the Watergate break-in; I told of the way the CIA had maneuvered its case officers after the break-in; I listed the Pennington matter, the CIA pipeline from Bennett, and the post-August 1971 contacts we knew that Hunt had had with the Agency, including his requests for a lock-picker and a specialist in "entry operations."

Helms stared straight ahead and did not speak. Symington thanked me for my reassuring remarks, but I could not tell from his reaction whether he was aware of the incidents I had related. Later it occurred to me that he could have been shocked and surprised, reevaluating his position on the spot, or that he might have known about such activities but had not been aware that we did.

The remainder of the interview turned out to be much less eventful than the preliminaries. Helms' testimony, although at variance with other testimony we had received in some areas, was consistent with what he had said at our public hearing. Our inquiries since his appearance before our committee had not caused him to reevaluate his position. He held the hard line.

Although the suspicions were that we were working with the White House, in fact, we were getting no encouragement from the White House whatsoever. I felt that one of the possibilities was that the CIA was working at cross purposes with the

White House. However, if this was the case the White House was keeping very quiet about it. I asked Fred Buzhardt on two occasions whether the White House had any information that would shed light upon our inquiry. Buzhardt always replied in the vaguest of terms. They either had nothing, or they were not willing to impart anything of substance.

I arranged an interview with Ehrlichman in the office of his attorney, Frank Strickler. I put the same question to him. He replied that they did have trouble with Helms on one occasion. He stated that pursuant to the president's instructions, he, Ehrlichman, had requested Helms to submit to him a report of a secret in-house investigation on the CIA's role in the Bay of Pigs. He said that Helms stalled and finally told Ehrlichman that he would have to talk to the president directly about the matter. After Helms and the president conferred, a report was submitted to Ehrlichman. However, much later, they found that the report was not complete.

Ehrlichman stated that except for that one instance, the White House relationship with Helms had been good. I wondered why, if the relationship had been so good, Helms had been removed as director of the CIA and sent to the other side of the world as ambassador to Iran.

Ehrlichman's brief comments took on new significance as I, along with the rest of the country, read the release of the June 23, 1972, presidential tape transcript. The discussion centered around utilizing the CIA to help shore up the deteriorating White House position. The president told Haldeman he was sure that the CIA did not want to expose the Bay of Pigs matter. Nixon suggested guidance for Haldeman's discussion, apparently with Helms and Walters:

When you get in—when you get in (unintelligible) people, say, "Look the problem is that this will open the whole, the whole Bay of Pigs thing and the President just feels that, ah, without going into the details—don't, don't lie to them to the extent to say there is no involvement, but just say this is a comedy of errors, without getting into it,

the President believes that it is going to open the whole
Bay of Pigs thing up again.

What could the Bay of Pigs matter be? Everyone knows that
the CIA was involved at the Bay of Pigs. What was yet to be
uncovered? Whatever it was it seemed that neither the CIA
nor Nixon was willing to disclose it. Nixon also said, "We
protected Helms from one hell of a lot of things."

In view of our cool reception from White House aides and
Nixon's comments on the transcript, my assessment to Senator
Baker was, "They've got so much on each other that neither
side can afford to talk."

Our credibility with the CIA oversight committees did not
improve. As we prepared a report on our findings, there were
no inquiries from the committees on what our investigation
had turned up, although they should have been the first to
want to know. After we completed our initial report Senator
Baker presented it to Senator Stennis. Stennis told Baker he
wanted it understood that he was "only agreeing to receive the
report." Later he returned it to Baker with the notation that he
had not read it.

Simultaneous with the CIA's increased intimacy with its
oversight committees was its public relations campaign with
the press. The Agency's power to get its story across simply by
dropping the right word in the right ear was awesome. At a
time when the American press was being heralded throughout
the world for its role in breaking the Watergate case, the
developing story of the CIA's clandestine activities was receiving hardly any attention. One reason for this was our refusal to leak the story piecemeal. When it became obvious to
me that the CIA was selling its side of the story to powerful
representatives of the news media, I urged Senator Baker more
than once to relate what we had learned to at least one responsible reporter, with the understanding that nothing would
be printed until our findings had been fully developed. As I
saw it, we would be playing the game by the CIA's rules to

keep ourselves from becoming completely isolated. Baker was reluctant to adopt this course.

We heard that, immediately after his arrival in the United States from Iran, Helms met with top officials of both *Time* and *Newsweek*. We also had heard that Colby had had a long, "off the record" conversation with Seymour Hersh, investigative reporter for *The New York Times*. Later Hersh acknowledged to me that Colby had met with him, but he insisted that he had not been "neutralized" on any CIA story.

Shortly after Helms' return to the United States, the syndicated columns of Tom Braden and Evans and Novak carried anti-Baker, pro-CIA articles suggesting that Baker was pursuing the CIA matter for personal political reasons and that Baker and the minority staff were seeking to undermine the Agency. It is common knowledge in Washington that Braden—himself a former CIA employee—and Evans are friends of Helms' and members in good standing of a select group in Washington society composed primarily of ivy league alumni who now hold important positions in the government, the intelligence community, and the press.

Throughout this press campaign, Baker insisted that we ignore it and continue our work. Our job, he kept telling us, was to write our report and to get it declassified by the CIA; after that, the report would speak for itself.

Of all those who watched this CIA-press maneuver, no one was more irritated than Charles Colson. Each time he saw evidence of it, Colson would call me and stress the need for us to play the same game. "We're being done in," he would say; "they're killing off any possible story before the facts are in." I agreed with him in part, but I knew that Baker wouldn't play that game.

After our group repeatedly refused to leak information in defense of our effort, Colson evidently decided to do it on his own. Les Whitten, columnist Jack Anderson's associate, called me frequently; it was apparent that Colson had been talking with him. Colson also was trying to interest other reporters in his position that our investigation had turned up matters of substance. But instead of promoting our cause, Colson's efforts had the opposite effect; reporters, mindful of Colson's reputation, viewed his theories with great suspicion. Colson never seemed to realize the extent to which his credibility had been damaged with the press. One reporter, admitting to me that Colson had pushed his CIA story with a number of reporters, said that Colson had commented that "Thompson is a good man but he doesn't know how to work the press." Ironically, "working the press" in an effort to damage Daniel Ellsberg's public image was at the heart of the charge to which Colson pleaded guilty and went to prison.

We considered the *Washington Post* a constant threat in the campaign against us. We were well aware of Robert Bennett's report to his CIA case officer in which he said that he was cooperating with a "suitably grateful" Bob Woodward. After we interviewed Bennett, he told a *Washington Post* reporter that our staff had the memorandum that mentioned Woodward. The *Post* immediately took Woodward and Bernstein off the CIA phase of the Watergate story. From what we heard, the *Post*, too, was concerned. Baker and I discussed interviewing Woodward, but took no action. The problem was solved for us when Bernstein called Baker, who agreed to talk with Bernstein and Woodward. Baker asked that I attend the meeting, which turned out to be a tense session marked by mutual suspicions. Even though Bennett had told us that his relationship with Woodward had been "blown out of proportion" in his memo, we had still not resolved the strange behavior of the Agency in response to our inquiry.

As many people have observed, Bernstein and Woodward are a markedly contrasting pair. Bernstein, with his reputation as "tough guy" of the two, looked the part, with his long hair and dark features; Woodward was the very model of the patrician Yale graduate with a Republican background.

Woodward opened the session by saying he understood that we had information about his relationship with Bob Bennett. Baker replied, after a pause, that although he would not disclose committee information, Woodward could assume that was the case for the purpose of our conversation. Bernstein assured us that he had made no deal with Bob Bennett to protect the CIA. He seemed uncomfortable and concerned; it occurred to me that these now-famous young men, for perhaps the first time were the interrogated, not the interrogators.

For fifteen minutes the Baker-Woodward-Bernstein conversation continued. It was a fencing match in which the two reporters insisted that there was nothing to whatever we had heard about them. After they left, it was clear that we had not convinced them that our motives were pure and that they had not completely allayed our suspicions. The encounter did nothing to improve our relations with the *Washington Post*.

On the afternoon of April 12, 1974, I saw Woodward walking ahead of me on a Washington sidewalk. I called to him, and we chatted; despite the antipathy that our respective positions appeared to have created, we always got along well personally.

Woodward asked how the CIA investigation was going; I replied that it was nearly complete and that if people like him would press the CIA to declassify it, he could read it and decide for himself. The whole affair "must raise questions about your investigation," Woodward said.

On the contrary, I replied, it must raise questions about the press, which appeared oblivious to any possible wrongdoing on the part of the CIA but spent a great deal of time questioning the motives of the minority staff. Woodward said that Baker's public statements contained nothing but unsupported implications. What Baker had stated, in fact, was that he felt there were "animals crashing around in the forest" that he could hear but not yet see. In light of what we knew, I considered that an understatement. Woodward said, "If he's got the facts, why doesn't he go ahead and lay them out?"

"Bob," I replied, "we're dealing with classified material. If we made a statement about them at this stage of the game, before they were declassified, we would be irresponsible. On the other hand, you guys are constantly asking him if there is anything to his CIA investigation. What do you want him to say—'No, it's all a waste of time'? Obviously he's got to talk in generalities."

Woodward went on, "There's really no story here unless he can really prove the CIA was directly involved in the Watergate break-in."

"What do you mean there's no story? You people have such tunnel vision about the Watergate break-in that not only does everything have to be related to the break-in, but you have to have ironclad proof before you will even make any inquiries of your own."

"But let's face it," he said, "the break-in and the White House cover-up is the story in this town."

"Obviously, but it's not the only story in town. You're certainly making the criterion for a reportable story in this area more narrow than in any other area I know." He agreed that this might be true to a degree.

In our fencing exchange, I was sure he was deliberately downgrading our efforts in an attempt to get me to divulge more details. And he must have realized that I was trying to give him enough of a scent of what we were doing to head off an attack on us by the *Post*. We spoke for a few more minutes, shook hands, and parted.

Finally, because of the support the CIA was receiving from its oversight committees and because of the lack of interest in the press Colby sent word to Senator Baker that no further documentation would be produced. What was in the "Mr. Edward" file, the Pennington file, and the Watergate file? It seemed to us now that probably no one would ever know. The door had been slammed in our faces, and we had no leverage to reopen it. Baker instructed us to pull our materials together and prepare a report, although it would, of necessity, have to be incomplete. Liebengood, Madigan, and I did this, and Senator Baker started the long and arduous process of trying to get the CIA to declassify the report. After many requests, a number of which were totally ignored, the Agency agreed to the public release of a sanitized version of our report.

In its final form, our report, although it drew no conclusions that the CIA was involved in the break-in, cited much of the evidence we had marshaled, and a lot of it we considered newsworthy and new. It cited most of the major elements of our investigation. Also, it contained evidence of a variety of apparent domestic activities by the Agency, including the activities of Lee Pennington, whom we labeled as possibly being a "domestic agent," and the activities of Martinez in monitoring the actions of possible demonstrations at the Republican and Democratic National Conventions. The Agency maintained a file on columnist Jack Anderson, and had an investigative interest in Robert Maheu.

We decided to release the report at 9 A.M. on July 2, thus giving the *Washington Star*, rather than the *Post*, the opportunity to publish it first in the capital. To our great disappointment, the *Star's* account of the report was carried on page 5. *The New York Times* had a thorough account on page 1 the following day, but radio and television coverage was no more than moderate.

On the afternoon of July 2, a *Star* reporter came to see me. He was angry and dejected and complained about what he considered his paper's inadequate treatment of what he considered a very significant story. "You know, of course," he said, "that Helms is a good friend of some of our top people." I didn't know it, but I might have guessed.

The winding up of the CIA investigation was a lonely time for Baker. Because of his persistent inquiries he seemed to have placed himself at odds, not only with the CIA, but with the White House, the press, and the rest of the committee.

Months later, as we were writing the committee report, I submitted the Baker-CIA report to Dash for inclusion in the report. Not long after we received the news we had been expecting. According to Dash, Senator Ervin had decided that the CIA report would not go into the main body of the committee report. Senator Baker could have it printed in his separate views, or he could submit a minority report. Ervin seemingly did not want to dignify the Baker report or in any way put his stamp of approval on it. Baker directed that the CIA report be printed as a part of his separate views.

Over a year later, on December 22, 1974, Seymour Hersh evidently became alarmed over the information he had been discounting and he reported a story that "informed sources" said that the CIA had 10,000 domestic intelligence files on American citizens. The story seemed hardly startling in view of the wide range of specific activities that we had documented, but it seemed to strike all the major newspapers and television networks like a bolt of lightning. Reporters virtually leaped for their note pads and ran for their nearest sources. This produced an avalanche of stories, each reporting various domestic indiscretions on the part of the CIA. The Baker report suddenly became a red-hot item.

Two factors accounted for this new swarm of activity. The first was that Nixon was now safely out of the way, and the result of any CIA inquiry could in no way inure to his benefit. The second was simply that *The New York Times* decided to make the CIA story news by running it on the front page under a Seymour Hersh by-line. Shortly after the Hersh article, President Ford formed a presidential commission to investigate domestic CIA activities, and select committees were formed in the House and in the Senate to investigate U.S. intelligence activities. I had never seen a clearer example of the power that a major newspaper has to perhaps even shape the course of events in this country by the manner in which it treats a news story.

# Chapter VIII · Partisan Rumblings

By the end of 1973 I began to seriously doubt for the first time that Nixon could survive. The adverse public reaction to the "Saturday Night Massacre" on October 27, 1973 precipitated by the firing of Special Prosecutor Archibald Cox had been overwhelming. In my own thoughts I had wrestled with the question of Nixon's guilt or innocence from the very beginning. It was the progression of the battle for the tapes that finally rekindled my prosecutor's skepticism to its fullest. Although it was not very persuasive to most legal scholars, it appeared to me that Nixon did at least have a legal argument for refusing to release the tapes that the Watergate committee and the special prosecutor were demanding. There was no Supreme Court precedent that covered the situation. However, it was clear to me that no politician, not even a president, would forever stand upon constitutional niceties to prevent the disclosure of facts that would save his own neck.

On October 31, a White House lawyer disclosed that two of the nine tapes subpoenaed by the special prosecutor did not exist and that Nixon had known this fact for nearly a month. Then in late November a White House spokesman disclosed that an 18½-minute gap had been discovered in an important taped conversation between Nixon and Haldeman, on June 20, 1972, three days after the Watergate break-in.

For me the question finally became not, "Are the tapes damaging?" but instead, "How damaging are they?" However, developments inside the committee again intervened to take my mind away from those thoughts.

From the outset of our investigation, the committee was

determined to present a united front, to avoid at all cost the appearance of internal, partisan bickering. For the most part, in the public sessions this objective was achieved; in private, however, things were becoming less and less harmonious.

The focal point of the committee's investigation never changed: the Watergate break-in and the cover-up that ensued. But as our work proceeded, the committee staff divided into small groups and looked into other aspects of political wrongdoing. And it was in some of these areas that acrimony developed at times.

One group of majority staff members pursued the so-called milk investigation. On March 12, 1971, the secretary of agriculture, Clifford Hardin, announced that the price of milk for the 1971–1972 marketing year would be supported by the federal government at approximately 80 percent of parity, an arbitrary figure based on the price experiences of past years. Dairy farmers, through their trade organizations, had already undertaken a campaign to raise a substantial contribution for Nixon's reelection campaign. On March 23 Nixon met with representatives of the dairy industry, and on March 25 the secretary announced that the level of support had been raised to 85 percent, an action that obviously pleased the dairy groups.

For the investigators the question was simple: had the increase been granted in exchange for a political contribution? The appearance of administration impropriety could not have been stronger if a dairy official had been seen leaving a black bag in the White House rose garden; on the other hand, many members of Congress at the same time were backing legislation that would have compelled the president to raise the price-support level to 85 or even 90 percent of parity.

Another group of majority staff members looked into what became known as the Hughes-Rebozo contribution. Early in Nixon's first term Charles (Bebe) Rebozo, the president's "best friend" and Richard Danner, a representative of Howard Hughes, discussed a campaign contribution to the president. Danner and Rebozo had long been friends, dating from Danner's service as FBI agent in charge of the Miami area. Subsequently Hughes contributed a total of $100,000 in two equal installments to the Nixon campaign, a gift made through Rebozo in 1969 or 1970.

Rebozo told committee investigators that the money had never been spent, but had been kept in a safety deposit box and returned intact to Hughes in June of 1973. It had not been used, he said, because he had become concerned about the "appearances" of the contribution. The majority staff members suspected that Rebozo had indeed used the money, probably for Nixon's personal benefit, and that the money was later replaced in the safety deposit box after the Internal Revenue Service had begun looking into the matter. The majority staff members also explored numerous avenues by which Hughes could have gained benefits as a *quid pro quo* for the $100,000 contribution, but all their leads ran into dead ends. Staff members working in this area had a limitless number of theories, often a theory a day. One that was widely held—and dutifully picked up by the press—was that, because Lawrence O'Brien had once been employed by the Hughes Tool Company on a retainer basis and was a friend of Robert Maheu, a former associate of Hughes who had been fired amid considerable acrimony and lawsuits, O'Brien might have knowledge of the $100,000 Hughes gift, through Maheu or other Hughes associates. Fear that the contribution might be disclosed, the theory went on, could have been the reason for the tapping of O'Brien's phone and the burglary of his office. To take the theory its final mile, only Rebozo and the top echelon at the White House knew about the contribution; thus, the orders for the break-in would have to emanate from the top. This was a possible way to link Nixon directly to the break-in.

These two areas were among a large number that, in my opinion, reflected abysmally bad judgment on the part of the White House. In the overall picture of White House wrongdoing, I considered them relatively mild, but the investigations that arose from them offered superb insight into the mentality of committee staffs. Each area had been little explored, and each involved Nixon. Here was a way for a young man on the staff to make his mark in history, possibly even to bring down a president. For several months extraordinary amounts of money and manpower were expended on these efforts. Members of the majority staff became highly competitive, because the one who achieved the breakthrough might be able to question witnesses at a public hearing. This same desire for glory—for the key that would unlock the Watergate mystery—required that the hearings be prolonged. So staff members passed the word to the press and to senators on the committee that a breakthrough, like prosperity in the Great Depression, was just around the corner.

Senator Ervin, a kind man in almost all his dealings with people, permitted some members of the majority staff to approach him privately in his office, often without Dash's knowledge. These staff members impressed on him the importance of their investigations and the need for further hearings, at a time when it was almost universally agreed that our day in the limelight was long past.

During this process of staff politicking, the elements of fairness and respect for individual rights frequently suffered. Rebozo was a particular target and an easy one. By the time the staff concentrated on him, Nixon had been severely wounded, and no one stepped forward to defend the rights of Nixon's best friend for fear that he might be accused of being soft on Nixon.

Staff members made four trips to Miami to interview Rebozo. They traveled in pairs, sometimes in threes. Sometimes one team would interview Rebozo for four, five, or six hours; a few days later another group would arrive and go over the same material with Rebozo, seemingly unaware of what their colleagues had just done.

Rebozo was called to Washington for interviews on three other occasions. As many as twenty staff members would attend the interviews and sit and gawk at him.

Rebozo investigators interviewed the members of Rebozo's family and all of his business acquaintances over a six-year period; they subpoenaed the business records, not only of

Rebozo but also of all those with whom he had done business for six years. They interrogated all the people he had written checks to over that period. At a committee meeting, when I asked what six-year-old business records had to do with the 1972 presidential campaign, I never received an answer. By this time the staff members had realized they were really answerable to no one.

They obtained the toll records for eleven telephones that Rebozo had had access to for this six-year-period and questioned him on over 400 telephone numbers, asking him whom he talked to and what they talked about. Young committee staffers unable to get the answers they wanted told a respected trust officer in Rebozo's bank, "We'll see that you get immunity if you'll tell us the truth."

William Frates, the Miami lawyer who later defended John Ehrlichman at the cover-up trial, was Rebozo's counsel. He had taken the position from the start that the truth ultimately would benefit Rebozo, and he gave the staff almost total access to his client's records. It soon became almost routine, after a batch of Rebozo's records were examined, that newspaper reports would appear quoting sources "close to the committee" and referring to the Rebozo investigation in ways that were damaging to Rebozo. One day Carmine Bellino examined the records of all of the loans Rebozo had made over a period of several years. The next morning at 9:30 the *Miami Herald* began calling each of the lending banks to verify information the newspaper had about the loans.

On another occasion a customer entered Rebozo's bank in Key Biscayne and told an employee that he feared a holdup was imminent. He pointed to two mysterious-looking men in a car down the street, slouched down so that only the tops of their heads were visible. It turned out that a couple of young committee staff members were casing the joint, checking on everyone who entered or left the bank. Still another time staff members followed an executive of Rebozo's bank from his office to his home, and they knocked on the door to interrogate him about the stops he had made on the way.

One afternoon when three committee staffers arrived at the Key Biscayne Bank to continue their interviews, an ABC truck and film crew just happened to arrive at the same time and filmed the staffers going into and out of the bank.

Frates complained bitterly and constantly to Dash and me. Dash, although sympathetic to many of Frates' objections, appeared to be losing more and more control over some of his staff members. Once the staff members knew they could see Ervin when they wanted to, Dash's authority was diminished considerably.

After all this, and after still another angry telephone call from Frates, I decided to evaluate the situation firsthand. Unlike the majority staff, we on the minority staff had never gotten Rebozo's position on the matters at issue. Richard Shultz of our staff (a former FBI agent) and I interviewed Rebozo in Frates' office. He was friendly and spoke so quietly that at times his words were barely audible. While a question was being asked he kept his hand in front of his mouth as if to shield himself from what was happening. As he talked about the things that had happened to him since the investigation began, he did not sound embittered, only astounded.

Midway through our interview, Frates' secretary entered the room to announce a local telephone call for me. When I spoke on the phone, the caller hung up. I had told Dash of my plans to interview Rebozo in Miami; I learned later that two majority staff members were in Miami at the same time, and it was apparent that one of them had called to check on my whereabouts.

As we were gathering our papers after the interview, Shultz, who had a rather unconventional sense of humor, remarked, "Well, Mr. Rebozo, I guess you'll just have to start choosing your friends a little better." I cringed; Rebozo managed a weak smile.

Shultz was attempting to keep abreast of the majority's Hughes-Rebozo investigation, but the majority staff far outnumbered him. I brought the matter before the committee more than once. In view of the fact that the Senate had limited our investigation to the 1972 campaign, I asked, what gave staff members the authority to investigate a private citizen's business life? What about the private-eye tactics and the leaks to the press? Ervin usually replied that he understood matters would be clarified in a week or two.

One afternoon, after such a session, Leslie Stahl of CBS dropped by my office and asked, "Why have you become Rebozo's defender all of a sudden?" The question was not related to fairness, or even committee rules, but to my role as a roadblock. Whoever had briefed Stahl was sending me a not-so-subtle message: stand in our way and you will pay for it. This tactic was one of the most effective ways in which the press was used by the staff—even against members of the committee.

Nearly every member of the committee wanted to conclude our investigation weeks before it actually ended. However, any indication of such a desire, or any question that was raised about the tactics being used, invariably found its way to the press, with the implication that it evidenced either a lack of courage to pursue the inquiry or an attempt to cover up wrongdoing. Because Ervin permitted as many as fifteen staff members to attend executive sessions, there was no way to trace the source of such a press report.

Dash appeared to have no control over Lenzner, and Lenzner lacked control over his subordinates. As a result, those in the lowest echelon of the committee's staff were able, in effect, to make policy for the committee—a situation I had never encountered.

Rebozo was not the only one who felt the heat from the investigation of the $100,000 contribution. Gen. Alexander Haig, then Nixon's chief of staff, was summoned for an interview. It turned out that he knew almost nothing about the Watergate matter. Nonetheless, the president ordered Haig to invoke executive privilege and refuse to answer the staff's questions, a patently untenable position because the questions involved possible criminal acts. All those present when Haig appeared understood the situation, and he was asked only a few questions for the record to provide a basis for later action by the committee. As expected, Haig respectfully declined to answer. The next morning the *Washington Post* reported that Haig had refused to answer "over 200 questions," implying that Haig himself might have some legal problems.

That night Haig called me for the first time. The *Post* story had depressed him, and he appeared anxious just to talk about it. "You know," he said, "my reputation is about all that I've got." He asked whether I thought it would be wise if he issued a strong denial; I replied that I would not try to advise him but that I thought such action would do little more than draw additional attention to the original story. He seemed to agree.

The Internal Revenue Service staff was still another target of our committee's staff. Five IRS agents had already spent fourteen weeks investigating Rebozo and had orally given him a clean bill of health. Members of the majority staff had demanded the income tax returns of numerous individuals, including Rebozo, as well as several "sensitive case reports." Because of the record of leaks to the press, IRS officials were understandably reluctant to turn over such sensitive information. Ironically, it was still another leak that pried loose the information. Lenzner drafted a long memorandum to the staff, implying that IRS and its employees had been too easy on Rebozo in the past and that they were now covering up. Copies of the memorandum were delivered to all the senators on the committee, and the result was predictable: within forty-eight hours the substance of the Lenzner memo was in the newspapers. The IRS, now forced to prove its innocence, reluctantly turned over the information to the staff.

Senator Ervin, who was acting more and more as though he wished the entire investigation would go away so he could get back to a fishing hole in North Carolina, allowed himself to be placed in still another embarrassing situation because of staff excesses. According to a Jack Anderson column, Anderson had furnished information to the majority staff indicating that Nixon's personal attorney, Herbert Kalmbach, had significant information about the Rebozo matter. Kalmbach, of course, had already been a target of our investigation because of his role in raising and distributing the hush money after the Watergate break-in.

Whenever I thought of Kalmbach, I always thought of his attorney, who early in the investigation tried to arrange a meeting of Baker and Kalmbach in Baker's office. The senator referred the matter to me, and the lawyer later brought Kalmbach to my office and suggested that we become better acquainted. Kalmbach was completely innocent, the lawyer said, and I would soon find that this was the case. I told him that we had best limit our contact to the lawyer and me, alone, at my office.

Later, of course, it turned out that Kalmbach not only had raised the hush money but that he had also been a negotiator for the sale of certain ambassadorships. The attorney evidently thought he could help his client by getting close to Baker and me. It was an example of some of the dangers that confronted everyone on the committee and the staff.

After receiving Jack Anderson's tip, Lenzner and his staff aides called in Kalmbach for another interview. It was a secret session in Ervin's office; even Dash did not know about it. Kalmbach's attorney made it clear that Kalmbach was willing to say that Rebozo had told Kalmbach that he had given some of the $100,000 to Nixon's brothers, to Rosemary Woods, Nixon's secretary, and others. However, it was also Kalmbach's position that Rebozo was seeking Kalmbach's advice as an attorney-client privilege. Staff members obviously had that information, because they had Rebozo secreted in another room on Capitol Hill. Members of the staff shuttled between the two rooms. They asked Rebozo, without mentioning Kalmbach's name, to list the attorneys he had retained in the past. When Rebozo did not mention Kalmbach's name, word was sent back to Ervin that Rebozo was not claiming any attorney-client privilege with Kalmbach. Thereupon, Ervin ruled that no privilege existed and he ordered Kalmbach to testify. Kalmbach proceeded to make his accusation against Rebozo, a statement that was later denied by Rebozo, Miss Woods, and Nixon's brothers, Edward and Donald. This development produced subpoenas for the business records of both Nixon brothers.

Frates was now becoming increasingly hostile toward the committee staff; he refused to comply with any more subpoenas. When he learned that his client's rights had in effect been waived by Ervin, he filed a motion with the committee to quash all remaining subpoenas. One of his arguments was that information had been derived from an improper waiver of Rebozo's attorney-client privilege.

After Frates had acquainted the committee with the matter and left the room, it was evident that his concern was shared by others. Weicker questioned the staff members involved. Dissatisfied with their responses, he finally lost his temper and shouted, "I just want one straight answer for a change. Did you or did you not specifically ask him if he ever had such a relationship with Kalmbach and whether he was waiving his privilege?" The answer was no.

Turning to Lenzner, Weicker said, "Goddamn it, Terry, this is the very sort of thing that we have been dealing with at the White House for over a year. It's not fair and it's not right."

His statement, though directed at Lenzner, was really a criticism of Ervin. The chairman tried to explain his reasoning for his ruling that no attorney-client privilege existed. Regardless of the legal niceties, however, there was a general feeling that this matter had an odor about it. Unemotionally, Baker stated the other side of the legal argument; the committee faced a vote on the Frates motion to quash the subpoena. A vote to quash would clearly be a criticism of both Ervin's interpretation of the law and his judgment, but it appeared that exactly that was about to happen.

Rufus Edmisten left to fetch Talmadge, who had left the committee room to return to the Senate floor. Edmisten, realizing a partisan vote was in prospect, needed Talmadge's presence. When the matter was explained to Talmadge, he drawled, "What I want to know is what the hell are we doing faced with a problem like this when the committee is already supposed to be writing a report and going out of business?" No one seemed to have an answer. Talmadge gave his proxy vote to Ervin, as usual, and left.

Ervin appeared embarrassed and concerned. I had mixed feelings; I was glad that someone finally had blown the whistle on questionable methods, but I believed that Ervin had acted without malice and that his problem was primarily a result of allowing the committee staff to go unchecked. Moreover, with the committee winding down its operations, all its members appeared to intensify their efforts to avoid situations that would harm the committee's work. I did not believe that any of the three Republicans would relish the prospect of casting a vote that would reflect adversely on Ervin's judgment. Moreover, I concluded, if I could resolve the matter quietly it would give me some leverage with Ervin later when we would be fashioning the committee's report.

"Mr. Chairman," I said, "why don't you give Sam Dash and me a chance to talk to Mr. Frates privately about the matter? I think it might be resolved without taking a vote." Ervin looked at Baker, who was nodding his head affirmatively. I felt that Ervin did not know what I had in mind, but that Baker did.

"All right," Ervin said in a soft voice. "We'll give you a few minutes."

Inouye gave me the keys to his Capitol office, a small room that adjoined Ervin's. Dash and I were joined by Frates and Lenzner, along with Mark Lackritz and Scott Armstrong, who had been working with Lenzner on the Rebozo matter. Frates and the Lenzner-Armstrong team, who had fought many battles before, began exchanging sarcastic insults before I could speak. Frates was livid. Armstrong managed to keep cool.

After the atmosphere calmed down a bit I told Frates it was obvious that the committee was reluctant to vote on his motion, which had created embarrassment. I said I thought that if he would simply withdraw his motion to quash, the gesture would be highly appreciated; I said I did not believe the committee had any intention of pressing the subpoenas at this point. Frates did not like the idea.

"These guys have harassed us and leaked everything we

have given them and demanded stuff they are not entitled to, and I'm not going to put up with it any longer," he said firmly.

"Bill," I answered, "when it comes down to a vote you're probably going to lose anyway. It would be a smart thing for you to do."

Lenzner and Armstrong did not seem to think much of the idea either. They wanted it expressly understood that the subpoena matter would be pressed fully. I found myself arguing simultaneously with Frates and with Lenzner and Armstrong. I told the majority staff members that they had put Ervin on the spot and that now they were not willing to help him. "You might as well face the fact," I said, "that Rebozo is not going to be cited for contempt even if he doesn't comply with the subpoenas. What you guys have done over the past few months has insured that. You've lost your support."

Then Frates and Armstrong locked horns again. "Rat fink! Rat fink!" Frates was shouting at Armstrong. "You're nothing but a rat fink!" We all started yelling at once.

I turned back to Frates. "Bill, damn it, if I were you I would drop this motion and get out of town as fast as I could. You know after everything that's gone on your man's not going to be held in contempt." We had agreed earlier on several portions of the subpoenas with which Frates and Rebozo were willing to comply. Therefore the subpoena fight had become largely a symbolic struggle. "Bill," I said, "send us what you have agreed to send us. My guess is that that will be the end of it."

This time the staff members remained silent. Frates, by now composed, agreed. We returned to the committee room and Dash announced that Frates had agreed to withdraw his motion to quash the subpoenas. An expression of relief came over Ervin's face. Weicker said, "Sam, Fred, good job." Rebozo heard little more from the committee.

In checking on the milk-fund investigation, we discovered that members of the majority staff, when interrogating witnesses, were confining their questions to Republican campaigns. Although the resolution that established our committee called for an investigation into all improper campaign activities in 1972, it was clear to us that improper Democratic campaign activities were not being looked into with anything like the gusto or detail that was being used in examining the Republicans. Don Sanders, who already was investigating Democratic campaign activities, was assigned to the milk-fund matter, with instructions to see that the Democrats received equal scrutiny. The minority committee members had decided to look into all aspects of the various Democratic campaigns, including those made in the primary elections by Senators George McGovern, Edmund Muskie, and Hubert Humphrey, John Lindsay of New York, and Rep. Wilbur Mills of Arkansas.

What really started us moving in this area was a committee colloquy during the testimony of Maurice Stans, former secretary of commerce and chairman of the CRP finance committee. Ervin questioned Stans critically over the fact that certain campaign records relating to the period before April 7, 1972, had been destroyed by the Republican National Committee. Prior to that date, the law did not require even that records be kept. After Ervin noted that the law did not require that the records be destroyed either, Baker suggested that the committee also examine the practices of the Democratic candidates prior to April 7.

Following this, our minority staff began interviews with Democratic campaign treasurers and other campaign personnel, and we sent out blanket subpoenas for campaign records. Sanders soon discovered that, like Stans, Humphrey's campaign chairman, Jack Chestnut, had destroyed many of his records for the period before April 7. Over the next several months the minority staff systematically produced findings that were later incorporated into the committee's final report. One key finding was that "improprieties in campaign finances were not limited to any particular candidate or party."

We discovered that approximately $340,000 of McGovern's leftover presidential campaign funds were transferred to his Senate campaign. Although this was not illegal in itself, it was

*Senator Ervin points out a passage of scripture to Majority deputy counsel Rufus Edmisten. "Sam is the only man I know," said Senator Baker, "who can read the transcript of a telephone conversation and make it sound like the King James version of the New Testament."*

done at the same time that McGovern's campaign creditors were being asked to accept a compromise settlement of their bills. Of this group, thirty-seven corporate creditors accepted reductions in indebtedness that amounted to $35,000. In short, it appeared that the McGovern campaign directors were asking their creditors to take less than full payment while transferring money that could have been used to pay them in full into a different political campaign. The transfers began within a month after the 1972 election.

Some members of the majority staff seemed to be as concerned about the Democrats' improprieties as they were about

Nixon's. One of these men, with whom we worked well and closely for several months, was David Dorsen, who had primary responsibility for the milk-fund investigation. As we were writing our report Dorsen indicated his belief that the McGovern transfer of funds was a violation of at least the spirit of the law that prohibited corporate contributions to political candidates. It seemed to Dorsen and to us that settling a corporate debt, after the election, at fifty cents on the dollar, when funds were available for full payment, was as much a corporate contribution as if corporate money had been given outright before the election. The minority had the primary responsibility for drafting this part of the committee's report, and we incorporated Dorsen's suggestion that an apparent "violation of the spirit" of the corporate-contribution law had taken place.

We also discovered that an official in the Muskie campaign had made an arrangement with Hertz Rent-A-Car under which automobiles would be leased to the Muskie forces without charge. This struck us as an outright corporate contribution. Hertz had engaged in an elaborate but apparently quite common scheme to disguise this arrangement. Bills for car rentals in excess of $4,000 were accumulated by a Hertz official, who then solicited contributions to cover the amount from various attorneys who represented Hertz. In turn, the attorneys appeared to have recovered their outlays by billing Hertz for services the lawyers never performed. Because of our limited manpower, the minority staff was spread thin; but it seemed that everywhere we looked there was an array of campaign irregularities waiting to be discovered. In New York we found that two paving contractors had contributed $5000 each in cash to the Lindsay presidential campaign, having been solicited by city highway maintenance officials. The cash was delivered directly to Lindsay's campaign manager in an envelope that showed the identity of the donors; a few months later the same contractors received a $1.7 million award to provide asphalt to New York City.

Because we could not undertake a full-scale investigation of each of the Democrats who entered the presidential primaries, we focused on three—McGovern, Humphrey, and Mills. In the cases of Humphrey and Mills we concentrated on the milk contributions because both men favored increased milk price supports and both had received contributions from representatives of milk producers. While the majority staff's attention was directed at the administration's role in increasing the price support, we decided to explore the congressional pressure, primarily from Democrats, to achieve the same goal.

We found that Humphrey's presidential campaign had received at least $25,000 in apparently illegal corporate gifts from dairy cooperatives, in addition to $17,225 that was given legally by the industry's trust fund. Our investigation showed that three weeks before the government announced the change in the price-support level from 80 to 85 percent of parity, Humphrey had made a speech on the Senate floor in favor of a 90 percent support level. There was no indication that the Humphrey contributions were made in exchange for his support of the milk producers' cause, but we considered the link no more tenuous than the one the Democratic staff members were making about the milk gifts to Nixon and his action on price supports.

Some of the campaign-financing discoveries were hardly earth-shattering, but we were compiling an impressively long list. Ten officers of Minnesota Mining and Manufacturing bought $100 tickets to a Humphrey fund-raising affair; the money, we found, had come from a secret corporate fund. John L. Loeb, senior partner of Loeb, Rhodes & Company, the investment bankers, gave Humphrey a $50,000 contribution. But instead of making the contribution in Loeb's name, as required by law, Loeb had several of his employees write personal checks totaling the $50,000 and then reimbursed them.

Prior to April 7, 1972, federal law prohibited anyone, with some exceptions, to give more than $5,000 in any calendar year to a presidential candidate. We documented more than $500,000 in contributions to the Humphrey campaign in the form of individual gifts that exceeded $5,000. Humphrey used assets from a blind trust that he had created to provide separate sums of

$23,000 and about $86,000 to his own campaign in January and February of 1972. It did not seem logical that the law actually intended to prohibit someone from contributing to his own campaign, but the law appeared to provide for no such exception. So we added that item to our list of apparent Humphrey campaign violations.

Congressman Mills, chairman of the House Ways and Means Committee, was considered one of the nation's most powerful men. He became a presidential candidate on February 11, 1972, although efforts on his behalf began early in 1971. His ill-fated campaign illustrates, possibly better than any other, the pitfalls facing a candidate who begins with a relatively small base of support. The temptation is to align oneself with at least one of the country's major money interests, and that seemed to be the case with Mills and the Associated Milk Producers, Inc., with which he had long enjoyed a friendly relationship. In addition to apparently legal contributions totaling $55,600 from the political-action arms of the milk producers, there was evidence that Mills' presidential effort had received up to $75,000 from the corporate assets of AMPI, $15,000 from the corporate assets of another dairy cooperative, Mid-America Dairymen, and $40,000 in donations from members, employees, and officers of AMPI, for a total of about $185,000 from dairy-producing sources. This constituted about 38 percent of Mills' entire campaign revenues. Mills helped AMPI in its organized drive to persuade the administration to increase milk-price supports. He had numerous meetings with the producers and their lobbyists; he arranged a meeting at which the House speaker suggested that members of Congress be contacted to co-sponsor the bill increasing price supports and to urge officials of the Nixon administration to act in the producers' interest.

In addition, several AMPI employees worked in the Mills campaign. We had sworn testimony that Mills asked AMPI to arrange a rally in Iowa in October 1971 to provide him with a forum to address Iowa farmers. AMPI paid the bill—about $45,000. Corporate funds of AMPI were used to buy "Mills for President" bumper stickers. If the Democrats wanted to link political contributions from the milk industry to support for legislation favorable to that group, they could try on the case of Wilbur Mills for size.

We also discovered that a vice president of Gulf Oil Company had personally delivered $15,000 in cash from corporate assets to a Mills fund raiser.

Our investigation received little attention in the press, but our findings were well known to the political figures involved. And they were not exactly cooperative.

We subpoenaed Jack Chestnut, Humphrey's campaign manager, and Joe Johnson, who had the same job for Mills. Observing congressional protocol, we suggested to Ervin that he write Humphrey and Mills, requesting that they make themselves available for interviews. Humphrey said he had no personal knowledge of the matters we were exploring and, therefore, declined to appear. Mills failed to reply to two letters sent by Ervin.

As might have been expected, our activities in this area did not interest many of the Democratic staff members. Copies of drafts of staff reports were readily available to both the majority and the minority, but there was no rush to examine ours for possible additional action.

McGovern supporters evidently had been advised of what we were doing, for McGovern wrote a letter to Ervin that complained bitterly about our activities, particularly the language in the draft report citing an "apparent violation of the spirit of the law" in regard to the arrangement under which some corporations settled their campaign debts for less than the full amounts owed. McGovern's letter castigated the minority staff, likening us to Haldeman and Segretti. The senator obviously did not know that the language to which he objected most had been drafted by Dorsen, a member of the majority staff—language with which we, of course, wholeheartedly agreed.

The *Washington Post* quoted a member of the McGovern staff as saying that his group would attempt to change the language of the report before it was approved by the committee in final form. A few days later, Dick Shultz told me that he had heard from a member of the majority staff that Ervin had passed the word that the phrase "apparent violation of the law" was not to appear in the report. In the final report the language to which McGovern objected was deleted, but we used the fact as a bargaining weapon to obtain the inclusion of other matters we wanted to retain.

Perhaps the most intensive lobbying effort of this kind was one by a Democratic member of the House, Jim Jones of Oklahoma, who had been an aide to President Johnson. While examining AMPI records Sanders discovered a letter from Jones to AMPI, written before Jones was elected to the House. The letter complained that AMPI had stopped paying a retainer to Jones, a retainer that began shortly after he left the Johnson White House. In effect, the letter said that because Jones had persuaded Johnson to act on matters of interest to the milk industry, AMPI had agreed to place him on retainer and that now AMPI was backing out of the deal.

When our staff contacted Jones about the letter, he faced a painful decision. He had to admit either that he had improperly used his influence while serving in the White House or that, to keep the retainer, he had misled AMPI about his efforts in AMPI's behalf. He told us that the latter situation was true—that he had not really provided any of the help for AMPI that was spelled out in his letter.

For weeks afterward, Jones called several senators on the committee, including Ervin and Baker, and several members of the staff, among them Dash, Sanders, and me. He did not want his letter mentioned in our report. The committee's majority finally decided that the Jones matter did not fall within the committee's jurisdiction. This ruling, in my view, was not consistent with the committee's action on other matters of our investigation, including Rebozo's dealings. I believed that the Democrats were using the jurisdictional issue to bail out one of their Democratic colleagues.

I also believed that this same double standard was applied with regard to the minority staff's investigation of the financial operations of the Democratic presidential campaigns. When we uncovered improper financial practices that could not be clearly linked to the 1972 presidential campaign, the majority staff always headed us off, knowing they had the support of a committee majority. Dash acknowledged to me after we were finished that he had received several calls from Democrats, asking what we were "trying to do" to Humphrey, or McGovern, or other Democrats under investigation.

As the realities of life with the committee became clearer to me and as the partisan infighting intensified, I began to employ the leak for my own purposes. Reporters would periodically call me for verification of a story they had obtained from a majority staffer. Often they would have only half a story—the half most damaging to the person the staffer was trying to put the heat on. I would supply the other half of the story, which often cast the reporter's original information in an entirely different light.

When Dick Shultz told me that Ervin had directed that the reference to the McGovern campaign's "apparent violation of the law" be removed from the report I called a UPI reporter and informed him of Ervin's action. The reporter's inquiries to Democrats on the staff put them on the defensive for several days and improved our bargaining position.

When it became apparent to me that some of the Democrats on the committee were trying to suppress some of the essences of Democratic wrongdoing, I seriously considered leaking the entire contents of the reports we had compiled on the Democrats. I decided against that, however, because I believed it would ultimately defeat our purposes. The source of such a leak would be pretty obvious, and the Democrats would use it to put us on the defensive and further whittle down our final report.

As things turned out, we took more precautions to prevent leaks of the material we were developing against the Democrats than we did in other areas of our investigation. We did not distribute the drafts of our reports until they had been rewritten several times to insure that every allegation in them could be fully substantiated. Then we distributed the material only to the Republican senators. For one thing, we could never predict Weicker's reaction; he had developed a close rapport with the Democrats through his expressions of outrage about White House "horrors," and we thought he might be unwilling to pursue Democratic improprieties for fear that he would be accused of attempting to justify the wrongdoings of the Nixon administration.

However, when a member of Weicker's staff called Sanders on June 26 to request additional copies of our reports on the Democratic campaigns, we knew that we had passed the Weicker test. We also surmised that copies of the reports were probably being distributed to reporters, and our guess proved accurate. Leslie Stahl had obtained copies of our entire package, and the next day she was calling members of the committee and the staff for clarification of various points.

On Friday afternoon, June 28, 1974, Dash, Lenzner, Armstrong, and I were in Dash's office negotiating the language of the Hughes-Rebozo section of the report, which Lenzner's group had prepared. Ervin had been concerned that this section might be leaked, as other reports had been, because he believed it contained some serious accusations and implications that could not be supported. We tried to work out a compromise that could be presented to the commiteee as a joint product of both the majority and minority staffs.

In the midst of our labors there was a telephone call for Dash. He looked somewhat pale as he hung up the phone after a brief conversation. "That was Senator Inouye's office, Fred. They want you and me to come up there to meet with Senator Humphrey." It was hard to believe; we were being called on the carpet by Humphrey himself.

Humphrey was standing in the waiting room when Dash and I arrived at Inouye's office. With Humphrey were his attorney, Joe Walters; his administrative assistant, David Gartner; and Senator Inouye and his assistant. After the usual preliminary small talk, ranging from the beauties of Hawaii to the gangrene that had cost Inouye his right arm, Inouye turned to Dash and me—we were seated side by side on a small sofa—and said he wanted to discuss a matter that was of some concern to him.

"I admit that it is partially due to personal friendship with Hubert Humphrey and the regard I have for him," Inouye said, "but I must say that I am concerned that this report that I have just read makes it look somewhat like my friend is a crook." He spoke softly and slowly, measuring his words well; the approach was similar to the one he used in questioning Watergate witnesses.

Humphrey, seated across from Dash and me, had said little until then. But now, as he began to talk at some length, it was obvious that he was angry. He said he had two objections to the staff report as it referred to him: the implication that there was something wrong about his personal contribution to his own campaign and what he called the unfair implication that his support for milk-price legislation was somehow linked to the contributions he had received from milk-industry sources.

"Furthermore," he went on, "Dwayne Andreas [the trustee of the blind trust that was used to transfer Humphrey's personal money to his campaign treasury] is my neighbor and my friend. I am the godfather to his son and there is nothing wrong with our transferring my money to my own campaign. I'll give my own money to the damn Republican National Committee if I want to." His voice rose and he seemed to generate his own heat as he went along, in much the same manner that I had seen on television during his 1968 presidential campaign. To my surprise, he seemed to be looking directly at Dash nearly all the time.

"And on dairymen, I'm for them. As far as I'm concerned, this 80 percent parity is too damn low. I'm for 100 percent. I've always supported them. I'm not a law violator," he said, his face flushed. "I can't stand to have that on my record." In addition, he declared, when he found out about the destruction of his campaign records, he had raised "holy hell" about it.

Dash began his reply by apologizing for the leak of the report on Humphrey's finances, explaining that nearly all of our work had seemed to spring leaks, and that we would certainly be willing to speak with Humphrey or his attorney on those points that the senator regarded as unfair.

Dash was in a difficult position. He had already assured me that he would fully support my pursuit of Democratic campaign improprieties. I had kept Dash fully informed of our work because I knew our group was basically vulnerable in getting its findings reported and that I might need his help when the showdown arrived—which it evidently had. A few others on the majority staff had cooperated with us, perhaps just enough to protect our position.

Then Senator Inouye's aide interjected himself. Apparently anxious to impress the senators with his toughness, he related a series of personal objections to the report and, looking directly at me, concluded by saying caustically, "Just what do you think you're trying to do?"

I must have risen halfway out of my seat. I was infuriated that a staff member would try to take such advantage of a tense situation. "You don't ask me that question, or anything else," I said. He looked down and began to shuffle his papers. "If we have problems to work out, we'll do it with the senator or with his lawyer. You and I don't have any more to say to each other."

Senator Humphrey stepped in. "Thank you, Fred, that's good," he said. "I appreciate that." I thought he was making a sincere effort to bring about a peaceful solution.

Turning to Senator Humphrey, I said, "Senator, let me explain my situation in this matter. As you probably know, the minority staff has been carrying the ball in this investigation. I think that we're all probably caught up in a Watergate syndrome. The Democrats have been investigating the administration for a year and a half now, trying to prove that Nixon was bought off with a milk contribution. I don't know whether it's true or not but I do know that our committee was supposed to investigate all presidential candidates, including those in the primaries, and it has fallen to me to push these investigations."

As I spoke, Senator Humphrey's features seemed to soften, and I thought I could detect his head nodding slightly in affirmation. He seemed to understand my position and to realize as well as I that once an investigation tiger is let out of the cage it is destined to rattle a lot of people before being caged again. The whole procedure had turned into one of, "Okay, you boys investigate our people and if they are guilty, so be it; but in the meantime, we're going to investigate your people with no holds barred."

Looking at the matter objectively, all the points that Humphrey had raised were arguable, and I would have made them myself if I had been representing him. Dash and I then had a brief discussion with Joe Walters and Dave Gartner about a question of law concerning a candidate's contributing to his own campaign. We all shook hands and agreed to meet Walters later to discuss the legal points with him. As we walked into the hall, I told Walters, "Joe, Sanders or I and Dash's people will meet with you anytime, but leave that Inouye aide at home." He agreed.

The confrontation with Humphrey had ended more pleasantly than I expected, and I thought that we might have cleared the last major hurdle before completing our job.

# Chapter IX · Unanswered Questions

The story of the Watergate break-in contains so many extraordinary elements—including amateurish bungling and remarkable coincidences involving those who took part—that it is difficult to accept a straightforward chronicle of the events as fiction, let alone fact. It also raises some unanswered questions that were explored by the Watergate committee's minority staff, questions that remain unanswered to this day.

That five men, most of them with CIA experience, were caught in an office at the headquarters of the Democratic National Committee, without any provision for escape, without having either subdued or subverted the security force at the Watergate building, and after the group had twice left tape over the locks of the doors leading to the office they were entering, tape that could be detected by any passerby—all these elements of the escapade raised immediate suspicions on the part of investigators.

On the night of June 16, 1972, the Watergate burglars taped the door at the rear of the Watergate complex to facilitate their entry later that night. When they returned, sometime after midnight on June 17, they discovered that the tape had been removed. Instead of abandoning the mission, they inexplicably decided to tape the same door and proceed. Hunt said later that Liddy had insisted that they go ahead. The Cuban-Americans said McCord made the decision to carry on, speculating that "probably a mailman" had removed the tape. As it turned out, of course, the tape was discovered and removed by a Watergate guard—Frank Wills.

After they entered the building, McCord, the last man to

enter Democratic headquarters, was supposed to remove the tape. There was no use for it once the group had entered; the door did not lock from the inside. Martinez told us later that he had asked McCord if he had removed the tape, and that Mc-Cord had answered yes. But McCord had not, and when the guard spotted it for a second time he called the police, which happened to have a plain-clothes unit, working overtime, in the neighborhood.

Because of the White House involvement in the scandal, questions surrounding the break-in and speculation that some-one apart from the burglars and a small group in the Nixon reelection committee might have had advance knowledge of it received little attention, even as a matter of historical interest. Although I was not above trying to drag out any embarrassing skeletons the Democrats had hiding in their closet, I saw minimal possibilities for partisan advantage in pursuing these questions, even if we developed irrefutable proof that, say, Lawrence O'Brien had held the flashlight for the burglars. It wouldn't bear on the guilt or innocence of anyone at the White House or the CRP. Yet the questions were intriguing.

Much of the early speculation centered on the possibility that Alfred Baldwin was a double agent. Baldwin was sta-tioned at the Howard Johnson Motor Inn across from the Watergate; his job the night of the break-in was to inform the burglars of any suspicious persons who entered the building while they were in the Democrats' offices. Even though the policemen who arrived there were dressed in civilian clothes, it struck us that Baldwin had been unusually inept in not alerting the group at once when a group of men left a car and ran into the Watergate. At an executive session of our committee in September 1973, Hunt strongly voiced his suspicions about Baldwin and about other circumstances surrounding the break-in. These received little attention until we learned of what appeared to be collaboration, within weeks of the break-in, between Baldwin and attorneys for the Democratic National Committee.

On September 11, 1972, Woodward and Bernstein wrote in

the *Washington Post* that the Democratic party had an informant who had participated in the illegal Watergate activities, and that the informant was the source of the details of the break-in that were made known by O'Brien, then the Democratic national chairman, at a news conference on September 7, 1972.

Our committee staff interviewed O'Brien on October 3, 1973. He told us that the source of his statement at the news conference a year earlier had been Joseph Califano, who served as counsel to the Democratic National Committee from 1970 to March 6, 1973.

When we interviewed Califano, he said that Baldwin had contacted his office through Baldwin's Connecticut attorney, John Cassidento. Califano gave the committee copies of notes of an interview with Baldwin that contained extensive information about Baldwin's activities. The material based on an all-day interview with Baldwin contained background information on McCord's employment of Baldwin, Baldwin's work as a security guard for Martha Mitchell, details on the monitoring of the phones of O'Brien and Spencer Oliver in Democratic headquarters, a discussion of the aborted break-in at McGovern headquarters, and a description of the delivery of the transcripts of wiretapped conversations to the Nixon reelection committee before, as well as shortly after, the break-in. Was there a deal in which Baldwin and the Democrats agreed to have Baldwin participate in the break-in operation and then dutifully report to them?

On October 11, 1973, Baldwin was interviewed by Liebengood and Madigan in the committee's offices. When Liebengood mentioned Baldwin's cooperation with the lawyers for the Democratic committee, Baldwin appeared genuinely surprised. He said he had never been in contact with lawyers for the Democratic National Committee.

"You mean you didn't give information to them?" Madigan asked.

"Me give information to them, Democratic attorneys? Of course not. I would never have given information to them."

Liebengood and Madigan were astounded. Califano had stated flatly that his office had interviewed Baldwin and had produced notes to prove it. How could Baldwin possibly deny such a meeting? Baldwin was pressed further, and he continued his vehement denial that he would ever collaborate with the Democrats. He did recall, however, that at one point he had spoken to a couple of men whose identity he did not know.

Interviews with Baldwin's own attorneys, shed some light on the mystery. Cassidento said he had arranged an interview of Baldwin without informing his client of the identity of those who were going to question him. In that interview, for reasons never made clear to our staff, attorneys from Califano's firm posed questions to Cassidento, who repeated them to Baldwin, whereupon Baldwin would reply to Cassidento, who repeated the answers to Califano's associates.

The more we learned, the less Baldwin struck us as a double agent, and the more like a perfect participant in the Keystone Cops caper on June 16–17 at Democratic headquarters. Immediately after the burglars were caught, for example, Hunt raced across the street to Baldwin's room at Howard Johnson's, where the wiretapping was being monitored. Hunt told Baldwin to get rid of the bugging paraphernalia, and then Hunt ran out the door. According to Hunt, Baldwin, who had been promised a trip to Miami as part of his work, shouted after Hunt, "Does this mean I don't get to go to Florida?"

Although we had no evidence that Baldwin had deliberately informed anyone prior to the break-in, several things led us to believe that he could have unwittingly given the operation away. Using an alias, Baldwin reconnoitered Democratic headquarters on the pretext that he and Spencer Oliver had been classmates at law school and that he was a nephew of John Bailey, a former Democratic chairman. Baldwin offered to buy a $7.50 book, containing the names and addresses of persons associated with the Democratic committee, with a new $100 bill that no one could change. After he left the Democratic offices, Baldwin came back to ask O'Brien's telephone number in Miami. When O'Brien's secretary left the room, Baldwin, fearing his masquerade had been exposed, asked directions to the men's room and left again. Later, he called O'Brien's secretary, explaining that he had gotten lost in the Watergate complex, and obtained O'Brien's phone number.

Furthermore, Baldwin told us that, while staying at Howard Johnson's and using a room registered to McCord to monitor the Democrats' telephones, he had given the desk clerk his real name. He also told us that once he invited a buddy from Connecticut to spend the weekend with him while he was at the Howard Johnson's. And finally, he made several additional visits to Democratic headquarters to see a secretary there. All in all, we considered Baldwin a most unlikely double agent. He was more like a built-in disaster for a clandestine operation.

Other tantalizing bits of information appeared as our inquiry proceeded. For example, both Martinez and Hunt told us that McCord was on good terms with the Watergate security force. In fact, Martinez said that prior to one of the Watergate entries, McCord chatted with one of the guards, whom he appeared to know. In addition, we discovered that Louis Russell, once an employee of General Security Services, which provided the security guards for the Watergate, was an old friend of McCord's. In March of 1972, Russell worked three weeks as a night watchman for the Nixon reelection committee, for which McCord was director of security. Russell was paid for his work with a check drawn on McCord's account, not the committee's. Russell told us that on May 31, 1972, he was put on retainer by CRP and given a $706 advance, but that his job had been terminated with McCord's arrest. An associate of Russell's told us that he had rented living quarters to Russell, whom he described as a Democrat extremely critical of Nixon. On the night of the break-in, it turned out, Russell had had dinner at the Howard Johnson's across from Watergate. On July 1, 1973, before we could interview him further, Russell died of a heart attack.

Some information that raised intriguing questions came to us without solicitation. On May 18, 1973, Carl Shoffler, one of the plainclothesmen who answered the call to the Watergate after the break-in was discovered, came to my office following his public testimony to the committee. He said Edmund Chung, an acquaintance with whom Shoffler had served in the U.S. Army Security Agency in Warrenton, Va., had approached him early in 1973, a week before the trial of the original Watergate burglars, seeking information. Shoffler said Chung had hinted that he was somehow involved with the group that had been arrested and appeared to be seeking advice and help. Chung indicated, Shoffler said, that he was to report on his meeting with Shoffler, which lasted three hours, and that Chung's "people" would not be pleased with the results.

Shoffler said he met with Chung a second time, and Chung asked if there was any way it could be made to appear that a double agent had been on the roof of the Watergate during the break-in. Chung suggested that Shoffler might admit prior knowledge of the burglary. As soon as Shoffler left, Don Sanders and I discussed his story; we agreed that it seemed likely that agents of the reelection committee were trying to use Chung to involve Shoffler in some kind of entrapment theory. If this was true, we had a blatant attempt to solicit false testimony, another variation of a cover-up.

But when Sanders interviewed Chung on May 20, 1973, he turned the story completely around. He denied any knowledge of efforts to conceal Watergate-related facts or to induce others to change their testimony. He denied knowing any of those arrested at the Watergate or anyone associated with CRP. He conceded that he had had dinner with Shoffler, whom he said he had contacted after reading Shoffler's name in a newspaper. Chung quoted Shoffler as saying, in the course of the evening, that he had not told everything he knew. Shoffler, Chung said, indicated that he was familiar with some of those who had been arrested. And Chung said he got the impression that Shoffler had had advance knowledge of the break-in, that Shoffler had said that Baldwin had given him leads, and that if Chung checked the records he would wonder why Shoffler was on duty the night of June 16–17.

Now we were truly perplexed. Did this mean that Shoffler

had advance knowledge and had come to us to negate the impact of Chung's testimony? Checking Chung's record, we found that the nature of his military duties had been classified and that he held a top-secret crypto clearance. All his associates and prior employers held him in high regard.

So, Liebengood and Shultz again interviewed the police officers on duty the night of the break-in and examined the police department logs to see if there was any indication of unusual circumstances. They found an unvarying story. Shortly after midnight on June 17, Shoffler, having concluded work with the narcotics squad at about 10 P.M. the night before, volunteered to accompany Sgt. Paul Leeper and Officer John Barrett in an unmarked police vehicle. The car left the station at about 12:20 A.M. and was cruising in the Georgetown neighborhood when a dispatcher called for assistance at the Watergate. Shoffler immediately grabbed the phone in the car and volunteered his unit's assistance. He did not check with Leeper, who said this was not an unusual procedure. Both Leeper and Shoffler insisted it was simply a case of being at the right place at the right time (not to mention the right kind of clothing and the right kind of car to prevent being spotted).

We would not immediately pursue these matters as we plunged into the committee's hearings, which posed issues that we considered of more importance to the country. Nevertheless, many people around the nation were obviously asking some of the same questions; from time to time we were contacted with "hot information" on the subject, but in nearly every case it turned out that the information had already been reported in the press or that we were dealing with a crackpot.

In June 1973, Liebengood received information from a Floridian named Bill Howell that a friend of his was also a friend of Watergate burglar Frank Sturgis. This friend, who was referred to by the pseudonym Ed Morgan, had prepared an affidavit, which Howell forwarded to us, which indicated that Sturgis had been in touch with columnist Jack Anderson about his clandestine activities prior to June 17, 1972. I asked Liebengood to look into the matter, although both of us felt that the information was highly suspect. We had known for some time that Anderson had visited Sturgis at the District of Columbia jail shortly after the Watergate arrests, and we had heard rumors about Anderson meeting Sturgis at National Airport in Washington on the afternoon of the final break-in. We understood that Anderson had been an acquaintance of Sturgis' but we had no link between Anderson and the Democrats. We noted that Anderson had the reputation for writing scalding stories on Democrats and Republicans alike and prided himself on being disliked by both. Nonetheless, Howell kept Liebengood's telephone lines lit up with information that became increasingly intriguing, including the name of another individual—a Cuban who was very close to Sturgis and who was willing to provide us with another affidavit detailing regular Sturgis-Anderson contact prior to the break-in. With this, we decided Liebengood deserved a trip to Miami.

"This investigation may take eight or nine months," Liebengood said as he grinned and packed his bags. "I ought to be back by the time you guys write your final report." However, Liebengood soon found out that Miami consisted of different worlds from the one he had seen in the travel brochures. As he entered the Miami airport, Howell met him with a wide, semi-toothless grin and hustled him to his airport hotel room. Here Liebengood clustered with Howell and Ed Morgan, who looked as though he might have been the sole survivor from a nuclear holocaust. He was barefoot and dirty and sported an ugly burn on his leg, which Liebengood understood had been suffered on a recent "training mission." It was obvious that Morgan was one of the ardent anti-Castroites who had been involved with Sturgis in plans to recapture Cuba. After sending out for rum and Coca-Cola, Liebengood learned that Morgan had been active with Sturgis in Cuba exile efforts for over three years. In particular, Morgan recalled a telephone conversation that Sturgis had with Jack Anderson in Sturgis' home in the spring or early summer of 1972. Sturgis told Morgan that there were plans to create a disturbance with the Vietnam Veterans Against the War at the Republican convention, and it was

Morgan's opinion that this was the subject matter of the Anderson telephone call. Although the story sounded far-fetched, Liebengood dutifully took notes and made the most of the situation. Besides, he was buying the rum and Coke. The interview droned on into the night while Morgan propped his feet on the wall above Liebengood's bed and Liebengood wondered how he would explain the footmarks on the wall should anybody ask.

The next morning, Howell and Morgan ushered Liebengood, a survivor of the all-night session, to the home of a member of the anti-Castro Cuban community near Miami Beach. It was this individual who provided Liebengood with information that opened his sleepy eyes. In particular, Liebengood was told that this person knew Sturgis extremely well (a fact that Sturgis himself was to confirm later); and that Sturgis often spoke to him about "a big project" that required frequent Sturgis trips to Washington. This individual stated that he drove Sturgis to the airport on June 16, 1972, and that Sturgis indicated that the "big project" was about completed and that soon they would have enough money to liberate Cuba. He stated that Sturgis was very close to Jack Anderson because Anderson had assisted Sturgis in regaining his citizenship and that they talked regularly on the telephone. He was confident that Sturgis was in contact with Anderson about the "big project" and knew that Anderson had been in touch with Sturgis and his wife after the Watergate break-in.

Most important, he advised Liebengood that, while Sturgis was out on bond, he asked to be driven to the DuPont Plaza Hotel in Miami to see Jack Anderson. He had then driven Sturgis to the hotel and waited in the car for approximately twenty minutes. When Sturgis returned, he displayed a stack of fifty-dollar bills and advised that the trip had been successful and that the money came from Anderson. Arrangements were made for another affidavit. Liebengood was impressed with the affiant's credibility and was anxious to get back to Washington. However, before he could leave town, there followed a semiclandestine meeting with a leader of the anti-

Castro underground and an abortive effort to make contact with Manuel Artime, the local hero of the Bay of Pigs fiasco. All of this left Liebengood somewhat unnerved and as he scrambled for the airport, he contemplated the quantity of paper he would have to eat should his flight be hijacked to Havana.

Liebengood's visit to Miami took place on July 10 and 11, 1973. In the July 22 issue of *Parade* magazine in his first disclosure of the matter, Anderson wrote that he and Sturgis were friends of long standing. Anderson wrote that Sturgis had introduced him to Bernard Barker, another Watergate burglar, in Miami, and had spoken of "Eduardo" (E. Howard Hunt). Anderson's article also said he had visited Sturgis in jail after Sturgis' arrest and had sought to have Sturgis paroled in his custody.

Furthermore, the article told of a remarkable coincidence on June 16, 1972, less than twenty-four hours before the break-in: Anderson happened to meet Sturgis at the Washington National Airport; the two chatted briefly and went their separate ways.

Although we had tried consistently to avoid developing a "conspiracy mentality" about Watergate, we were intrigued by the fact that Anderson had kept this incident to himself for more than a year. A few days later, while we still debated the relationship of Liebengood's interviews in Miami and the appearance of the Anderson article, I received a phone call from Les Whitten, Anderson's associate. It was my first conversation with Whitten, but he spoke as though we were old friends.

"Hey, Fred," he said after a few pleasantries, "we understand that you have certain information that could be damaging to Jack. The information is not true, incidentally." I did not respond, and after a short pause Whitten continued. "I felt maybe you could turn it over to us. We were afraid that it might leak from the committee and we need to be prepared for it if it does."

I laughed at the idea that Jack Anderson of all people would be afraid of leaks. Without either verifying or denying that we had such information, I denied his request. Whitten laughed and said, "Well, you can't blame me for trying." Now we understood that not only did Anderson know what information we had, but also that it concerned him.

We called in Sturgis for an interview. He said he had known Anderson since 1959, when Sturgis testified before a Senate hearing on Communist infiltration in Cuba, and that he had been the subject of several Anderson articles in *Parade*. Sturgis also said that he had been in contact with Anderson during the Bay of Pigs episode in 1961, and that Anderson had helped him to get political prisoners out of Cuba by providing letters of introduction to the presidents of Bolivia and Colombia. Evidently, Anderson's influence was not confined to the United States.

Yes, Sturgis said, he accidentally ran into Anderson at National Airport on June 16, as he arrived from Miami with his fellow Cuban-Americans for the Watergate break-in. But Sturgis denied that he had given Anderson information about the break-in that was about to take place, and he rebutted most of the allegations contained in the Miami affidavits. He said he never received money from Anderson.

Liebengood, Madigan, and I described our interviews to Baker, who listened with great interest. "What do you think it all means?" he asked. Liebengood and Madigan were convinced they were onto something. Liebengood said, "There is so much information floating around. So many potentials for leaks from Baldwin, from McCord and his relationship to Lou Russell, from Sturgis, and from others. It was just too coincidental that those cops were in the neighborhood working overtime just at the right time. I believe that someone tipped off the DNC."

"Maybe we ought to have a talk with Mr. Anderson," Baker replied in a manner that indicated he was concluding the discussion for the time being. Two days later, Baker called to tell me that Anderson was coming to his office. "He'll be here at 2 o'clock. Give me a little time with him alone and then I want you to come in."

"I'll be there," I replied.

When I arrived at Baker's office, he and Anderson were already there. I waited about fifteen minutes, then walked in, and Anderson and I exchanged cordial greetings. From the conversation I heard as I entered, they were discussing the broader issues of Watergate. Anderson said, "I know the president didn't know anything about the break-in beforehand. I have access to one of the people who was with him when he found out about it, and the president raised holy hell."

Baker gradually shifted the conversation to the matters we were interested in. He said, "Fred has a few things he'd like to talk to you about."

I began, "We have information that you were in contact with Frank Sturgis before the Watergate break-in and that you may have given him some money. Is that true?"

Anderson's reaction was neither surprised nor hostile. "Yes," he said, almost casually, "I know Frank Sturgis, but I've never given him any money. I've never paid for a story in my life." After a short pause, he added, "I've offered to loan him money, but I've never given him any."

I asked if Anderson had spoken to Sturgis about a plan to create a disturbance with the Vietnam Veterans Against the War at the Republican national convention in 1972. Anderson said he had not. He was vague about how many times he had had contact with Sturgis in the year before the break-in. His meeting with Sturgis at the airport had been wholly coincidental, he said, and he had not received any advance information about the Watergate break-in. Nor had he had any contact with Larry O'Brien.

As Baker closed the door after Anderson left, he broke into a broad grin. "I didn't know you were gonna put him on the grill quite like that," he said.

However, we had gained little, if anything, in getting at the truth of the matter. I suggested to Baker that we call in Anderson for a more intensive interview, under oath. Baker agreed. Liebengood arranged the interview for November 12, 1973; I said I would be home in Tennessee on that date, but told Liebengood to conduct it without me.

In his session with Liebengood, Anderson said he first met Sturgis shortly after Castro took power in Cuba, and that he had helped Sturgis retain his United States citizenship following Sturgis' defection from Cuba. Anderson said he was in touch with Sturgis throughout the Bay of Pigs episode and had kept contact after that, with Sturgis calling regularly "to tell me about his projects." Sturgis had Anderson's home and office telephone numbers. Anderson recalled his visit to Sturgis at the Washington jail, as well as his offer, in court, to take custody of Sturgis with the intention to "get him into my house where I would be able to talk to him at great length and try to find out what he had been up to." Anderson also recalled a meeting with Sturgis and his attorney at which he said he had urged Sturgis to plead not guilty and tell his full story.

Asked if he had received information from Sturgis at any time regarding either the Democratic party or the Democratic National Committee, Anderson was vague. "I would think not. I would not want to say that he never mentioned it. It is possible that he could have said something but I do not recall it, and I rather doubt it." However, Anderson categorically denied that Sturgis provided any information regarding the Democratic National Committee from January to August 1972. He said he knew that Sturgis was strongly anti-Communist and that he believed some leaders in the Democratic party were a little soft on Castro.

When Liebengood asked what he was doing at the airport when he met Sturgis on June 16, hours before the break-in, Anderson said he was on his way to Cleveland for a speaking engagement. But he could not remember where he had spoken in Cleveland. By the time I returned from Tennessee, Liebengood had tried to check the Cleveland report, but there was nothing in the Cleveland newspapers at the time that had any reference to an Anderson appearance. Liebengood and Madigan briefed me on the Anderson interview. Referring to Madigan in mock rage, Liebengood said, "This character has just guaranteed us all coverage in the Jack Anderson column for the next twenty years." When I asked why, Liebengood explained that he had handled Anderson with kid gloves and tried to ask all the right questions in an inoffensive manner. Then, he explained, Madigan walked into the interview late and called Liebengood outside for a briefing. When they returned, Madigan proceeded to bore in on Anderson, giving the interview the appearance of the old Mutt 'n' Jeff police interrogation. "It was unbelievable," Liebengood said. "He chased Anderson all over the room." Liebengood was talking with exaggerated motions and pointing to Madigan, who was rolling with laughter. We all had a good laugh, but we watched Jack Anderson columns closely for the next few weeks.

All we had, though, were suspicions and uncorroborated allegations. Anyway, what if Anderson did know of the break-in in advance? There was no evidence that he had informed anyone at the Democratic committee. But there was one other line of inquiry we needed to check out before closing the book on the matter.

In his article in *Parade*, Anderson mentioned that he had received some information in April 1972 from William Haddad that indicated knowledge of plans for the illegal Watergate operations. Haddad was the editor of the *Manhattan Tribune,* a neighborhood newspaper in New York. In another odd coincidence Haddad wrote in that paper's July 21 issue, the day before Anderson's article appeared in *Parade*, that he too had received information about plans to break into the Watergate, and that he had passed the information to Jack Anderson. So, after thirteen months in which both men had remained silent, both had alluded, twenty-four hours apart, to what they knew.

With Haddad we found a possible link between Anderson and the Democratic National Committee. Haddad, an official of the Office of Economic Opportunity during the Kennedy administration, was a friend of Larry O'Brien and others in the Democratic committee. Before we contacted Haddad, we interviewed O'Brien. He appeared to be perfectly candid and produced a letter Haddad had written him, dated March 23, 1972, almost three months before the break-in, that read as follows:

> I am hearing some very disturbing stories about GOP sophisticated surveillance techniques now being used for campaign purposes and of an interesting group here in New York where some of this "intelligence" activity is centered. The information comes from a counter-wire tapper who helped me once in a very difficult situation in Michigan and who had come to me highly recommended from two lawyers, Gallagon and Shapiro.
>
> Can you have someone call me so you can get the info first hand and take whatever actions you deem necessary. If you want, I will go a little deeper into the situation, but I would prefer that you evaluate the same information I have received, and from the same source, before taking any further steps.

O'Brien said he had instructed John Stewart, director of communications for the Democratic National Committee, to follow up the letter. O'Brien said he became acquainted with Haddad during the Kennedy campaign of 1960, and that he knew Haddad well enough to realize that he would not have written such a letter without some basis. He acknowledged that his referral of the matter to Stewart indicated that it had not been treated routinely, but he denied any foreknowledge of the Watergate break-in.

On the following day we interviewed Haddad. Asked about correspondence with officials of the Democratic National Committee, he produced this letter to Stewart, dated April 28, 1972:

> I talked to Woolston-Smith.
> Yes, he does have good information; and, yes, he did want to cover expenses for producing it in an acceptable

way. He explains that he wasn't looking for payment for his services, but to cover what looked like necessary expenses to tie down his theory with factual presentations (like checks, etc.).

Instead of pursuing this with money, I decided to see what a good investigative reporting operation could do with it now. So I went ahead along these lines. If they draw a blank, I'll be back to you on how to proceed, and I'll keep you informed.

My own journalistic judgment is that the story is true and explosive. It would be nice for a third party to uncover it, but if they fail due to the type of inside work required, I would move back to Woolston-Smith.

Haddad told us that Woolston-Smith was a private investigator who had reported that he had overheard conversations in New York's intelligence community indicating that Democratic headquarters in Washington was about to be bugged, that the bugging activity was linked to the November Group (an ad hoc advertising agency working for the Nixon campaign, based in New York) and to certain Spanish-speaking or Cuban individuals. Immediately after he sent his letter to O'Brien, Haddad testified, Stewart flew to New York and met with Haddad, Woolston-Smith, and Ben Winter, a friend of Haddad's who happened to be in Haddad's office at the time. Haddad said Woolston-Smith's information had been "spotty"; there might have been some mention of Cubans, he said, but he really could not remember.

Haddad also said that John Mitchell's name had come up at the meeting. He testified that he had sent his entire file to Jack Anderson in April 1972, but he could not remember what was in it. In fact, Haddad said, he sent material to Anderson twice, but had kept no copies. Madigan, Liebengood, and I looked at one another; all of us found the story hard to accept. Haddad said the purpose of sending the material to Anderson was to obtain independent validation of Woolston-Smith's information. Noting that caution was essential, Haddad said, "The fact of asking the questions might have stopped everything." Then Haddad tried to soften the statements made in his article in the *Manhattan Tribune,* in which he mentioned the possible involvement of Cubans. He really didn't think he had been that specific, Haddad told us.

Jack Anderson had acknowledged receipt of the material from Haddad concerning plans for the break-in, but he said he had since lost it. The man who made his living exposing the frailties of others had somehow managed to lose two files dealing with the same subject matter. We wondered what there was that was "true and explosive," as Haddad had put it in his letter. Whatever it was, it was in the files sent to Anderson, and they did not want us to know its contents.

Liebengood and Madigan interviewed Ben Winter, the vice president of a New York bank. Winter said that Woolston-Smith had displayed a "sophisticated bug" at the meeting and had handed it to Stewart and Haddad. According to Winter, the information revealed by Woolston-Smith appeared to be hard evidence of surveillance, not just a theory. Winter said he got the impression that the investigation was to proceed and that those looking into it would "get the whole ball of wax" before making it public.

For us, the possibilities were multiplying as fast as the complexities. We recalled that McCord had testified that he had checked the telephones of the November Group, which feared it was being tapped or bugged. Had McCord been guilty of loose talk around the November Group, talk overheard by someone who then linked the bugging plan to the advertising agency? Had someone bugged the November Group?

It seemed clear to us that the Haddad group knew (1) of a plan to bug the Democratic National Committee, (2) that it involved Cubans, and (3) that McCord was related to the operation in some way. What else did it know? The answer undoubtedly was in the files that Anderson had "lost" and that Haddad had not bothered to copy before sending on.

The mystery surrounding the November Group appeared to deepen after Liebengood and Madigan interviewed some of its former members. Paul Muller, senior vice president in charge of finance and administration, who was McCord's security liaison in the New York office, gave us another new detail: Gordon Liddy was one of the three original directors of the November Group. Furthermore, he said, he recalled a problem in the November Group's offices involving mix-ups on the inter-office telephones, as well as concern about the telephone apparatus in a hallway panel outside the Group's suite of offices. A telephone strike was under way at the time, he said, and this panel was often open, with nonuniformed repairmen working on it occasionally. Muller believed that McCord had checked the panel, along with all November Group phones, in April of 1972. He thought that the telephone company, and perhaps McCord too, had made subsequent visits to check strange happenings on the phone lines, including one on June 16, 1972, when an office conversation on the WATS line was interrupted by an unknown third party breaking in and making anti-Nixon comments.

Now it appeared that both McCord and Liddy had links to the November Group and that any skilled "wire men" probably could have had access to its telephone lines.

After each new development, Liebengood, Madigan, and I met with Baker to discuss the possibilities. The only thing on which we could agree was the amazing series of apparent coincidences. Baker emphasized again that we proceed with caution. Any leaks of the startling bits of information we were gathering before we knew exactly what we were dealing with could jeopardize our efforts. If it appeared that we were trying to sell a story without proof beyond a reasonable doubt that the Democrats had had prior warning of the Watergate break-in, the press would attack us for attempting to divert the investigation from the Nixon administration. Clearly, our minority staff would be held to a standard different from that of the majority staff. We needed solid proof.

In my office I would often agonize over the possibility that we were wasting time, that we were headed down a one-way street. Even if what we suspected was true, no one would step forward and admit it. However, Madigan and Liebengood, who had done most of the interviewing and thus were in the best position to evaluate the credibility of witnesses, were convinced that we were onto something. And even though I sometimes referred to them, tongue in cheek, as "conspiracy nuts" I bowed to their judgment. And their judgment kept looking better all the time.

The next nugget they turned up was the deposition of John Stewart of the DNC. He had given the deposition on February 28, 1973, in connection with the civil suit by the Democratic National Committee against the Nixon reelection committee that arose from the Watergate break-in. It appeared from the deposition that Stewart had been very hesitant to divulge the fact of the meeting with Woolston-Smith in Haddad's office. Under questioning, he recalled that he received a telephone call from Woolston-Smith prior to June 17, 1972, warning of rumors that the Nixon campaign would attempt to bug the DNC. He said the information was "so unsubstantiated that it certainly was not the basis for any action on our part." Then he was asked if he had had any further contact with Woolston-Smith. Stewart said that several days after the break-in he called Woolston-Smith to determine if the latter had any further information, and Woolston-Smith said he did not. Finally, a question was put to Stewart that he could not dodge. Did he ever *meet* Woolston-Smith? Stewart then told of the meeting in Haddad's New York office. According to Stewart, he was in New York "on other business" and had called Woolston-Smith to determine if he had any additional information; Woolston-Smith suggested that they meet. At the meeting, Stewart testified, Woolston-Smith indicated he had no further information. We found it intriguing that Stewart had apparently sought to avoid an admission that a meeting had even occurred and that he had tried to downgrade the importance of the meeting.

In addition, Stewart's version of the meeting was certainly not consistent with that of Winter, a disinterested witness, who told of "hard evidence of surveillance" and said he understood the investigation was to continue. Also, it was inconsistent with Haddad's letter to Stewart two days after the meeting that said "my own journalistic judgment is that the story is true and explosive."

The time had come to interview the only remaining participant in Haddad's office—Arthur James Woolston-Smith. After many futile attempts, an interview was finally arranged by Liebengood and Madigan in Woolston-Smith's New York offices on October 10, 1973. The basic questions were what information he gave at the meeting and where he had obtained the information.

Woolston-Smith was a short, paunchy, bald man who spoke with a pronounced British accent and smoked a pipe. He was good-natured and appeared at ease and in full command of the situation. It was obvious that he had been around. He testified that he was a private investigator in New York City, a citizen of New Zealand with experience in British intelligence, and a permanent resident of the United States. He acknowledged that he had excellent contacts in the intelligence community and said his New York offices had been used by the CIA, after the Bay of Pigs, as a clearinghouse for those returning from the invasion brigades. This information was consistent with what we had determined from other sources. Woolston-Smith was a most mysterious person; there were indications that he had connections with both British and Canadian intelligence, although we could never determine the exact relationship.

Woolston-Smith said he had told William Haddad of the possibility of Republican media control through the November Group as early as December 1971, and that they had discussed the Group many times before the meeting of April 26, 1972. He knew enough about the operation, he said, to know that Gordon Liddy "ran the show." He confirmed that on one occasion he visited the building where the November Group had its offices, but had stayed in the hallway without entering the suite. His information concerning a possible tap of Democratic National Committee phones, he said, was "very general" and he had picked it up from word going around the "intelligence community." He said he could not remember any specific person as the source of the information.

Liebengood and Madigan were not buying his story. Was this the kind of information that caused Stewart to rush from Washington to Haddad's office? What was the story that Haddad, two days after the meeting, called "true and explosive"? Woolston-Smith smiled. He did not know. But some later questions turned up surprising answers.

Woolston-Smith said his first contact with Stewart was a call he placed to arrange Stewart's trip to New York. This, of course, was inconsistent with Stewart's deposition, in which he said he was in New York on other business and had happened to call Woolston-Smith to see if there was any new information. Woolston-Smith, confirming the April 26 meeting in Haddad's office with Haddad, Stewart, and Winter, said it was Haddad who first focused on Democratic headquarters as the specific target of the wiretap. The more Woolston-Smith talked, the more he directed attention to Haddad. Haddad, he said, had information at the meeting that was independent of his own intelligence gathering. For instance, he said it was Haddad who suggested at the meeting that "little Cuba in Miami" was involved in that the Republicans were searching for something to indicate that the Democratic party received money from Cuba.

To use an overworked Watergate expression, this was a "bombshell." Six weeks before the break-in, Haddad cited the same reason that the Cuban-Americans gave later for their participation in the Watergate entry: they said they had been told that the Democratic National Committee had received money from Castro. How could Haddad have known? Liebengood and Madigan both recalled that the Cubans in Miami had told Liebengood about Sturgis' contacts with Jack Anderson; and they recalled, too, all the unanswered questions surrounding Anderson, including the disappearance of the material that Haddad had sent to him.

"Did Haddad indicate that he had been talking to Jack Anderson?" Woolston-Smith was asked. "Yes, as a matter of fact he did," was the reply. Woolston-Smith went on to say, without prodding, that on the basis of Haddad's conversation he believed some of Haddad's pre-Watergate information had come from Anderson.

Woolston-Smith said he had taken his information to Haddad originally because they had had previous dealings in matters of public interest and because Haddad was a former official in the Kennedy administration with many "contacts." Woolston-Smith was "pretty sure," he said, that Haddad knew someone in the CIA, but he added that Haddad never mentioned the CIA as a source.

Despite Stewart's indication that Woolston-Smith's information had never been taken very seriously at the Democratic National Committee, Woolston-Smith said that Stewart was "very interested" in Haddad's information about the Cuban money and the Democrats. After the meeting, he said, he and Stewart talked frequently on the phone, perhaps as often as twice a week. Asked if Stewart's interest had waned as the contact continued, Woolston-Smith said, "It was hot right up until the end and after the end." He could not recall exactly his last pre-Watergate conversation with Stewart, but "it was along the lines of something-is-about-to-happen." After the Watergate arrests on June 17, Woolston-Smith said, Stewart attempted to call him, finally reaching him on the following Monday, June 19. Stewart was elated over the arrests.

Months after the Watergate arrests, Woolston-Smith recalled, an attorney for the Democratic National Committee called to ask him if he was "going to do anything about the Watergate committee." The lawyer also advised him that Stewart had given his name to the FBI, and he told Woolston-Smith that any correspondence between him and Stewart was a personal, privileged, private communication. Woolston-Smith acknowledged that he had sent one letter to Stewart shortly after the Watergate break-in but he could not find his copy. Later, Stewart told us he could not find the letter. Another missing letter, another missing copy.

Woolston-Smith also said that after Stewart's deposition in

the civil suit, a reporter called Woolston-Smith, who then called Stewart. Stewart told Woolston-Smith to "play it cool." Whatever the Democratic National Committee knew, it did not want the information disclosed.

When Liebengood and Madigan discussed Woolston-Smith's testimony with me, we agreed that he was not telling us all he knew. I told them to try to get him to my office so I could question him myself. Several weeks later, we arranged an interview in my office. I laid it on the line, telling him it was clear that he knew more than he was telling us and that we wanted the whole story—right now. I had been confident that my "tough guy" approach would open him up at least a little, but I was wrong. Woolston-Smith merely smiled, and reverted to the same generalities that characterized the early stages of his first interview with Liebengood and Madigan. In a good-natured way, he was telling me that I was not dealing with a gumshoe. I got nowhere.

Our exploration had covered many months and many witnesses, from Edmund Chung to Arthur James Woolston-Smith. We looked into an aspect of Watergate that had not been explored before—or since. Liebengood, Madigan, and I all came to one conclusion: several people, including some at the Democratic headquarters, had advance knowledge of the Watergate break-in. An obvious effort had been made to conceal facts, including the meeting in Haddad's office and what was discussed there. But did we have proof—proof beyond a reasonable doubt? The answer, reluctantly, was no. Additionally, for our suspicions to amount to anything conclusive, we would have to tie this advance knowledge to McCord, or someone else on the inside of the Watergate break-in team, or at least to the plainclothesmen on duty the night of the break-in. We had no such link.

Did McCord, for whatever reason, deliberately leave the tape on the door? Did someone alert Shoffler? Did Baldwin give the plan away inadvertently? Did the information pass from Sturgis to Anderson to Haddad to the DNC, or had the offices of the November Group been bugged, with information from conversations of McCord or Liddy, or both, combined with Haddad's "other sources" to put the story together before June 17? Or was it some combination of these things? And why had Jack Anderson been so mysteriously quiet?

We agreed that we had come close but that we had fallen short. To borrow still another Watergate expression, we had been unable to find the smoking gun in anyone's hands. Because of the press of the Watergate business, we knew that we could not justify the expenditure of any more time, effort, and money on a matter that, even if our hunches turned out to be true, might add up to a finding of historical interest only. We realized that we had played out the string, and we let the matter drop, reluctantly, and with a gnawing feeling in our stomachs.

Because nearly all our information stemmed from testimony taken under oath, Liebengood and Madigan prepared an elaborate, thoroughly documented report on their investigation. We drew no conclusions. We made one major effort to include it in the Watergate committee's final report. As we had expected, Ervin accepted the majority staff's opinion that the report was "too speculative." It was never published.

# Chapter X · The Press

The Watergate affair provided for the nation's press some of its finest hours, and some of its worst. Coverage of the scandal by newspapers, magazines, radio, and television appeared to escalate the battle that had been raging for some time between the press' defenders and its detractors. This process of polarization gave reporters an image of pure virtue or pure sin, obscuring the fact that they were as varied a group as the people and events they were following.

When it became apparent with the leak of James McCord's testimony before our committee that the story of the century was developing, Capitol Hill was transformed, in the eyes of members of the news media, to an objective to be captured, as in open warfare. About 285 accredited correspondents and about 105 radio and television technicians—cameramen, soundmen, and the like—were assigned to our committee's hearings, and at any given time during the sessions a great many of this number could be seen milling inside the Caucus Room. The reporters ascended Capitol Hill by the dozens, and they roamed the halls of the Senate buildings individually and in packs, foraging for scraps of information that they later shared with their colleagues in the hope of piecing together a story. Each of them was forever seeking that one friendly senator or staff member who would provide that one big story requiring little work that would gain immediate nationwide attention.

In dress, they ranged from holdovers of the beat generation to J. Walter Thompson button-down types. Some wore suits with vests. Some wore sneakers and no socks. There were many representatives of the major television and radio networks and the major daily newspapers, and there was also an assortment of freelance "street people" who came to Washington to expose corruption and become famous. There were seasoned veterans and kids on their first assignment. Some were clean-shaven; some sported shaggy beards. Some were grandparents and some were mothers of infants. All were looking for gold.

For all the variance, there were certain things they had in common: a higher-than-average intelligence and a dislike, often bordering on detestation, for Nixon and his administration. Most of them felt that the press had been deceived and misled not only by Nixon, but also by Lyndon Johnson and his associates in connection with the war in Vietnam. And as more of their reports attributed to "sources" turned out to be accurate, they pushed harder and harder.

The single, compelling need for each element of the news industry in a situation like Watergate and its investigation is a story—not a story shared by everyone else, but an exclusive. For a major daily newspaper nothing is more anathema than printing a juicy front-page report that must be credited to another paper. And the need for reporters is not just for a single exclusive story, but for a steady stream of them. The intensity of the competition, which probably distinguishes the American press from any other in the world, amazed me. The anti-Nixon comments of some reporters were mild in comparison with the remarks some of them made about one another. It was competition, not ideology, that drove them on—the instinct for survival, the need to get more information, faster information than the competition. The columnist Joseph Kraft spoke of a "shark frenzy"—the urge among some newsmen and newswomen to "rush in to get a bite of the bleeding body in the water."

When Les Whitten, Jack Anderson's associate, was calling around for verification of some secret document he had obtained, one of his most frequent questions was, "How long do you think it will hold?" It took three or four days after they were written for Jack Anderson columns to get into print, and

Whitten was constantly concerned that he might be scooped. It was a common argument of the press, in justifying the use of reports about secret information, that the people had a right to know. But the need could wait until an individual reporter had a chance to print it in his own newspaper first.

Most of the reporters I knew hardly bothered to deny the White House charges that the Washington press corps had an anti-Nixon bias. As Daniel Schorr of CBS said in my office one day as we relaxed with our pipes, "Watergate doesn't make that much difference to me as far as my attitude toward Nixon is concerned. I don't like him, but I have never liked him." Schorr had a personal reason—he was on the White House "enemies" list, and the FBI had conducted a security check on him on the bogus pretext that he was being considered for a job in the Nixon administration. Yet CBS assigned him to the Watergate story, when he often had to report developments on the very enemies listed that contained his own name, an awkward situation that is hardly conducive to the objectivity most reporters profess. To Schorr's credit he displayed his seasoned professionalism and maintained his objectivity better than most of his colleagues.

Seymour Hersh of *The New York Times*, who uncovered the My Lai massacre and was regarded as perhaps the best investigative reporter in the country, made no effort to hide his feelings about Nixon. "I hate him," he was reported to have said. Hersh always referred to Nixon as "the Trick," his own corruption of "Tricky Dick."

Contact between reporters and committee members and the staff was continuous and took many forms. While the hearings were in progress, a constant stream of notes was passed up from the press table to staff aides, who served as messengers for the senators. The notes usually contained suggested questions for whatever witness was testifying. After I had solicited from Richard Helms, the former CIA director, the fact that Eugenio Martinez, one of the Watergate burglars, was still on the CIA payroll at the time of the break-in, a reporter for United Press International passed me a complimentary note on what he called a "front-page story" and urged me to press the matter further.

Mary McGrory, a columnist for the *Washington Star News* and other papers, would seek out senators on the committee and voice her opinion as to how the investigation was progressing. The afternoon after Bart Porter testified, McGrory interrupted a conversation Baker and I were having in his office with a telephone call praising the senator lavishly for his pointed questioning of the young man. Baker thanked her, but noted immediately afterward that she undoubtedly expected him to tear into every witness, and he predicted a short honeymoon. He was correct; later in the hearings, when he sought to counteract some of the extremely partisan behavior in the Caucus Room, McGrory wrote that Senator Baker, whose "star had shone so brightly when the inquiry began" now seemed to be "falling." In all the months that the hearings lasted, I never saw McGrory smile; hers was an all-consuming mission of vengeance, with every committee member graded by the number of verbal lashes he administered across the backs of White House witnesses. It occurred to me that her attitude was probably colored by the fact that, alone among the major columnists in the country, she had predicted victory for George McGovern in 1972.

By suggesting questions for witnesses and by trying to influence the course of the proceedings through informal contacts, many reporters were clearly stepping over the line that separates reporting the news from participating in it. Had the White House engaged in such participation with the committee, the reporters would have considered the activity highly improper. Nearly every day I was asked if the White House was feeding me questions. This amused me, because it indicated that the press believed there were certain magic questions that could either break the case or successfully cover up wrongdoing. Moreover, it took no account of a lawyer's ego, which leads him to believe no one can frame a question better than he can.

Despite the shortcomings of some, however, I found most

"name" reporters and commentators notable for their professionalism. Moreover, many of them had worked on the Watergate story so long and so diligently that they had a better mastery of the facts than anyone on the committee or the staff. It was difficult for them to sit and watch as pertinent questions, based on their own detailed analysis of the case, went unasked. I also learned that the risk of being misquoted depended almost totally on the experience and talent of the reporter, and had nothing to do with his political viewpoint. The bush-leaguers and the fly-by-nighters invariably would take comments out of context and "hype" an account to produce good copy. The good reporters, whatever their political leanings or anti-Nixon attitude, usually would give an accurate report. It became enormously important, as the hearings continued, to know whether you were dealing with a professional or an amateur.

Reporters, as a group, were likable as well as knowledgeable. They were skeptical of almost everyone and rarely idealistic. They had "street savvy." They had been used, cultivated, lied to, and cursed by experts from all shades of the political spectrum. They had observed so much hypocrisy in politics that honesty and candor were what they sought most in a news contact; their livelihood, of course, depended on the accuracy of the information they received. Anyone who lied to one reporter was instantly suspected by all of them; the word that someone was giving out false or distorted information spread among them faster than the latest Watergate rumor.

Despite the many excesses of the press and their dislike of Nixon, most of the top reporters who covered Watergate, men such as Hersh, Woodward and Bernstein, Jim Weighart of the *New York Daily News,* Jim Squires of the *Chicago Tribune,* Dan Thomason of Scripps Howard, Sandy Smith of *Time,* and Nick Harrock of *Newsweek,* prided themselves in being apolitical. They would agree with Squires, who told me more than once that "I consider myself a critic of government. It doesn't make a damn who's in power."

Reporters are the most interesting conversationalists a person could find. Once I determined which ones among them I could trust, I enjoyed immensely our "off-the-record" conversations, in which we would swap opinions on who was lying and who wasn't and speculate on what would happen next. Not once did an off-the-record comment return to haunt me. For example, my relationship with Walter Pincus, editor of the *New Republic,* one of the nation's most liberal magazines, developed to the point that he understood when our conversation went off the record without my having to say so. I never divulged anything of great substance, but many of my comments about personalities and my own prejudices could have been extremely embarrassing had he (or others) betrayed my confidence.

From my first days in Washington, I was pleasantly surprised to discover that reporters and commentators recognized their individual prejudices and tried to deal with them responsibly. At a dinner of radio and television correspondents, which I attended soon after arriving at the capital, I spent a good part of the evening in private conversation with John Chancellor of NBC. I was impressed with what struck me as his genuine concern with Watergate's impact on the nation and with the problems involved in pursuing an investigation thoroughly while simultaneously giving fair treatment to the principals involved.

Carl Stern, another NBC reporter, is also a lawyer. He called me often for background analysis of the legal issues facing the committee. Although he obviously would have accepted any information I cared to give him, he never pressed me for material that he knew I would not disclose. At lunch one day shortly after the Saturday Night Massacre in which Archibald Cox was fired as special Watergate prosecutor, Stern confided to me his concern about whether he had reported the episode responsibly. Everyone in the news media considered Nixon's actions an affront to all Americans and the ultimate "cover-up." Carl shared that attitude, but he was fearful that he might have displayed his sentiments while reporting the event.

Reporters, even the best ones, approach their job in different ways. In contrast to the cool, somewhat detached approach of Dan Schorr and Carl Stern, for example, were the frantic pursuits of Leslie Stahl. When Stahl was on the trail of a story, it was as if the recess bell had just rung at grade school and she was determined to be the first to get the volley ball. When you heard the click of high heels on the marble floors of the Senate office buildings, it was not necessary to turn around or try to dodge. Stahl was in full trot, moving in for the kill. Once within earshot, she fired nonstop questions: "What went on at the meeting? Is it true that you and Dash got into an argument? Who's going to be the next witness?" Stahl, an attractive and highly intelligent person, was sensitive to the many rebuffs she received because of her aggressive approach; but she was a young woman in a hurry, in direct competition with her CBS colleague, Schorr. So if she did not get the story she wanted immediately, she would scurry off in search of another source, always looking for the scintillating tidbit that would be a surefire, one-minute attention-grabber on the evening news.

I soon discovered the pressures enveloping the reporters and their superiors in the home office. Reporters chasing a lead would telephone senators and staff members at 2 or 3 o'clock in the morning. Moreover, just as we on the committee and the staff showed increasing fatigue and irritability as the proceedings wore on, the reporters displayed many of the same signs. Like us, they began to get more and more criticism from people who had previously praised their performances. Sen. William Proxmire, the Democrat from Wisconsin, pilloried the press for "grossly unfair" journalism and "McCarthy-istic destruction." Harry Reasoner of ABC said he had "had it with *Newsweek* and *Time* magazines and their unprofessional handling of the whole Watergate story." Reasoner said, "Week after week, their lead stories on the subject have been more in the style of pejorative pamphleteering than objective journalism, and since they are highly viable and normally highly respected organs of our crafts, they embarrass and discredit all of us." Archibald Cox criticized *The New York Times* for "downright silly reporting."

Every reporter I talked to was embarrassed and somewhat defensive after the *Wall Street Journal* reported that Nixon had "soundly slapped" a man's face during an appearance near Orlando, Florida. The man who supposedly had been slapped said, when questioned, that he had been amazed at the furor aroused by the incident, which he described as being "like a pat you give a basketball player after he's made a basket." The man went on to describe Nixon as "one of the greatest presidents we've ever had."

Such instances of distorted coverage were sought out eagerly and constantly by the White House public relations staff, which used them to the fullest extent possible in their war against the press. What Reasoner and some others appeared to be complaining about primarily was the intensity of some of the coverage. No matter what else was happening in the country, certain elements in the press could turn the most mundane Watergate week into a lead story.

In the haste to get the news and to get it first, several totally inaccurate reports got into print that not only were brutally cruel to the persons unfairly accused, but would have been prejudicial legally had any of those named subsequently gone to trial. The *Washington Post* repeatedly reported as a fact that Alfred Baldwin, the Watergate lookout, had identified three officials of the Nixon reelection committee—Robert Odle, Jr., J. Glen Sedam, and William Timmons—as persons to whom he had delivered transcripts of Watergate wiretaps. The charges were never substantiated, and Baldwin always insisted that he had never made such a statement. Another serious, unsubstantiated charge, printed in both *Time* and the *Washington Post*, said that federal prosecutors were told in April 1973, that Charles Colson, the former special counsel to Nixon, knew in advance of the Watergate bugging plans and urged that they be expedited. And *Newsweek*, seeking to be the first to report what John Dean would say as a witness before the Watergate committee, reported that Dean would testify that White House officials considered the assassination of Panama's head of government, Omar Torrijos, because of his uncooperative attitude.

This sensational report was erroneous, but it was picked up and repeated by hundreds of newspapers.

Neither did the reporting of the "milk fund" scandal reflect the greatest of times for American journalism. Calling on sources on the House Judiciary Committee while they were in the midst of considering Articles of Impeachment, the *Washington Post* reported on June 6, 1974, under the headline "Tape Shows No Nixon Tie to Milk Gift," that "House Judiciary Committee Members listened yesterday to a taped conversation in which President Nixon decided on a 1971 increase in milk price supports and generally agreed it provided no evidence that he acted in response to a promised two million dollar campaign contribution."

*The New York Times* on the same day reported under the headline "Nixon Tape Is Said to Link Milk Price to Political Gift," the following: "The House Judiciary Committee heard yesterday evidence suggesting that President Nixon conditioned his 1971 decision to raise federal milk price supports upon a reaffirmation by dairy industry leaders of a pledge to raise two million dollars for the President's re-election campaign."

Such stories demonstrated pointedly (and painfully) a fact that most people in Washington had known for a long time: the "truth" often depends on who you talk to and the axe your source has to grind.

Stories such as these, and the sources of most sensational Watergate accounts, were products of the "leak." The phenomenon of the news leak and the ethical and legal questions it engenders have been debated for years. The leak, in one form or another, has produced most of the major news developments in Washington for many years. As I learned late in the investigation, the device can neither be praised nor condemned categorically, because it can take many forms and spring from many motivations. A leak can be loose gossip at a cocktail party or documents copied or stolen in the dead of night. The leaker can be a frustrated bureaucrat who has witnessed wrongdoing and seeks to correct an injustice; he can be an administration employee who seeks to change national policy by creating pressure from the news media; he can be a president who wants to get a "trial balloon" before the public before making a final decision on an important issue. The leaker also may be someone aiming to settle a score with an enemy or relishing the thought that he or she has the power to originate a report that will receive nationwide attention. A leak can disseminate important information that might otherwise never be known; but it can also jeopardize an investigation that is already under way.

Most of the major leaks in the Watergate case occurred after our committee was at work, after the appointment of the special prosecutor, and after several grand juries had been convened. Each of these bodies was just as interested in getting to the facts as was the press, and each was doing so in a fashion that took into account the rules of evidence and some concept of fairness to those who might be unjustly accused. The reporters covering Watergate, in general, also subscribed to these lofty ideals, but each one operated on the assumption that someone would break the story if he did not and all of them lived by the media's Eleventh Commandment: "Thou shalt not be scooped." As Senator Baker said, the Watergate committee did not invent the press leak, it merely "raised it to its highest art form."

*Newsday,* the Long Island daily, reported that two senators on the committee had approached Ben Bradlee, executive editor of the *Washington Post,* suggesting an exchange of information. "They wanted to play a little show and tell," Bradlee was quoted as saying. "I told them to buzz off." Bradlee, whose job was to produce news from whatever source, could see the impropriety of such a marriage, even if the senators could not. In addition, the senators on the committee had unanimously adopted rules strictly prohibiting such disclosure.

Reliance upon leaks must have presented some moral problems for those reporters who made their living pointing out the shortcomings of others. Leaking information is a very effective way of buying protection. I have never known a reporter to criticize a good source in print. It would be a sure way to lose the source. So the best protection a congressman, a staffer, or a bureaucrat can have is to tell whatever he knows to as many reporters as possible.

Ironically, it was several months after I left the committee staff before I realized the penalty that one sometimes must pay for depriving a newspaperman of the basis of his livelihood. In January of 1975 William Safire of *The New York Times* was still trying to get his hands on the Sullivan memos and the results of the minority staff's investigation on past abuses of the FBI. Along with substantive information, the Sullivan memos contained several titillating scandalous accusations of a personal nature, which have never been published. Safire called a Baker aide, who told him that I probably still had access to this information but that I would not give it out. Safire, an avid Nixon defender who was probably still upset (and rightfully so) that I had allowed the majority staff to shield the Sullivan memos from me for a period of time, launched into a diatribe against me to Baker's aide. Safire then called me in Nashville, but I was unavailable. Having learned of his comments about me, and enjoying my role as a private citizen who was not at the beck and eall of newspapermen, I did not return his call.

For this little indiscretion I was made the subject of an Op-Ed Safire story in *The New York Times,* which was syndicated across the country. According to Safire I was leaking information about the FBI investigation piecemeal to other reporters in order to cover up my "bumbling" and "inept" questioning of the witnesses.

As a matter of fact I had not released the information. Furthermore, I had not even been present during any of the interrogation of witnesses in this investigation. Safire probably considered it a good guess, but he printed it as fact, evidently to teach a lesson to anyone who would rebuff *The New York Times.*

To me, one of the most serious leaks of all was the breaching of grand jury secrecy. For several days in succession, Jack Anderson's column carried verbatim excerpts from testimony before a Watergate grand jury. Several newspapers ran editorials chiding Anderson for invading the grand jury room in the same issue in which their news pages were using Anderson's articles with the excerpts from the testimony.

Reporters always pointed out, with some justification, that the White House had lied to them systematically for months, and that the officials they were writing about were hardly helpless in being able to make public their rebuttals. The constant argument of the news media was the people's "right to know."

One night, after Nixon had resigned and Gerald Ford had taken the oath as president, I heard a group of reporters discussing Ford's choice for a vice president. It was apparent that each of them had tapped every one of his sources for any hint as to whom Ford would select. They had written their stories, made their predictions, and now they were sweating out the final result. I could sense the pressure and realized the joy for those who guessed right and the depression for those who did not. I thought back to the "right-to-know" argument; knowing Ford's choice twenty-four to forty-eight hours before the formal announcement had very little to do with the right to know; it had everything to do with the never-ending need to get the story first.

Capitol Hill had become a place where a career could be made within the scope of a few months. By the time the Watergate affair had ended, Woodward and Bernstein were rich. Seymour Hersh was a near folk hero. Jim Squires had become chief of the *Chicago Tribune*'s Washington bureau. Jim Weighart had become chief of the *New York Daily News* Washington Bureau, and Jack Nelson had become Washington Bureau Chief for the *Los Angeles Times*. Reporters who couldn't keep up the pace saw their careers suffer.

Many reporters disliked the games they were playing. As Daniel Schorr told me one day, "You know this is really not my bag—standing around in the halls, hoping someone will slip me a piece of paper. It's demeaning." Even so, he played it as well as anyone. One day, just after several committee members had deplored still another time the steady flow of leaks from the committee, Schorr stood outside the Caucus Room and told his audience, "Thanks to one of these much-publicized leaks, I have here in my hand a copy of Donald Segretti's interview."

It was well known that several reporters had easy access to the committee's files. One day I wrote a memo to Baker listing the many areas in which the CIA had failed to cooperate in our minority inquiry of CIA involvement. The memo said CIA representatives were refusing to let us see pertinent reports. Baker sent the memo directly to William Colby, the CIA director, along with a covering letter. Within twenty-four hours a copy of the memo had reached Lawrence Meyer of the *Post,* who tried to reach Baker for verification.

Our first thought was that Colby had provided the memo to Meyer. Then Joan Cole recalled that she had made a typing error in preparing the memo, and that she had corrected it on the original but not on the two copies. I had one of the copies and Howard Liebengood had the other. If we could see Meyer's copy we could tell if the leak was from Colby or someone else. Several days passed before Meyer called me for verification; I insisted on seeing the document Meyer had, and I noted immediately that it contained the typing error. I confirmed to Meyer that the document was, in fact, a memo from me to Baker, but that I would have nothing further to say about it.

Because my copy had been locked up, it was apparent that someone had removed Liebengood's copy from his desk and had reproduced it. A little checking around turned up the fact that a member of the majority staff had been in Liebengood's office, and that he had been making inquiries about what the minority staff was doing. Since this person was known to us as a notorious leaker, we were convinced we had the answer. I called the staff member and dressed him down, barring him from our offices. He insisted he was innocent, and it occurred to me, in the next few days, that I might have made a terrible mistake. So I sent word to him that if Woodward called to assure me that the staffer had had nothing to do with the matter, I would apologize. This was a procedure that Dash used frequently and with success. I knew that Woodward would call if the man I had accused was innocent. The call never came.

Some reporters use ingenious techniques in developing stories and achieving good relations with their sources. Of those I dealt with, Les Whitten and Seymour Hersh were the masters.

One of Whitten's devices was to float a trial balloon—a report that had no substance—to test a source's veracity. One day, in the midst of our inquiry into possible CIA involvements with Watergate, I agreed to let him come to my office to present three reports he had heard, so he could "run them by me."

Whitten's quick movements and rapid chatter befitted a man with a perpetual deadline. "First," he said, "I understand that you have proof that Howard Hunt was a spy either for the CIA or the Democrats and that he was placed on the White House staff for that purpose."

"Les, I don't have any proof of that," I said.

"Fine," he replied, and then he moved on to the other points he wanted to cover. Although the Hunt story had been rumored, it was obvious to me that Whitten knew I had no such proof but that he was testing me, assuming that I probably wished it could be proved that Hunt was indeed a spy. Since I did not lie to him on that matter, he might have some confidence in whatever else I might tell him.

Whitten, like many other investigative reporters, also employed the carrot-and-stick technique in dealing with prospective sources. He always asked me, for example, if I was going back to Tennessee to run for public office. "Jack Anderson and I have been talking," he would say. "We need to support some good Republican candidates." That was the carrot.

On another occasion, an Anderson-Whitten column reported that Charles Colson had been cooperating with the minority staff in developing the CIA inquiry. Baker said Colson had not been cooperating with him. Whitten considered this a denial of his original report so he called Baker's office and told the senator's press secretary that he had prepared a column that called Baker a liar. Whitten told me later that Anderson had vetoed his rebuttal to Baker, and read me passages from it. That was the stick with the implication that it could be used at any time.

Once Whitten's habit of implying complete and intimate knowledge of a secret meeting tripped him up. Following our interview with Richard Helms, the former CIA director, a Whitten-Anderson column spoke of the "secret transcripts" of that meeting and said Helms had "chain-smoked" while deftly answering our questions. I called Whitten and advised him that no transcript of the Helms testimony had been prepared prior to the publication of his column; furthermore, I said, Helms, who had puffed away steadily during his public appearance before the committee had given up smoking. Whitten laughed. "Dammit," he said, "I told Jack we were taking a chance on that one." He took his lumps in stride and in good humor. I couldn't help but like him.

Of the major investigative reporters covering Watergate Seymour Hersh was one of the most effective; he was certainly the most devious. I never met Hersh, but his shotgun chatter became familiar to me after he entered the Watergate fray, as *The New York Times* brought up its biggest gun in an effort to match Woodward and Bernstein. Hersh would call me, apparently as a last resort, after he had worked all his other sources. I was told that he had contacts in the White House, the CIA, and all other major governmental agencies.

He called Dash regularly. One day Dash told me Hersh had called him the previous night and had implied, very broadly, that I had already given him my version of a story and Dash had better get his version out to balance the record. So I called Hersh, put Dash on the extension phone, and asked Seymour if he wanted to set the record straight. There must have been some misunderstanding, Hersh said; he hadn't really meant to say that.

Playing Dash and me against each other was a fairly common tactic among reporters. They complained to me about Dash and I am sure they were complaining to him about me. Had we risen to the bait and bad-mouthed each other, we both would have been quickly destroyed. So, even during our most violent disagreements, neither of us ever criticized the other to the media.

Seymour Hersh struck again one day as the hearings were nearing a close. He called me at home in Nashville one weekend. "Look Fred," he said, "I've just been talking to Howard." (It was always "Howard," never "Senator Baker.") "I've got the story on the guy you interviewed yesterday, but Howard couldn't remember his name and thought you might help."

I knew it was most unlikely that Baker had either disclosed the details of an interview or had told Hersh to call me to get a witness' name. "Wait a minute," I said. "Do I understand you to say that Senator Baker told you to call me to get the name of the person we were interviewing?"

"Well, we talked," Hersh said, "and I've got the details. All I need is the name and we thought you would remember it and could give it to me."

"I tell you what," I said, "let me call the senator and verify that and I'll call you back."

"Well," he said "that's not really necessary. Maybe I didn't have it exactly right. I'll call you later." I knew I had seen the old Hersh whipsaw in full operation.

However, while watching and dealing with the country's best reporters I developed respect (albeit sometimes a grudging respect) for their ingenuity and ability.

Although a reporter sometimes gets a "handout"—a complete story from a good source that requires little verification, good stories are usually much more difficult to come by. Many, if not most, of the best Watergate stories were developed along the following lines: a reporter would accumulate scattered pieces of information. He would have nothing really solid. He would take a look at it and try to determine if possibly there was more to it than met the eye. He would develop a hypothesis. He would draw a "logical conclusion" and decide for himself what probably "really happened." He would make this determination on the basis of his knowledge of human nature and of the personalities he was dealing with. He would then call a bureaucrat, a staff member, or someone else in a position to know the true facts, and ask him if he could verify a story off the record. Then the reporter would present his conclusion, not as a guess, but as hard fact. Most people will not lie to a reporter under these circumstances, especially if the truth does not damage them personally. If the reporter has guessed right he can smell it the minute the source starts to answer. The source will probably either verify the story or nervously reply, "I can't comment on that." Either way the reporter knows he has a story.

For a reporter this process requires ingenuity, perseverance, and an extraordinary amount of brass. It's something that can't be learned from a textbook.

# Chapter XI · The End of the Affair

The death of the Watergate committee was slow and pro-longed. Like an aging athlete who cannot realize that time and events have passed him by, the committee—more particularly, its staff members—kept trying for a comeback, for one more day of glory. Mostly because certain staff members kept prom-ising a breakthrough on the Rebozo fund, the milk contribu-tions, or some other area, the committee requested and re-ceived two time extensions from the Senate (the committee's lifespan was originally to be one year, expiring in February 1974) as well as a supplemental appropriation of $1 million in addition to the original budget of $1 million.

The committee's demise began as soon as the break-in and cover-up phases of its investigation were completed at the end of September 1973. The later exploration of dirty tricks and illegal campaign financing never gripped the public in the same way. "No sex appeal" was the comment we heard most frequently. Indeed, listening to how Donald Segretti trickily ordered pizza for a Muskie rally was not really the kind of thing that most viewers wanted to hear in place of "The Edge of Night." A number of grand juries had been convened to look into various aspects of the Watergate affair; the special pros-ecutor's office was hard at work, and it was clear that the House of Representatives would consider a step of the gravest national consequence in 100 years: the impeachment of a pres-ident. As Baker said publicly, it was time for the Watergate committee to relinquish the spotlight.

Despite the sporadic efforts of a few, the senators, the staff members, the subjects of the investigation, and everyone else on Capitol Hill who had been touched by the Watergate committee came to the gradual realization that the matter that had consumed our lives for what seemed an eternity was coming to an end. The abuses of the Nixon administration, along with certain fundamental weaknesses and strengths of our political institutions, had been exposed and made known across the nation. The issues and personalities involved had been debated in Congress and on street corners. It appeared obvious that whether Nixon personally had been shown guilty or not, his administration was damaged beyond repair. It clearly was time for our committee to write its report and fade into history.

In the committee's waning days in the late spring and early summer of 1974, a feeling of reconciliation appeared to emerge among all of those whose lives had been touched by Watergate. In a sense, every senator and every staff member on the committee had been on trial; each of our actions had been scrutinized, our professional abilities tested, our motivations questioned. There had been numerous opportunities for even the most innocent individual to be placed in a compromising position.

The background and the activities of everyone on the committee had been examined for any possible improprieties. On June 28, 1973, the *Wall Street Journal* carried an article charging that Senator Montoya had concealed the sources of "as much as $100,000" in contributions to his 1970 reelection campaign.

On July 30 the *Washington Star News* reported that Senator Talmadge was given a 1973 winter vacation by a major government contractor.

Jack Gleason, a former Nixon staff assistant, admitted that he had made requests for information on possible financing irregularities by Senator Weicker in his 1970 Senate campaign.

After the Watergate hearings were over it was disclosed that the special prosecutor's office had investigated Senator Inouye's reelection campaign. Subsequently Inouye's campaign committee pleaded guilty to failing to list $5650 in donations from George M. Steinbrenner, III, on its public reports during

*Sam Dash and I chat during one of the rare moments of Watergate relaxation. Despite our occasional public clashes, Sam and I almost always got along well in private.*

the Watergate hearings. Steinbrenner himself had been under investigation by the Watergate committee.

During my first month in Washington I had received a valuable lesson as to the scrutiny we were all under. After placing a call I had left my appointment book in a phone booth. Within five minutes I realized what I had done and returned to retrieve it, but it was nowhere to be found. Within a few days a Jack Anderson article appeared, referring to a "Kleindienst" notation in the book. The article implied that I was secretly meeting with then Attorney General Richard Kleindienst. I had in fact met with Kleindienst with both Ervin's and Baker's permission in order to facilitate the transfer of FBI documents to the committee.

I often wondered what might have occurred if, on arriving in Washington convinced of the president's innocence, I had called the White House and assured Haldeman or Dean that I could be counted on to see that Nixon got a fair shake. Dean, after his break with the White House, undoubtedly would have testified that Nixon's people were working with me behind the scenes. And the tapes probably would have contained a Haldeman comment to the president to the effect that "We've got the minority counsel in the bag." Such a naive and basically innocent action on my part would have destroyed my credibility and damaged my professional reputation. I am certain that similar thoughts went through the minds of everyone connected with the Watergate committee. So, as the committee's days wound down, there seemed to be a general feeling of relief, a sense that "at least we're getting out of this thing alive."

Much of this aura of at least guarded friendliness among the committee members and the staff reflected the personal qualities of Ervin and Baker. Both men were capable of fighting hard for their positions, and several times they found themselves at odds in private, but both were also basically sensitive to the feelings of those around them; both seemed incapable of harboring any kind of grudge that would hamper their effectiveness in presiding over our work harmoniously.

The senators, in keeping with congressional practice, assigned the staff the task of drafting various lengthy sections of the committee's report. Because staff members had pursued separate and sometimes unrelated investigations, we were actually drafting many reports, rather than one. Ervin and Baker instructed Dash and me to meet with our staff colleagues, study the various reports, and return, if at all possible, with recommendations that satisfied both of us. Considering all the heat that had been generated over the months, when Dash's staff and mine had often worked at cross purposes, such agreement appeared all but impossible. But it was clear that Ervin wanted a single report, not separate majority and minority reports. He wanted the committee's final act to be a document unanimously agreed upon that would provide a suitable capstone to his illustrious career in the Senate. Ervin had already announced that he would not run for reelection in 1974.

Baker shared Ervin's view about a single committee report. He told me early in the investigation that he wanted our minority findings integrated into the body of the report. Whenever it appeared that political differences might inflict substantial damage on the committee's work, Baker would say, "We have come too far to let this happen." He expressed the same opinion to me in private. It was a valuable contribution to the education of a headstrong young lawyer from Tennessee.

To accomplish our final job, Dash and I engaged in a series of almost around-the-clock sessions. Each of us would take part of the report and meet with one or two other staff members who had worked on that part of the investigation—the milk fund, dirty tricks, Hughes-Rebozo, the break-in and cover-up, and so on. We would go over the proposed drafts line by line, often word by word. We then bargained over content, substance, and language. It was something like the United Auto Workers and General Motors at the bargaining table, with each side knowing that stockholders and rank-and-file union members were demanding a settlement.

Members of the majority staff had prepared drafts for the

matters they worked on, and our side had done the same for the areas we had investigated. On both sides, the initial drafts were tough. Majority staff members cited conclusions of guilt throughout their reports, and the resulting publicity would certainly have damaged significantly those persons already awaiting trial. On the other hand, our report contained every Democratic impropriety and incident of wrongdoing we had discovered, even though we knew some of the items would be dropped over the issue of the committee's jurisdiction.

The bargaining commenced. We would demand that a conclusion of guilt be eliminated, and the majority team would insist that it remain. In the ensuing discussion, our side would agree that if certain Democratic improprieties were retained in our report, we would agree to their use of such language as "there is evidence to the effect that" someone had committed an illegal act, rather than stating a conclusion on a matter that a jury would soon have to decide. In this regard the minority staff had an advantage because we knew that Ervin felt strongly that the report should draw no conclusions of guilt or innocence. This attitude created some friction between Ervin's office and the Democratic staff members, but everyone knew that Ervin was adamant.

Every morning the minority staff would meet in my office, and the majority staff would assemble in Dash's office; each side would plan its strategy. We would discuss what the other side might be willing to yield on and what it would insist on retaining. Each side had padded its findings, knowing the other would whittle them down. Then, when face-to-face negotiations began, there would be a round of compromise, concession, shouting, and cajoling. Sometimes we argued for thirty minutes over a single word. Through it all, we discovered to our mutual surprise that we were accomplishing our goal. Despite past differences, we discovered that, seated across a table and forced to justify our positions, we could nearly always find common ground.

Most of the time we found that the toughest problems involved the attitudes of assistant counsels on both sides. Dash and I now knew each other well enough to understand how far the other would go on a point, and we could usually resolve our problems, often to the distaste of both assistant majority counsel and assistant minority counsel.

The bargaining sessions were not all serious bickering. When a new group of majority staff members entered to begin negotiations, I would often walk into Dash's office with a scowl on my face and say, "If you'll agree to burn your entire report, I'll agree not to have you indicted for conspiracy to obstruct justice." I would enjoy the momentary look on their faces. After one session, a Weicker aide called me and said the senator wondered if I had any objection to his naming me, in Weicker's separate views attached to the committee report, as an unindicted co-conspirator. I replied that I had no objection if the senator didn't mind if I put in the report that Weicker was on Howard Hughes' payroll.

One night in late June 1974, after a long negotiating session, Dash and I had dinner together at the Monacle restaurant. After nearly eighteen months in Washington, it was the first time we had dined alone together. We talked about committee business—about the change in the committee's atmosphere and of the progress we were making in negotiating the final report. And we talked about personal matters—about his leaving private practice to teach and his book on wiretapping. After a year and a half, we were finally becoming acquainted.

Our final report, as submitted to the committee, bore little resemblance to the original version of either the majority or minority side. Then the senators began their negotiations on the recommendations they wanted to make to the Senate on the basis of the report's factual findings. Here again, a spirit of conciliation and compromise emerged; the senators appeared more relaxed and down to earth, and they exhibited facets of their personalities that we had not previously observed.

At these executive sessions, Ervin and Baker always sat at the end of a long table, with Ervin next to Dash and Baker next to me. During lulls in these sessions, I occasionally had the opportunity to speak privately with Ervin. During one of these sessions the conversation moved to the grounds for impeachable conduct. Most legal scholars contended, in opposition to the president's assertions, that it was not necessary to prove criminal conduct to justify impeachment. But Ervin said, somewhat offhandedly, "You know, I think the president's right on that one: I think you do have to have an indictable offense before you can impeach him." The old constitutional scholar was still the strict constructionist, even if it meant aligning himself with his principal antagonist, Nixon.

One day, when the discussion wandered to the Internal Revenue Service, Talmadge, who seldom had much to say at committee meetings, stated his opinion and then gave a dissertation on the entire tax law, including its history. He had an extraordinary grasp of the law's intricacies, demonstrating to me for the first time why he is considered one of the Senate's most gifted members.

In the final week of our work on the report, Baker engaged in his favorite hobby—photography, at which he is quite expert. It appeared to me that he was snapping our rather plain-looking table, covered with our notes, pens, and pencils; he actually was making photos of Ervin's hands as they took different positions on the table. Months earlier, during our hearings, Baker called over a professional photographer before the start of a session and told him he was using an extremely complex camera in the wrong way. Baker adjusted a few of the settings, snapped a few pictures to demonstrate what he had done, and returned the camera to the photographer.

The evening after our report was completed I was eating at the Monocle when Dave Gartner, Humphrey's administrative assistant, walked in. "Is it all over now?" he said as he came over and sat down. "Yes," I replied, "and it's about time."

"You guys sort of gave us a hard time there for a while," Gartner said, "and I know it's something we all had to go through." We laughed and chatted about the Humphrey investigation, telling each other about behind-the-scenes maneuvers that had taken place while we were trying to dredge up whatever we could about Democratic presidential candidates and they were trying to cut us off at the pass. It was like two lawyers replaying a hard-fought trial, and I enjoyed the discussion.

I looked up to see Humphrey walk in. Gartner had told me he was to attend a Democratic function upstairs, and people were already waiting for him. The senator spotted Gartner and me and walked toward us. I braced myself for an encounter.

Humphrey, however, extended his hand, greeted me warmly, and asked if he could sit down.

"I wish you would," I said.

After waving and chatting with a few people in the room, he turned to me. "Fred," he said, "I just want to tell you that I appreciate the way you handled this situation. I know you had a job to do."

I thanked him for his comment. It was as I had suspected that day in Inouye's office: this "happy warrior" was a professional who knew the rules of the game. He recognized on the day the committee was formed that he was in for a share of the heat. He would fight, but he would bear no grudges against his opponents if the battle was waged fairly.

While his party continued to wait for him upstairs, Humphrey discussed how easy it is for things to go wrong in a political campaign no matter how much care a candidate takes. Innocent activities, he said, can appear much different later when viewed in a different perspective. As we chatted about politics in general, people who recognized the two of us walked by with puzzled looks. The committee was now out of business, and there was nothing I could do for or against Humphrey; even so, he seemed to want me to know that he did not consider himself guilty of any wrongdoing and that there were no hard feelings.

I recalled a conversation months earlier with Donald Segretti's attorney. Segretti had been found guilty of, among other things, distributing scurrilous literature that wrongly accused Humphrey and Sen. Henry Jackson of sexual misconduct. When Segretti appeared before the committee he admitted his sins and was contrite. He and his attorney decided to call on the two senators and apologize. When Segretti went to Jackson's office, his lawyer told me, Jackson was in no mood for reconciliation. "He gave us absolute holy hell," the lawyer recalled. A little shaken, the two men kept to their plan and visited Humphrey. The senator welcomed them, asked them to sit down, and accepted Segretti's apology gracefully. "No harm done" was his attitude. It was months later, when I was reading an old magazine back home in Nashville, that I learned for the first time that while we were applying the heaviest pressure on Humphrey, he was fighting cancer of the colon. I had never suspected he was ill.

As I think back on those hectic days, I recognize that our forays into Democratic campaign activities, the CIA investigation, and all the battles that accompanied them were almost welcome diversions that kept me from thinking about the impending doom that seemed to be hanging over the White House like a thick fog—the realization that the president himself was guilty of criminal offenses committed while in office. To those, like myself, who had considered such a state of events inconceivable, it was a tremendously difficult fact to accept. We certainly should have realized it earlier, because all the signs were there—the enemies list, the use of the Internal Revenue Service and other agencies, the overreaction to all criticism and dissent, and the conducting of the nation's business in isolation.

Two events appeared to serve as an ominous, but fitting, prelude to the downfall of Nixon: the conviction of Spiro Agnew and the indictment of Gurney for irregularities in the 1968 campaign. Most adults have their share of disillusionment and misjudgments, but for me, the thought that Agnew, the strong man, the man one could admire even when disagreeing with him, had accepted payoff money in the office of the vice president was more demoralizing than any of the disclosures of Nixon's misconduct. After Agnew's admission of guilt, the idea that Nixon might also be guilty moved much closer in my mind to the rim of possibility.

Gurney's situation was a much more personal matter for me. In the several months in which I sat next to him at the committee table, we had seen a full array of political misdeeds and a procession of men who had fallen from power and respectability. Although no one associated with the committee appeared close to Gurney personally, he and I exchanged many comments about such matters as the credibility of witnesses and the human tragedies that were taking place in front of us. Then one day I picked up a newspaper and learned that he was facing indictment. We had few opportunities to chat after that, but he expressed his innocence as ardently in private as he did in public. I wondered how long he had lived with the knowledge that he might be indicted. Now, with an invalid wife, with his own physical problems at the age of 60, his political career in ruins, he appeared to be in a position as tragic as that of most of the others we had seen in our investigation. Gurney's plight eradicated, for me, any of whatever fun or excitement remained as a result of my association with the Watergate committee. It seemed almost as if the earth would open up and swallow everyone in Washington.

Although the arrogance that often accompanies power and the centralization and misuse of government agencies were the antithesis of basic conservative principles and the principles of the Republican party, it was the sometimes hysterical and often hypocritical criticism of Nixon from some quarters, the application of a double standard, the instances of unfairness, the lionizing of Daniel Ellsberg—all these things—that kept me, and probably millions of others, from accepting for so long the fact that most of the charges against the president were true and that he had systematically lied to us all. In a way, I realize now that somewhere during the course of the investigation I had allowed Nixon's enemies to determine my feelings: I simply took a position opposite to that of some of his detractors. And now because of Nixon's plight, the excesses of his critics would soon be forgotten.

I had never been a great admirer of Richard Nixon, the man. (I imagine it would be difficult to find someone now who would say otherwise.) To me, Nixon's career and his policies seemed to evidence an all-too-familiar American political phenomenon—a man consumed by the desire, the need, for elective office, and the willingness to adopt the tactic and position to win. In him, as with so many others, I could find no underlying philosophy by which all things could be measured. In the end, I think that this, more than any other factor, caused his undoing. There was no anchor there; there were no roots. But to many people, he was a symbol; to others, he was simply the alternative to McGovern; to still others, he was "conservative." He received what he regarded as his mandate in 1972, and that must have caused him to believe to the end that he would survive.

As I watched Nixon's resignation speech, a million hazy thoughts crossed my mind. I felt neither joy nor sorrow, only relief. I was exhausted—physically, mentally, and emotionally. For me it marked the end, not only of the political life of Richard Nixon, but also of the most interesting period of my life. I thought back over the previous eighteen months. I suppose that in most historic events—when new nations are formed, when great nations disintegrate, or when wars are waged—the thoughts of those involved are primarily personal.

There was no single point at which the truth about Nixon dawned on me. I saw no bright light on the road to Damascus. It was more of a gradual realization. Even during the battle over the White House tapes, I could not conceive that the president could order their installation and then keep them if they were damaging to him. The answer to why he did so, more than any other, sheds the most light, I believe, on Nixon's perception of the presidency and of himself as president. He undoubtedly felt that the institution of the presidency, and he as the holder of that office, were so powerful that no force on earth was strong enough to make him relinquish the tapes. In this, the master politician misjudged Congress, the Supreme Court, and the American people.

When the White House transcript of the tapes was released on April 30, 1974, even though there was still room for die-hards to debate whether Nixon was personally guilty of the obstruction of justice that had taken place, the die was cast.

The knowledge that the president had even entertained the idea that the Watergate defendants should be paid hush money was a horrible blow to those of us who had sought to give him the benefit of the doubt. During the days that followed the release of the transcript, when the staff discussed the tapes, some of us would play devil's advocate. Was the president not faced with an unprecedented situation? Did he not confront an impossible choice, the prospect of bringing down all that his administration had achieved in the previous four years and the ruination of the lives of many of his oldest and closest associates? Could Kennedy or Johnson have survived this kind of scrutiny? I considered these questions. But late at night, when I was alone with my own thoughts, my mind kept returning to how I could explain to my children what the president had done. Any attempt to justify his actions would fly in the face of the standards that I hoped to instill in them.

Baker also agonized over the matter. He had not called for Nixon's resignation because of his strong belief that in the long run it is bad precedent for any president to resign under pressure. Even the agonies of impeachment, in his view, would be better. One afternoon, late in May, we discussed the deteriorating situation. Actually, he seemed to be talking more to himself. "You know," he said, "in spite of all I have said, I think he ought to resign." He looked out the window for a few moments. "No! Damn it!" he said as he threw a pencil at the wall. "He should be removed on constitutional grounds only. Anything else would be a terrible precedent." He paced the room.

The final card in the long game was played on August 8, 1974, when the White House released the transcript of a conversation on June 23, 1972, between Haldeman and Nixon. It revealed that Nixon had ordered that the FBI be directed to pull away from the Watergate matter. When the news came, I found Baker in a committee meeting. He stepped outside the door and I said, "Well, I guess this is finally it, isn't it?"

"Yes," he replied, "and it's time. He'll be gone by the end of the week."

## The End of the Affair

Later, as I watched Nixon speak of his sainted mother and come close to weeping, I was touched by the monumental dimensions of his tragedy. I also thought of the many others who had paid the price of loyalty to Nixon and who would continue to do so. I remembered that Rob Odle, the young aide to the Nixon reelection committee, had told me that secretaries and many others who had worked for the committee, completely innocent of any link to Watergate, could not get jobs because of their previous affiliation. Fred Buzhardt told me of one young White House aide who had been accused of nothing; he was interviewed so many times that his attorney's fees had already mounted to $25,000. I thought of people like Sen. Hugh Scott, who, like Nixon's own daughters, had been paraded out to rally the faithful. And I knew that solid Republicans in the House and Senate, as well as new Republican candidates, would pay their own price in the 1974 elections.

I thought of a chance meeting I had had with Rabbi Baruch Korff at the Nashville airport. It was a few days before the disclosure of the June 23 tape, and the rabbi had been on a television talk show in Nashville the night before, defending Nixon. I introduced myself, and as we bought our tickets and headed for the gates, he reiterated to me all the defense arguments I had heard him make before. However, just before we parted, he stepped closer and asked me, almost confidentially, "Do you really think I'm doing the right thing by urging the president not to resign?" Even Nixon's most persistent defender was voicing doubts; I didn't have the heart to give him a candid reply. I gave some kind of noncommittal answer and rushed off to catch my plane.

I wondered how many young people would drop out of the political process because of what had been revealed. I wondered what would happen to the concept of loyalty. At a time when loyalty among people, loyalty to a cause or principle, seemed to be something greatly needed in this country, the misplaced loyalty of a handful of people to Richard Nixon might mean that fewer people than ever would be willing to place their faith and trust in anyone or anything.

The next morning, I watched the swearing in of President Ford as I packed. I was finally going home for good. Most of the minority staff members had already left the committee and found new jobs. I had said my goodbyes to those who remained. The sky was dark and overcast as I peered out of the taxi on the way to the airport. Even though I had a reservation, I was not permitted to board when I reached the gate—the flight had been oversold. In thousands of miles of flying, this was the first time this had ever happened to me. I spent the rest of the afternoon sitting in a tiny office at National Airport, unshaven and showing the effects of only two hours' sleep. Finally I was assigned to another plane, and just as we were about to board the sky seemed to open up. It rained harder than it had in months, and I was drenched. It was an appropriate ending.

Once we became airborne, I tried to remember my thoughts when I flew to Washington a year and a half earlier to assume my duties. I have always tried to remember every detail about a beginning or an ending in my life. I had had no idea of what should happen during the life of the committee; I doubt if anyone did. And as I was leaving the job I was not sure that I could truly appreciate the significance of what had taken place.

It occurred to me that after such a national ordeal tribute would be paid to the boundless spirit of man and to the triumph of good over evil. But these were not my thoughts. More than anything else, I concluded, the experience taught me not that we had eradicated evil from the face of the earth, but that some things never seem to change. Lord Acton's admonition about the corrupting nature of power is as valid today as it was when he said it, and as it had been for centuries before. The admonition does not apply to presidents alone; when the most powerful elements of the news media, the Congress, the intellectual community, and the judiciary unite in a holy crusade, some individual rights are inevitably sacrificed. Concern for fairness too often depends on whose ox is being gored.

What happens when the prevailing philosophy is to make

the guilty pay at all costs can be seen in the Watergate trials that followed our hearings. Throughout our sessions, committee members kept saying that, even though many witnesses might be subjected to unfair pretrial publicity, several things could be done to insure fair trials at a later time. All of us pointed out, correctly, that the trial judge could grant a continuance until some of the Watergate fervor abated. Or a change of venue could be granted for the trial in a place less consumed by Watergate than Washington. Yet Watergate defendants were denied both continuances and changes of venue. The trials were conducted in Washington, which had voted over 70 percent for McGovern while almost all the rest of the nation was supporting Nixon. And the cases were tried before a judge who had been anathema to the liberal community until he won a national reputation (and became *Time* magazine's man of the year) by extracting confessions from the original Watergate defendants. And yet all of this seems to disturb almost no one's sense of fairness or propriety.

There was little to rejoice about, I thought as I flew home, at least not without a quiet realization that human frailties seem to manifest themselves as much when men attempt to eradicate evil as when that evil itself is being inflicted.

And yet one could not help but feel a certain amount of pride. At crucial points all along the way, the American people, their institutions, and their politicians responded. A few years ago, street riots might have been the response. Political partisanship and infighting were as common as ever on Capitol Hill, and I had become part of it. And yet it seemed to me that the partisanship was itself part of the system of checks and balances—a system that will work, no matter how hard the fight, as long as certain rules are followed.

I looked down on a quilt of clouds, bordered on the horizon by the blood-orange streaks of the setting sun. As the steady hum of the engine drowned out the chatter around me, I realized that I would probably be thinking about the implications of Watergate for the rest of my life. For the country, and for me, it had been a significant point in time.

# Index